Collecting African American Art

Collecting

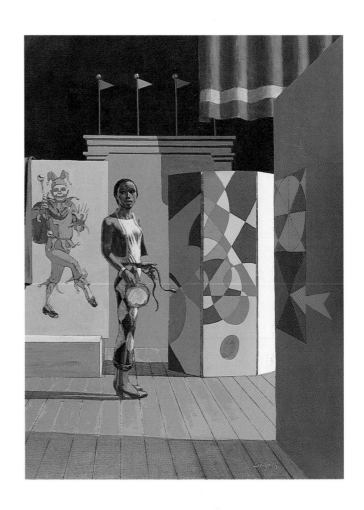

African American Art

WORKS ON PAPER AND CANVAS

HALIMA TAHA

With Forewords by **Deirdre Bibby** *and* **Samella Lewis**

Introduction by **Ntozake Shange**

CROWN PUBLISHERS, INC. • NEW YORK

To my parents, Khari and Ashaki Taha,

my beloved husband, Nuruddin Latif,

Denise K. Delapenha (1946–1993),

Laura Allen,

and Abner Sundell

Published by Crown Publishers, Inc., 201 East 50th Street, New York, New York 10022.
Member of the Crown Publishing Group.
Random House, Inc. New York, Toronto, London, Sydney, Auckland
www.randomhouse.com
CROWN is a trademark and Crown colophon is a registered trademark of Random House, Inc.

Printed in China

Design by Leonard Henderson

Library of Congress Cataloging-in-Publication Data
Taha, Halima.
Collecting African American art : works on paper and canvas / by
Halima Taha ; with forewords by Deirdre Bibby and Samella Lewis ; introduction
by Ntozake Shange. — 1st ed.
Includes bibliographical references and index.
(alk. paper)
1. Afro-American art—Collectors and collecting.   I. Title.
N6538.N5T34   1998
760'.8996'075—dc21   97-48739

ISBN 0-517-70593-1

10 9 8 7 6 5 4 3

Acknowledgments

The decision to write *Collecting African American Art: Works on Paper and Canvas* emerged in 1989, from an awareness that art enthusiasts, students, professionals, and collectors were interested in developing personal and corporate art collections. They were seeking answers to a variety of questions, needs, and aspirations. It seemed that interest, discussion, and debate had quickened and, like prisms, clarified a spectrum of approaches to collecting African American art: as a national patrimony, as a personal heritage, as objects in an art collection, as part of the study of art history, as an influence on twentieth-century art, and as historical materialism.

My knowledge of art has been formed over a significant part of my life, shaped by friends, family, and artists, teachers and students, writers and dealers, and others with whom I have shared time in studios, galleries, and museums. During the process of writing this book, inspiration and instruction came from many sources.

First, I am grateful to the Creator, whose guidance provided clarity and patience to endure the labyrinth of idiosyncrasies within the art and publishing worlds. Allahuakbar!

I am thankful to the many individuals, both intimates and strangers, who have in their own unique ways directly been a part of the creation of this book.

I am especially grateful to my husband, Nuruddin Latif, whose unconditional love and encouragement made the entire process a rewarding experience for me.

Thanks to Ashaki and Kofi Taha for reading many versions of the manuscript; Marianne Hoecker, for her patience and understanding; Frances Williams Taha, for making it possible to travel nationwide to interview collectors and dealers; to Sheik Hasan Cisse, Sheik Umar Job, Masamba "Papa" Khouma, Fatou

V

Sall, and Abu Diop, for their guidance, prayers, and inspiration to aspire to the highest standard; to Ndew Sall, for her generosity and many delicious meals of ceeb a jen; and to Ahmad Tijani Khouma, for reminding me about what is pure and beautiful.

Thanks to my friend Abner Sundell, for making a significant difference; to Roz Kirkland Allen, for providing insight and a sounding board; and to Hermine Maus, whose assistance enabled me to focus on deadlines.

Among the generous, I am thankful to contributors Deirdre Bibby, Dr. Samella Lewis, Ntozake Shange, June Kelly, and E. J. Montgomery, whose participation reinforced the importance of this book as a positive contribution to the art community (artists, dealers, collectors, curators, scholars, and auction houses). Among the talented, I thank the artists, whose commitment to make beautiful and meaningful visual statements has given this book purpose.

My gratitude to the following collectors for sharing their experiences and knowledge: Benny Andrews, Bill Arnet, John Axelrod, Dr. Leon Banks, Anthony Barboza, Juliette Bethea, Camille Billops, Jacqueline Bradley, Tom Burrell, Richard Clarke, Wes Conchran, Betty Davis, Dr. Robert Dearden, Thelma and Dr. David Driskell, Linda and Dr. Walter Evans, Dr. Dexter Fields, Tim Francis, Jerome Gray, Hermine Hartman, Vivian and John Hewitt, Corrine Jennings, Paul R. Jones, Harriet and Harmon Kelly, Professor Edward J. Littlejohn, Herb Nipson, Clarence Otis, Dr. Robert Perkins, Dr. Linda Rankin, Shirley and Edsel Reid, Dr. Richard Simms, Beauford Smith, Thurlow Tibbs, Dr. Nancy and Milton Washington, Joyce and George Wein, and Reba Williams.

Thanks to the dealers listed in the appendix for donating the art for this publication and for sharing their insight and expertise. In particular, Eugene Foney, hallie harrisburg, Jan Harrison, Larry Hilton, Corrine Jennings, June Kelly, Margeret Porter, Madeline Rabb, Michael Rosenfeld, Cheryl Sutton, Ellen Sragow, and Sande Webster.

During my research the following people provided a place to relax and reflect: Shani and Kwami Taha, Diane Strauss, Ntozake Shange, Robert Sengstacke, Cynthia and Johnny Simmons, Dr. Karima Joseph and Iman Salim, Faridah and Abdul Karim Muhammad.

I thank Joscelyn Wainright, Carl Horton, Karin Timpone, Robin Jarrells, Gail Kavenaugh, Mark Shamley, Louis Cunningham and Paula Silas for their support and belief in my work through their actions and deeds.

Thanks to Patricia Dunlea and Ellen LaManna of Hanover Services, whose professionalism and commitment were unparalleled. They and their staff—Vivian Buccari, Debra Burro, Lisa Castranuovo, Lillian Gallway, Helene Gonzales, Kathy Jetter, Loretta Pizzo, Joanie Narcisso, and interns Jennifer Gallway and Jennifer Corrado—transcribed and edited over three hundred interviews. I am equally grateful to my assistant, Hasanah Abdul-Mani, whose attention to detail and focus enhanced the administrative flow of this endeavor.

I thank those who helped in getting this project off the ground: Nance Sharpe, Adrienne Ingram, Carol Taylor, Lara Webb, and Gay Young, Esq.

Thanks to Frank Stewart, Burke Horne, Dorothy and Charles Johnson, Claudia Menza, and Richard Derus.

At Crown, a heartfelt thanks to Ayesha Pande, the last of three editors to guide this book to completion; talented Lenny Henderson and Mary Schuck, for the beautiful interior and elegant jacket design; Laurie Stark, Camille Smith, and Joan Denman, for making this book's production parallel the quality within; and finally to Steve Ross and Chip Gibson, for the courage to publish this book.

Contents

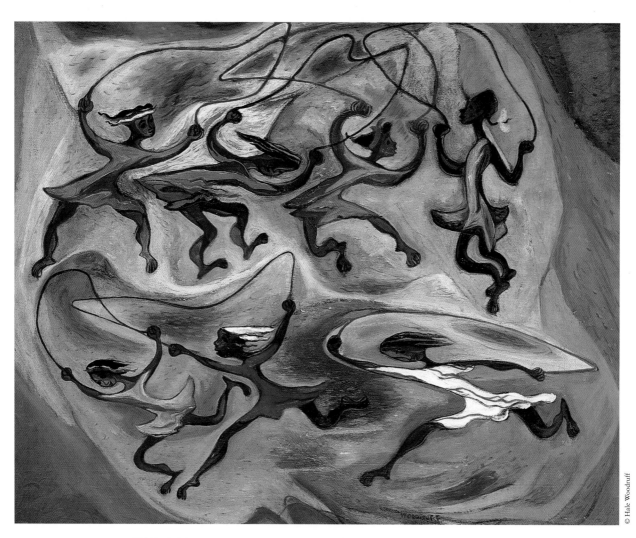

HALE WOODRUFF. *GIRLS SKIPPING*. 1949. Oil on canvas, 24 x 32 inches, signed.
Private collection, New York.
Courtesy of Michael Rosenfeld Gallery, New York.

Foreword by Deirdre Bibby

Until recently, dealers and collectors of twentieth-century art could be counted on one hand. John Quinn, Peggy Guggenheim, and Leo and Gertrude Stein are among those who shaped the history of collecting over eighty years ago. Though it is an exciting history, you will find that it does not include the work of African American artists. Although they were present and active during that time, they were excluded from the collecting market of early modernism. The unique tradition of collecting works by African American artists is being revealed here for the first time, and you will find it fascinating.

In thinking about this publication I could not help but recall some of my observations on the evolution of the collecting market for African American art. For me, it goes back to the sixties, a time more favorable to the arts than any other time in this country. Federal agencies like the National Endowment for the Arts and the National Endowment for the Humanities, and regional, state, and local arts agencies were actively funding the arts in response to the voice of America. During this period museums with a cultural and contemporary focus opened in response to the demands of the black community and its artists, who insisted on inclusion. The result was that museums discreetly added a few works by black artists to their collections or rushed to present temporary traveling exhibitions, while many of the older established museums responded by setting up community outreach programs. Other institutions opened satellite museums in underserved communities.

Concurrently, colleges and universities nationwide established black studies departments, while popular culture and media exploded with posters, magazines, books, television shows, and movies affirming African American contributions to world and American culture.

The 1960s saw the birth of black museums: the Studio Museum in Harlem, the Museum of the National Center of Afro-American Artists in Boston, the Anacostia Neighborhood Museum in Anacostia (just across the bridge from the District of Columbia), the DuSable Museum in Chicago, and the Museum of African American History in Detroit. Other institutions, such as the Schomburg Center for Research in Black Culture in New York City and historically black colleges and universities, served as intellectual centers hosting forums on local economic, social, and civic issues and conferences on Pan-Africanism, Negritude, and the new arts movement.

The art department faculty at black colleges attracted a wave of promising young artists, and mainstream colleges and universities throughout the nation were recruiting black artists to their faculties. Historically black colleges continued to collect works by black artists, many of whom were students and faculty. Laudably, these institutions had already acquired some of the most important works of African American art—stellar works by artisans, painters, and sculptors of the eighteenth, nineteenth, and early twentieth centuries. Their extraordinary farsightedness in forming these early collections has provided the nation and the world with masterworks chronicling what is now acknowledged as a crucial aspect of American art.

Two important private collections of museum quality were the Barnett-Aden and the Evans-Tibbs collections. The Barnett-Aden Collection, inherited by Adolphus Ealey, was developed in the late 1940s by art historians James V. Herring and Alonzo J. Aden. These two African American men were the first to establish a gallery for the exhibition of works by black artists, following the pioneering efforts of sculptor Augusta Savage, who opened the Salon of Contemporary Negro Art in 1939. Ealey actively added to the Barnett-Aden Collection, reshaping it over a period of twenty years. At the time of its sale the collection contained 140 works, including such major names as Edward Mitchell Bannister, Henry Ossawa Tanner, Romare Bearden, and Elizabeth Catlett, and a cadre of artists from Washington, D.C. Theodore Stamos, Jack Perlmutter, and Morris Louis were among the few white artists included in the collection. The Barnett-Aden Collection demonstrates the varying interests of African American artists, from regional landscape paintings to Abstract Expressionism. Purchased by the Florida Endowment Fund for Higher Education in 1989, the collection currently serves as the permanent collection of the Museum of African-American Art, which opened in 1991 in Tampa, Florida.

The Evans-Tibbs Collection was developed on much the same framework as the Barnett-Aden Collection and was recently acquired by the Corcoran Gallery of Art in Washington, D.C. Thurlow Tibbs, who is known for his high standards of connoisseurship, inherited his small collection from his parents and grandparents. During the past two decades he added significantly to the collection, which includes works by Henry Ossawa Tanner, Aaron Douglas, Hughie Lee-Smith, Lois Mailou Jones, Raymond Saunders, Betye Saar, and photographers James VanDerZee and Addison Scurlock.

Adolphus Ealey and Thurlow Tibbs, as collectors and art experts possessed of tremendous entrepreneurial zeal, have figured prominently in the formation of several newer collections. They have served as advisers to both seasoned and new collectors who wisely sought their guidance. Other art experts such as Terry Dintenfass, June Kelly, Merton Simpson, Linda Bryant, and art historians Regina Perry and David Driskell have served as consultants to museums nationwide and have continued to engage in the discourse on the value of collecting and preserving African American art.

The dramatic increase in collecting works by African American artists over the past twenty years is the direct outgrowth of more works appearing at auction, more museum acquisitions, and more professionals specializing in works by African American artists. Scholarly publications and reference sources have also increased, and important exhibitions have critically explored aesthetic issues and the work of individual artists.

Another factor has been the extensive visibility offered by television shows such as *Good Times,* where J.J., played by Jimmy Walker, is a budding artist, and the work of Ernie Barnes is used in the opening credits. In *The Cosby Show* pride and personal enrichment are expressed through the collections of art and jazz enjoyed in the Huxtable household.

The touring exhibitions of the private collections of Dr. Walter Evans, Harriet and Harmon Kelly, Wes Cochran, and Thurlow Tibbs also raised public awareness of great artists of the early twentieth century. Major corporations have purchased works and profiled African American artists through product marketing. Large cities, many of which have substantial black populations, have awarded major public art commissions, and mainstream museums have more aggressively acquired works by African American artists. Even a historically conservative museum like the Wadsworth Atheneum in Hartford, Connecticut, in keeping with its mission to serve its surrounding communities, has acquired a major collection of art and artifacts through a unique partnership with the black community. The museum furthered its efforts by establishing a curatorial department for African American art, hired a full-time black curator, and established two galleries for the exhibition of the Amistad Collection, which is on indefinite loan through the partnership venture, and a gallery for the exhibition of works by African American artists purchased directly by the museum.

One thing is for certain: To develop a good collection, you must have full knowledge of what it is you're collecting. Remember that collecting art is about seeing. You will need to develop and train your eye to determine stylistic and aesthetic qualities. You must also be able to judge the significance of art and objects against a myriad of factors—originality, age, rarity, market value, monetary value, provenance, and appeal.

I hope that this timely and authoritative publication will encourage you to establish personal standards and criteria, whether you collect for pleasure or for profit. When you do, your collection will have added depth and provide you with the fullest enjoyment possible.

Deirdre Bibby is a specialist in African American art and a noted curator and museum administrator. Currently executive director of the Amistad Foundation at the Wadsworth Atheneum and its curator of African American art, Ms. Bibby previously served as executive director of the Museum of African-American Art in Tampa, Florida; head of the Art and Artifact Division at the Schomburg Center for Research in Black Culture of the New York Public Library; and associate curator at the Studio Museum in Harlem.

CHARLES WHITE. *Looking Upward*. 1954.
Black ink on paper, 26 x 20 inches, signed.
Courtesy of Michael Rosenfeld Gallery, New York.

Foreword by Samella Lewis

To the many individuals, groups, and institutions who ask the questions "What is African American art?" and "What is black art?" I would like to respond with a question: What is art? If this question was posed to five individuals of different cultures, we would likely have five different responses. Some individuals may even find themselves puzzled at the question because in many of the world's cultures the word *art* simply has no meaning, nor do some languages even have a word for it.

In traditional African, Asian, and some American cultures the word *art* carries a different meaning from that intended in Western European society. Art marks a way of life; its signs and symbols are so integrated with everyday life, patterns, and beliefs that it is difficult, if not next to impossible, to separate art from life itself.

As an artist, I collect out of my own need to live my life fully. As an artist, I have a desire to share those inspirations and learning that have shaped my life. What we see, hear, think, and believe is important to how we value ourselves as African Americans, and art becomes a cornerstone to that endeavor for many.

I cannot recall a time when I was not in touch with the art that I collect. Although I grew up in New Orleans on the downside of economics, my life was still culturally rich and full. From the prose of Paul Laurence Dunbar to the music of Duke Ellington, Marian Anderson, and Dinah Washington, to the paintings of Jacob Lawrence and the sculptures of Elizabeth Catlett, I have had the enjoyment and satisfaction of being with and knowing about the works of some of the most talented people in the arts. Directly or indirectly, I was spoon-fed from a vast wealth of artistic influences that have given meaning and sustenance to my life and to others.

PHILEMONA WILLIAMSON. *The Logic of Solitude.* 1992.
Oil on linen, 48 x 60 inches.
Courtesy of June Kelly Gallery, New York.

We cannot deny the trigger response art has for the human spirit. It invokes in us memories and experiences that take us to new heights of understanding. It would be a crime to rob the world of art because of detractors and critics who, not being in touch with the spiritual essence that art has to offer, attempt to deny or destroy the credibility of an artist's works. That is why it is essential that books like *Collecting African American Art* continue to find their way into libraries and galleries across this continent as well as onto shelves in the homes of individuals who want to see art continue to breathe and exist in our lives. It is fitting and proper that we continue to touch the lives of people with every aspect of cultural expression.

Art represents the joys, sadness, and human experiences that have made my life one of satisfaction in being who I am—an African American whose people have given a culture to the world, which, in its basic ingredients, is surpassed by no other.

Samella Lewis, Ph.D., professor emerita of art history, Scripps College, of the Associated Colleges of Claremont, California, is an artist and art historian. She is also the founder and editor in chief of the International Review of African American Art, *published by Hampton University, Hampton, Virginia.*

Introduction by Ntozake Shange

What did I cover my walls with? What sat on my desk or by my bed to put me to sleep safely, to nurture my dreams, to validate my realities as a child? I vaguely remember very white, pale pink and blue dancers, colonial figures on their way somewhere, a daguerreotype of a not so distant but very serious relative. There's really nothing pernicious here or painful to the id. But something was clearly missing because my sister, Ifa, and I spent myriad early mornings when parents need quiet, the illusion of solitude; those times, we raided Daddy's bookcases and the extralarge shelves near the coffee table where art books or a small nimble child could fit easily. So sometimes we moved the books—many of them graphic medical books of human physiological anomalies, others lovely textured volumes almost as large as my torso wherein lay loose reproductions of Picasso, Modigliani, van Gogh, and Lautrec. Colors, unexpected forms, and light previously only imagined were immediately torn out and pasted to anything. I had no idea I was destroying images that were not only expensive but also precious to my parents for some of the same reasons I took them. This turned out not to be a good idea, taking others' images. I was instructed to make my own, but I would have to hear that many times before I began to understand how to create an aesthetic environment that was mine, even if the signatures and styles absolutely contradicted any narrative or thematic analysis.

I was in college before my walls were covered with posters of black, Cuban, and African revolutionaries: Che Guevara, Fidel, Lumumba, Huey Newton, Angela Davis. Here and there were photographs, very small, of friends, cousins, and assorted beaux. My "art collection" remained this way until I went on a date in graduate school with a guy whose take on the world I found fascinating enough to listen to casual comments intensely. He was leaving my apartment one night after an L.A. 1970s–type vegetarian dinner, when he turned to me and said: "I don't know why your walls are covered up with these people [Archie Shepp, Ayler, Holder, Fidel hanging in there, and Jimi Hendrix next to Du Bois]." "Why not?" I retorted indignantly. With a healthy cynicism I still respect, my friend replied with, I must confess, no small hint of condescension: "You have to be your own hero. Somebody is just making a lot of money off you."

That moment is actually the first time I felt my daddy's words about "making your own art"—so I did. I worked with wood first so I could have a totem. Then I spent hours weaving, and during my early twenties, weaving, crocheting, macraméing peculiar shapes and objects that pleased me. I made pieces of "found art." I made art out of my poems, the shapes and sounds. Since I was studying dance at the time, my sense of movement in stasis was evolving. I began to be able to look at other people's work and feel/see—not "read" as I'd been taught—the melody or depth of a piece of art or a tree stump, for that matter.

I still make pieces of my own, the most eccentric being a hanging of tree limbs I collected after Hurricane Hugo struck Philadelphia. I scoured downtown (one of the 1700s finest urban African American communities) and carried limbs that interested me home on my back. I accepted no assistance from men puzzled and genuinely concerned about the weight or unwieldy lengths of my ruptured, dying wood. These pieces were history. I carried them and somehow positioned them over my bed so that I would wake each day to "a world of my own making" that respected the spirits and dreams of others like me who had walked beneath them, sought shade from the sun or protection from those who would re-enslave a free people. Eight years later I still sleep beneath this assem-

blage. Sometimes I decorate it with lights or birds or small dolls who live there. Sometimes the bare branches alone are too beautiful to touch with anything but dreams.

Now I have all kinds of people from all over the world whom I rotate and move about depending on my needs. I place no more value on folk art by black Colombians than I do on my Haitian iron pieces or fotos by Adal, Louis Delsarte, Betye Saar, John Biggers, Romare Bearden, Coreen Simpson, Frank Stewart, Diallo Johnson, Savannah Shange Binion, Howardena Pindell, or Wopo Holup. These artists needed to create something, to let us see something no one had seen quite like that ever before, nor would that moment recur ever again. These paintings, altars, tapestries, sculptures, and solid poems are the world I enter each day. A world of carefully met spiritual and historical needs, needs for our "truth" and our "beauty," created by a disparate mess of folks, some living, some known to me, some strangers, some anonymous, some "been crossed over" to the other side, but they left me more than enough to get by with. I go into the "real world" nourished, protected, and inspired because I leave a realm of the worlds we create. I leave a home centuries old, continents broad, "all that and a bag a chips," as my daughter might say, because I decided to, because I allowed myself to be open to manifestations of "souls of black folks." When you visit me, I can honestly say: This is our world. Welcome.

A poet, playwright, novelist, and critic, Ntozake Shange is the author of for colored girls who have considered suicide/when the rainbow is enuf; Betsy Brown; Lilianne; Sassafras, Cypress and Indigo; Nappy Edges; A Daughter's Geography; *and* The Space Love Demands.

Collecting African American Art

ROBERT SCOTT DUNCANSON.

ON THE ROAD TO BEAUPORT, NEAR QUEBEC. 1863. Oil on canvas.

Courtesy of Robert Henry Adams Fine Art, Chicago.

1

COLLECTING ART

It doesn't have to be glitter to be gold.

ARTHUR ASHE

Collecting is a basic part of the human personality. We usually start out with toys, stamps, sports cards, or comics, then move on to books, music, and recipes. Yet, when we consider collecting art, we think that we have to be experts or extremely wealthy. To many beginning collectors, the art market appears to be a closed and forbidding community. If any of these misconceptions have kept you from or limited your approach to collecting art, you are invited to reconsider. This book will expose you to the talent of American artists of African descent and guide you through the art world's labyrinth of information. Essentially, *Collecting African American Art: Works on Paper and Canvas* is intended to nurture the development of informed collectors.

This book emerged from an awareness that what had once been an arcane topic of discussion—African American artists as the subject of critical discourse among art historians, critics, collectors, curators, auction houses, and dealers—has become, in recent years, cause célèbre, generating excitement, controversy, and optimism. As we approach the millennium, an expanding awareness of African American history and culture, increasing prosperity, and an integrated community of artists, arts professionals, entrepreneurs, and patrons of the arts have fueled the burgeoning interest in African American art.

JOHN BIGGERS. *MURAL SKETCH FOR CONTRIBUTION OF NEGRO WOMEN TO AMERICAN LIFE.* 1953.
Conte pencil, 16 x 48 inches.
Courtesy of Noel Fine Art Acquisitions, Charlotte, N.C.

Most Americans recognize that one of black America's greatest contributions to the twentieth century is jazz. There is a strong analogy between Earl "Fatha" Hines's rhythm of song and the Cubist innovations of the late 1920s, paralleled by the blues-drenched Pointillism of Count Basie and the angular Impressionism of Duke Ellington. And more recently, art enthusiasts have been realizing that the same people who developed this musical art form have also been creating its visual equivalent since 1780.

African American art has become a source of awe and attraction because of its unique history of African and European influences. Ultimately, though, the issue is not how the work of African Americans compares to that of their European peers, but to what extent it shows the artists' ability to create images that viewers, regardless of their background, can relate to.*

Collectively, the work of African American artists is not confined to one style or influence. These artists are no different from any other artist engaged in the creative struggle to express an individual sensibility, while simultaneously relating to the historical and cultural rhythms of time and place. Critical attention has positioned the work of African American artists among the most actively purchased and affordable American art because of its conceptual and aesthetic spheres of interest. Not only does black art in America possess a unique global characteristic by virtue of the rich contributions by artists from the African continent, the Caribbean, and the Americas, but it is in itself an exciting study of cultural diversity at its very best.

Excellent-quality drawings, paintings, and prints by established, mid-career, and emerging artists can be found to fit any taste and budget. You need nothing more than your interest, patience, and a steady income to begin collecting African American art. And since the established marketplace is still trying to catch up to what has already grown, prices are still affordable even for budding collectors.

There is no such thing as a "typical" art collector. Some collectors are just beginning their careers or decorating their first homes; some are ending their careers and looking for a new activ-

---

* *African American Visual Aesthetics: A Modernist View,* edited by David Driskell (Washington, D.C.: Smithsonian Institution Press, 1995).

CHARLES ALSTON. *BLUES SINGER #4*. 1955.
Oil on canvas, 40 x 30 inches.
Courtesy of Kenkeleba Gallery, New York.

HENRY OSSAWA TANNER. *Home de Jeanne d'Arc*. 1918.
Oil on wood panel, 20 x 24 inches, signed.
Courtesy of Michael Rosenfeld Gallery, New York.

ity to engage in in their retirement years. Some are professional art historians or curators; some have just begun to look at art for the first time. Some buy on a strict budget; others have unlimited funds. The thing they all have in common is an interest in owning and enjoying great works of art. Here are some reasons people collect art:

Decoration Art as interior decoration.
Status Collecting art may enhance social standing.
Hobby Collecting as an enjoyable activity: meeting people, going to museums and openings.

Creativity Assembling a good collection can be like making a good painting. Also, by supporting young, unknown artists, some collectors feel they are participating in their work.
Instinct Some collectors simply can't help themselves.

We all have personal reasons for thinking a particular work of art is more desirable and satisfying to own than another. Whether a selection is spontaneous, or based on knowledge of art history, art technique, market values, and current trends, every choice remains an individual one.

CHARLES ETHAN PORTER. *White Roses.* 1895.
Oil on canvas, 16 x 20 inches.
Courtesy of Essie Green Galleries, New York.

Just as a work of art communicates the thoughts and feelings of the artist, so an art collection reflects the collector's perception of what is beautiful, meaningful, or technically proficient. So always ask yourself: What do I see? What do I feel? What do I think or understand? What do I like or dislike about a work on paper or canvas? Do I like the colors, shapes, subject, or the way the imagery is broken up or put together? Why do I feel this way? *You must have a dialogue with yourself before you have one with anybody else.*

Keep in mind that the most significant function of taste is to amplify your enjoyment in your visual perceptions and experiences. Your reaction to a piece of art may not be anything like that of another observer—and this is to be expected. If you see a given work as an accomplished statement, add it to your collection regardless of trends or popular taste. In collecting art, you must begin to do something that many of us forget how to do—trust yourself and your instincts.

Beginning a collection of African American art also requires a sincere effort to gain knowledge from reading and observation. You must learn to adjust your visual perceptions to your changing levels of experience. As you understand what differentiates and identifies various media and styles

EDWARD MITCHELL BANNISTER. *RHODE ISLAND LANDSCAPE.* 1898. Oil on canvas, 18 x 22 inches.
Courtesy of Kenkeleba Gallery, New York.

of original art, you will react more critically to the strengths and shortcomings of particular oils, watercolors, collages, and prints. Chapter 2 offers a basic introduction on the distinctions between an etching and an aquatint, a lithograph and a charcoal drawing, and other media.

Use the illustrations in art historical texts to evaluate their relative aesthetic and historic merit within the stylistic period in which they were produced. This enables you to examine the painter's skill through a brush stroke, the application of paint to canvas, and the compositional style.

Once you are armed with a solid understanding of the various media and how to keep abreast of the art market and have begun to go to museums and galleries, you will be ready to decide where and from whom you want to buy your fine art. Chapter 3 will guide you as to how to choose a gallery and a dealer who is reputable and with whom you are comfortable.

Tasteful presentation of your new acquisition is an equally essential component of all your collecting activities. An understanding of the relationship between the matte, the frame, and the picture, as well as the environment in which it will live, is the basis for proper presentation. Chapter 4 discusses several guidelines to follow in selecting a framer and how to differentiate among the countless mattes, frames, and moldings that will enhance what you have so carefully purchased. This is one of the most exciting aspects of bringing home a beautiful piece of art.

Because African American fine art has been in existence for approximately 250 years, the basic economic laws of supply and demand apply. Auction prices, sales taxes, shipping and insur-

NANETTE CARTER. *Chiaroscuro*. 1992.
Oilstick, 53 x 53 inches. Courtesy of G. R. N'Namdi Gallery, Chicago.

ance costs, changing styles, trends, subject matter, signatures, dates of execution, and even tax deductions all contribute to the value and prices of African American art. Chapter 4 will also facilitate your understanding of these variables.

In addition to the aesthetic appreciation and personal satisfaction of collecting, the collector also benefits from the monetary value of works of art. Artworks, like stocks and bonds, can be traded at any time, as well as exchanged with or sold to a dealer or collector for current market prices. Anyone buying for investment would probably be wise to collect "old masters" like Henry Ossawa Tanner and Edward Mitchell Bannister, or important twentieth-century painters like Romare Bearden, Jacob Lawrence, and Horace Pippin, to name only a few. Collecting multiple originals on paper, like limited-edition

ROMARE BEARDEN. *MARTINIQUE RAIN FOREST*. 1985.
Collage, 13½ x 10½ inches.
Courtesy of Essie Green Galleries, New York.

PALMER HAYDEN. *Midnight at the Crossroads*. Circa 1940.
Oil on canvas, 28 x 34 inches, signed.
Courtesy of M. Hanks Gallery, Santa Monica, California.

lithographs by the same artists, can provide the average collector with the opportunity to own the work of more established artists at a fraction of the price of a work on canvas. One-of-a-kind and multiple originals should be distinguished from photographic reproductions (posters), originals having been made directly by the hand of the artist. Reproductions are much less expensive to buy, though, and are often an affordable entrance into the world of art collecting. It is important to begin within your means.

Also keep in mind that a well-planned collection includes both popular artists and less popular or unknown artists whose work is exciting or intriguing to you. For centuries collectors of world art have reaped the rewards and joys of discovering and collecting unknown artists with new styles and techniques. Try to keep up with gallery showings and trade and scholarly publications, as it is valuable to have some idea of who's who on the current scene.

Collectors are perpetual students, driven by passion, interest, and commitment, and, like students, they must be many things. As Kinshasha Holman Conwill, director of the Studio Museum in Harlem, eloquently affirms: "[A collector] must be an archaeologist, willing to dig deeply under the rock and sift the sediment that represents history's and society's changing cycles of interest in the art of African Americans. The student must also be a person of great patience, a Job-like figure perhaps, willing to remain steadfast in the face of resistance, opposition, or indifference. And finally, this student must be a visionary . . . he or she must be able to see the unseeable, think the unthought, imagine the unimagined."*

There are no more capable tutors of artistic merit than your own eyes and your own experience. Your spontaneous reactions will be enhanced by reading as much as you can about art history, techniques, and other related subjects. But what drives you will be your passion. Ultimately, it takes three things to master the joy of collecting art: personal interest, time, and money. Armed with these, anyone can learn about African American art and gain enough confidence to begin developing a meaningful and valuable collection.

---

* Kinshasha Holman Conwill, *Free Within Ourselves: African American Artists in the Collection of the National Museum of American Art* (Pomegranate, 1992).

CLEMENTINE HUNTER. *FISHING AT MELROSE.* 1950.
Oil on board, 14 x 18 inches.
Courtesy of Phyllis Kind Gallery, New York.

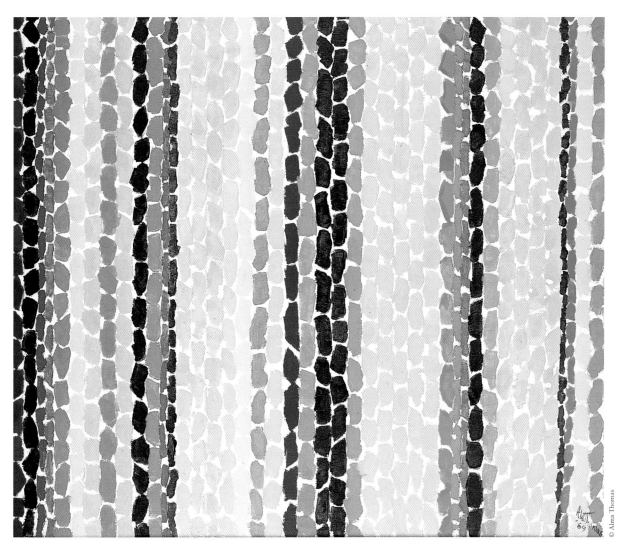

© Alma Thomas

ALMA THOMAS. *Forsythia Glow in Washington, DC.* 1969. Oil on canvas, 34 x 40 inches, signed.
Private collection, Pittsburgh. Courtesy of Michael Rosenfeld Gallery, New York.

NORMAN LEWIS. *WELCOME HOURS.* 1959.
Watercolor and ink on paper, 16½ x 23 inches, signed.
Courtesy of Michael Rosenfeld Gallery, New York.

RICHARD MAYHEW. *Santa Cruz #27.*
Watercolor and pastel on paper, 15 x 21¾ inches.
Courtesy of Sherry Washington Gallery, Detroit.

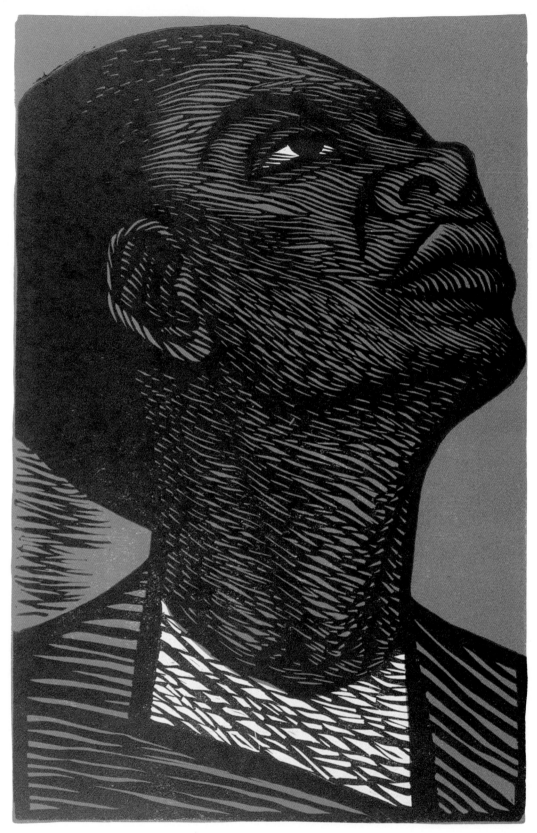

ELIZABETH CATLETT. *My Right Is a Future of Equality with Other Americans.* 1947.
Linocut, 9 x 6 inches. Courtesy of Sragow Gallery, New York.

JACOB LAWRENCE. *STRUGGLE SERIES NO. 21: TIPPICANOE . . . WESTWARD RUSH.* 1955–56.
Egg tempera on hardboard, 16 x 12 inches. Courtesy of D.C. Moore Gallery, New York.

FRANK BOWLING. *Smolts*. 1981–91.
Acrylic on canvas, 41 x 13 inches.
Courtesy of Kenkeleba Gallery, New York.

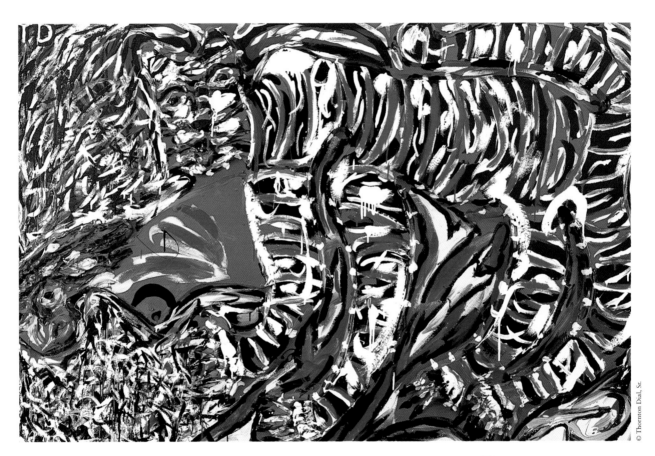

THORNTON DIAL, SR. *Ole Tiger Ain't What He Used to Be*. 1993.
Mixed media on wood, 48 x 60 inches.
Courtesy of Phyllis Kind Gallery, New York.

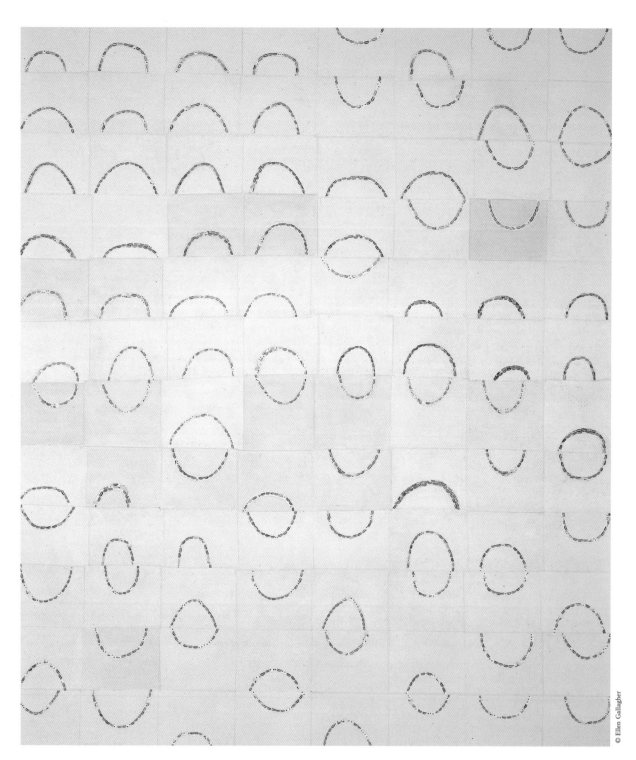

ELLEN GALLAGHER. *DY-NO-MITE*. 1995.
Oil and pencil on paper and canvas, 84 x 72 inches.
Collection of Denver Art Museum, Colorado.
Courtesy of Mary Boone Gallery, New York.

© Ellen Gallagher

JEAN-MICHEL BASQUIAT. *Untitled*. 1981.
Oil stick on paper, 20 x 16 inches, signed.
Courtesy of Dr. Robert H. Derden Collection, Chicago.

© Charles White

CHARLES WHITE. *The Preacher*. 1940.
Tempera on board, 30 x 22 inches, signed.
Courtesy of Michael Rosenfeld Gallery, New York.

2

BASIC TRAINING

Understand that excellence in education cannot

be achieved without intellectual and moral integrity coupled

with hard work and commitment.

NATIONAL COMMISSION ON EXCELLENCE

IN EDUCATION

If you know what you want,

you will recognize it when you see it.

BILL COSBY

uccessful art collecting is not difficult with preparation and common sense. It requires skills that you use every day in your professional and personal lives. Having a good eye for art—that is, being able to distinguish the strong from the weak—is also very important. Although few people innately have this ability, most people can develop it over time.

There are two approaches to collecting art: with your eyes—in other words, relying on your own instincts and judgment—and with your ears, relying on the advice of a few carefully selected dealers. The first approach is more interesting but tends to require more focus and work. The second is the frequent starting point for beginners, who worry that they lack sufficient taste and knowledge to buy wisely on their own. Each approach is legitimate, as is a combination of the two.

ED CLARK. *Taos Series.* 1986.
Acrylic on canvas, 79½ x 66.6 inches.
Courtesy of G. R. N'Namdi Gallery, Detroit.

Most people feel more comfortable starting slowly. Here is one approach toward cultivating your interest while also having a good time:

1. Spend a few months learning everything you possibly can about art. Direct your enthusiasm to the library or bookstore. Read a history of world art, a history of American art, and a history of African American art. *Art: African American* by Dr. Samella Lewis is an excellent place to begin. Subscribe to either or both of the major U.S. art magazines, *Art in America* and *ARTnews*, and to the *International Review of African American Art*. Visit museums and galleries to expose yourself to diverse styles, historical periods, and aesthetic techniques. Develop a feeling for dealers and the type of art they handle. Ascertain whether they are willing to help you choose the best work of art and whether they take pride in assisting you in developing your own expertise.

There is no need to try to become an "expert" overnight. Your main objectives in the initial learning process should be to focus on the types of pictures that interest you most; to learn to look at art; to get a feeling for local dealers and the types of paintings they handle; and to increase your knowledge. Take your time. Look at a work of art for a minimum of ten minutes and then venture an opinion. Notice the differences between artists and their techniques. Your appreciation of and sensitivity to art will become heightened.

2. Learn the various genres of art. The art market is vast. It encompasses hundreds of different submarkets, from Works Progress Administration (WPA) prints to nineteenth-century scene paintings, from American folk art to Surrealist drawings, from Abstract Expressionist paintings to nineteenth-century photography. The more you expose yourself to these differing genres, the more familiar you will become with the style and media of a particular culture or period and, ultimately, the more comfortable you will feel in assessing the aesthetic, historical, and investment value of African American art.

3. Buy a work of art. One of the ironies of the art market is that many people do not want to buy until they become experts, yet they cannot possibly become experts until they begin to buy. The easiest way to avoid this self-defeating cycle is to purchase one or two inexpensive pieces of art. This could be a $300 limited-edition print or a $2,500 painting on paper. The point is to buy something that appeals to your taste and budget. You may want to begin by setting a limit on what you will spend, and then try to find a work by a fairly well-known artist whose paintings you admire. Something usually turns up.

Some collectors start directly with a dealer. You might find a top dealer, explain what qualities you are looking for, and let the dealer make the choices for you. Advice on how to choose a dealer can be found in chapter 3. Your primary objectives here are to reach the point where you feel comfortable about spending your money on art and to get to know two or three good local dealers.

Now that you are aware of some of the advance preparation required to approach your journey intelligently and intuitively, it is time to become familiar with the terms, the media, and the techniques employed by artists.

An original work of art is one that comes directly from the hand of the artist. It may be a one-of-a-kind original or a multiple original. Oils, pastels, temperas, drawings, watercolors, gouaches, and monoprints are examples of one-of-a-kinds. Graphics—etchings, engravings, aquatints, drypoints, woodcuts, lithographs, and similar media—are multiple originals. To create

BENNY ANDREWS. *FIELD OF DREAMS.* 1990. Oil and collage on paper, 22½ x 30 inches.
Courtesy of Sherry Washington Gallery, Detroit.

WILLIAM H. JOHNSON. *JITTERBUGS III*. Circa 1941. Silkscreen on paper, 16 x 11 inches.
Courtesy of Michael Rosenfeld Gallery, New York.

BEAUFORD DELANEY. *Washington Square*. 1952. Oil on canvas, 40 x 60 inches, signed.
Collection of the Greenville County Museum of Art, South Carolina.
Courtesy of Michael Rosenfeld Gallery, New York.

original oil paintings, the artist conceives the image and completes the work on canvas. In the graphic arts the artist also designs a personal image but works it upon stone, metal plates, or blocks of wood. From these, a limited number of works are produced, each involving unique technical procedures and skills. Both forms of the original have been collected and prized. Henry Ossawa Tanner's etchings were widely collected by his contemporaries, as were his oil paintings. Elizabeth Catlett's prints are now as eagerly sought as her sculpture.

In the past, artists who excelled in one particular medium, or even in one form of the graphic arts, generally did not work in any other. Contemporary artists, on the other hand, often explore diverse media and may even use several techniques in a single work. We use the term *painter-printmaker* for an artist who works with

both single and multiple originals. So, if you like the style and feeling of an artist's work but cannot afford it in one medium, you can still enjoy his work in another medium that may be in keeping with your budget.

ONE-OF-A-KIND ORIGINAL ART

OIL PAINTING

The Flemish masters Hubert (ca. 1370–1426) and Jan (1395–1441) van Eyck have traditionally been given credit for the invention of oil painting. However, aside from several works by Leonardo da Vinci (1452–1519), it was the Venetian painters Giovanni Bellini (ca. 1430–1516) and Titian (1488–1576) who first explored the full possibilities of working in oil. The method quickly replaced the previously favored fresco (a technique in which pigments mixed with water are applied to walls quickly and decisively while the plaster is still damp so that the colors are absorbed; *fresco* is the Italian word for "fresh"). Today oil remains one of the most popular forms of original art.

Oil paints are composed of colored vegetable or mineral powders mixed with oil, which is the binding substance. The paints are thick, and they dry with the same consistency, but may be thinned by adding turpentine and benzene prior to application. Most contemporary oil painting is executed on stretched canvas; slate, marble, paper, paper on board, wood panels, copper, and tin are other surfaces to which oils adhere. To apply oil paint, the artist uses either a brush or palette knife, a flat tool with a flexible blade that closely resembles a kitchen knife. The artist may mix colors either on a palette before applying them to the canvas or directly on the painting surface. The latter method is called *al prima*. Artists may paint without a strict, laid-out plan, or as many of the old masters did, they may make careful preparations on their painting surfaces. The preparations might involve a detailed drawing or loosely painted forms on which color is eventually built. Often the artist allows the underpainting to show through, according to a prearranged scheme. We, as viewers of the finished picture, can then appreciate the total creative process. As a final step, certain masters like Henry Ossawa Tanner and Eldzier Cortor use glazes, transparent films of paint, to enhance the richness and luminosity of their work, and apply a coat of varnish both to protect their oils and to add a glossy finish.

As early as the sixteenth century, Titian and his followers developed the technique of impasto, the building up of layers of paint to add brilliance, texture, and three-dimensionality to paint surfaces. With its introduction, artists began to experiment extensively with the representation of light on canvas, which accounts for many of the varieties and subtleties of the oil medium. We can even say that in many respects impasto has been responsible for the unrivaled popularity of oil painting. Beauford Delaney, Sam Gilliam, David Driskell, Vincent Smith, Sylvia Snowden, Benny Andrews, Franklin White, and William T. Williams are artists who have worked with this technique.

PASTEL

Pastels were initially developed and popularly executed early in the eighteenth century. One of the first to experiment with them was the French artist Jean-Baptiste-Siméon Chardin. Unlike most other media, pastel is a completely dry technique. In its earliest stages it involved the thin application of pastel chalks, which were gradually blended and rubbed, usually with the fingers. Fragile, extremely delicate effects of surface and line were the result. Pastels, with their exquisite finish and polish, rival the effects of oils and watercolors. It became common to use pastels in place of oils. Pastel technique changed, however, during the nineteenth century; whereas artists had formerly blended and rubbed the chalk, they now began to apply color within networks of *lines*, the effect of which is an arresting combination of surfaces.

One easy way to recognize pastels is to examine the papers on which they are drawn. Since the middle of the eighteenth century, artists have been using tinted papers to help produce desired effects of light, shade, and depth. In addition, artists often select a specific type of paper, either smooth or rough, to give texture to pastels and structure to the drawing.

The most fundamental characteristic that distinguishes pastels from other media is their prominent chalky smell and their nonglossy, or matte,

HUGHIE LEE-SMITH. *TEMPTATION*. 1991. Oil on canvas, 48 x 36 inches.
Collection of Jarman and Barbara Holland. Courtesy of June Kelly Gallery, New York.

JAMES LITTLE. *HOMAGE EL SHABAZZ #5.* 1986.
Oil and wax on canvas, 34 x 34 inches. Courtesy of Janet M. Harrison.

finish. Also, often traces of pencil with which artists begin their drawings are visible. Later the drawn contours are accented with their chalks. Most evident is the wide range of pastel colors, varying from light and tinted hues to brilliant contrasts. The method of chalk application determines both color contrasts and surface textures. A soft, velvety, blended surface may be obtained in several ways, the most popular of which is crosshatching, first fully developed by the French artist Edgar Degas. In this method, colors are first stroked at an angle and covered with a fixative to dry; then the second layer of colors is placed at an angle to the lower layer. These strokes are separate and distinct from those of the layers below.

Sometimes, rather than crosshatching, artists prefer to use parallel diagonals to obtain flat tones and space. Corresponding colors in

BEVERLY BUCHANAN. *Summer*. 1988. Oil and pastel on paper, 38½ x 50¼ inches.
Private collection. Courtesy of Steinbaum Krauss Gallery, New York.

the spectrum give brilliant effects when juxta-posed. Orange, for example, is more brilliant when next to yellow. This is the intriguing quality of pastels. They can be soft and subtle, or, by contrast of color, they can be brilliant. Some pastels are slight and suggest much more than they state; others are highly finished works of art. Pastel drawings that merely hint at the subject matter seem to be most attractive to collectors. Studies of a head or of hands or of an unfinished nude are particularly popular.

Because pastels never adhere permanently to the surface of the paper, you should handle these works carefully. Glass and a variety of fixatives are most often used to protect them. Adverse chemical reactions of fixatives may, however, change the original tones of the pastel. For this reason, glass is usually the best protection.

James Porter, Jean-Michel Basquiat, Richmond Barthé, William Pajaud, Beverly Buchanan, Aaron Douglas, and Nanette Carter are artists who have used pastels.

TEMPERA

Tempera is a quick-drying paint made by mixing ground pigment with egg yolk or egg yolk plus egg white, and diluting it with water. Tempera was the most significant medium for painting on panel in Europe from the twelfth century until the fifteenth century, which saw the rise of oil paint.

History tells us that tempera, the medium used by the ancient Egyptians, is the oldest form of painting. A binding of colloidal or gelatinous material is necessary to make tempera paint.

Today's technique, which also utilizes egg yolks, is a direct, quick-drying process frequently favored for sketch work. Like pastel, tempera has gone through a revival during the last fifty years.

Tempera paints have a body like that of oils but tend to be more translucent. Color is of paramount importance. Generally, white is the solid background of tempera paintings, since it functions as light and is the neutral against which colors are blended. Unlike oils, which are mixed colors, tempera paints are usually pure colors. The artist generally blends them directly onto his surface, not on the palette. He blends them horizontally or vertically, often with crosshatching, so that you can see colors of one layer combined with those layers beneath. You can always detect the brush strokes, which delineate soft, subtle modeling and tones. Sketches or drawings, which are the artist's notes about placement and color, usually accompany the tempera painting.

Many artists execute temperas on cardboard or wooden panels, which often are better than absorbent canvases in achieving smoothness and richness. Also, the hard, immobile surfaces of cardboard and wooden panels are less liable to crack than canvas.

Tempera rarely reflects light and is therefore one of the best media for photographic reproduction. However, for the artist, it is a tedious and demanding medium; what an oil painter can do in one hour might take a tempera painter weeks to accomplish. Clementine Hunter, Bill Traylor, Sister Gertrude Morgan, Rex Gorleigh, Lois Mailou Jones, and Jacob Lawrence are some artists who have worked with tempera.

DRAWING

Drawn contours, outlines, and isolated marks distinguish our earliest pictorial images, those eloquent statements by prehistoric man. Drawing continues to be the truest record of the artist's thought, imagination, and personality. What the artist expresses in the finished oil is first stated, very likely with greater candor, in the preliminary drawing. Collecting drawings was of secondary interest at the turn of the cen-

WILLIAM PAJAUD. *TIGNON.* 1992.
Pastel, 14 x 31 inches.
Courtesy of M. Hanks Gallery, Los Angeles.

tury, but people now seem to have more appreciation for them.

Drawings are usually executed in pen or pencil, or the two combined. Artists often heighten or accent the features of a drawing with colored ink or sepia, an ink with a warm brownish tone. A coat of wash or water over a drawing makes it appear spontaneous, luminous, and transparent, much like a watercolor. Sepia affords extraordinary effects of light and atmosphere. Drawings may be rendered on any kind of paper—old or new, tinted or plain—with a surface able to retain pencil lead or ink.

A good original drawing should have movement, compositional order, a sense of depth, and an accomplished degree of modeling. Unlike graphics and painted art, a drawing has the ability to suggest more than is actually stated, or may lend an alluring animation to forms through precise and penetrating detail.

When drawings are studies for oils, they should have many of the characteristics of the finished oil. The drawings of Henry Ossawa Tanner, for example, have the same lush atmospheric quality as his oils. An artist seeks to delineate the essentials of form and action and, in this endeavor, may do thirty or forty drawing studies for an oil painting. It is important to keep in mind that artists are working out aesthetic problems and laying the foundation for their finished product, so distortion and exaggeration are not uncommon. Norman Lewis, Benny Andrews, Camille Billops, Charles White, Carole Bayard, Romare Bearden, Louis Delsarte, Eldzier Cortor, and Robert Blackburn are artists who have made beautiful and profound drawings.

WATERCOLOR

Watercolor is a pigment ground in gum, generally gum arabic, and applied with a brush and water to paper. Watercolors are transparent, which differentiates them from the more widely used, and thicker, oils. An oil painter produces his "white" and light with impasto, or layers of paint, but the watercolor artist usually does so by letting you see the white of his paper. Romare Bearden was a master of this device. The subtlety of the watercolorist's art lies in leaving out much of what the oil painter might amplify.

Good watercolors are fluid and fresh. Their composition holds a special delight for the viewer. You can usually distinguish the range of a single color within one watercolor, depending on the amount of water added in the primary color. Special atmospheric effects and textures can be achieved by wetting the paper before beginning work, or by applying the watercolor with a sponge or razor blade. Many artists draw their compositions in pencil before applying watercolor. Pencil marks are often visible beneath the surface of the watercolor. This in no way detracts from the finished work but presents an interesting linear contrast to the sensitive washes of color. While watercolors can be executed on almost any paper, rag papers of varying weights are best. The ability to recognize heavy rag papers ranging from fifty- or sixty-pound to two-hundred-fifty-pound weights will help you distinguish original watercolors from facsimiles, which are usually on a less textured, lighter paper. To attain the spontaneous quality of a good watercolor, the artist must create a first image that is essentially true, for compositions in this medium are hard to change. As a rule, the artist must try many times before completing a watercolor. Yet, like drawing, the watercolor is a medium that artists often use to execute major studies for important oil canvases. Watercolor is considered one of the most difficult media to master. James A. Porter, Richard Mayhew, Charles Davis, Lois Mailou Jones, Palmer Hayden, Charles Alston, and Hale Woodruff are artists who have works in this medium.

© Lois Mailou Jones

LOIS MAILOU JONES. *DESIGN FOR CRETONE DRAPERY FABRIC*. Circa 1932.
Tempera on paper, 30 x 21¾ inches.
Courtesy of Michael Rosenfeld Gallery, New York.

ELDZIER CORTOR. *PORTRAIT OF A WOMAN*. Circa 1947.
Pen and ink, 20 x 14$\frac{1}{2}$ inches.
Courtesy of Robert Henry Adams Fine Art, Chicago.

GOUACHE

Although the gouache is becoming a favorite medium among contemporary artists, it is in no way a modern medium. It has been used by artists for several centuries, and its name derives from the old Italian word *guazzo*, meaning puddle, or muddy pool. A gouache is essentially a quick-drying, opaque watercolor containing a special filler. The colors contain the same ingredients as watercolors, plus inert pigments that give a heavier and stronger appearance. Unlike watercolors, which should be executed quickly and without change, fast-drying gouache is an easy medium to handle.

Gouache has a paint quality produced by the thickness of the medium. A coat of varnish is often used over its fiberlike surface to enhance color intensity and enliven dark colors. Vivacity and freshness of color are the most easily recognizable qualities of this medium. If, however, the work lacks organization and development of form, spontaneity can become sloppiness. You must evaluate whether an original gouache achieves a successful balance of spontaneity and organization.

The amount of white paint and the degree of color intensity of a gouache determine the liveliness of color. As with oils, texture is paramount for gouaches; the three-dimensional layers of pigment enable you to see all the steps that have led to the completed picture. Since the medium dries quickly, the artist can work and rework the composition and achieve varied, unusual textures. Because of its versatility, artists often use gouache for experimentation and invention. Frequently the steps leading to creation of an oil painting include a drawing and a gouache. Gouaches originally used as sketch preparations are widely collected and highly prized. Jacob Lawrence is well known for his gouaches. William H. Johnson, Ellis Wilson, and Kara Walker have also worked in this medium.

MIXED MEDIA

Some artists combine oils, watercolors, pencil, pastel, and india ink within a single composition, often using guide lines for the drawing beneath. For instance, you will see drawings heightened with watercolor and further accented by colored chalks or gouache. Benny Andrews, Raymond Saunders, Jean-Michel Basquiat, Betye Saar, and Mary Lovelace O'Neal, among many others, work with mixed media.

PRINTS

Prints were first produced early in the fifteenth century. Prints are multiple originals and are more extensively distributed and easily secured than one-of-a-kinds. Today graphic prints are the most widely collected forms of original art. They are available at prices ranging from a few to thousands of dollars.

The beginning collector may misunderstand the term *print* because there are two popular uses: One refers to original graphic art, and another designates photographic reproductions. Prints that are lithographs, etchings, engravings, woodcuts, aquatints, and drypoints differ from photographic prints. The graphic artist does all the work on stone, the plate, or the wood block. Since the entire execution comes directly from the artist's hand, the work is unique and wholly original. Conversely, the artist has nothing to do with photographically reproduced prints that are used for posters. Printmaking will be explained in detail in chapter 6.

THE RARE PRINT

As a collector of fine prints, you should have an idea of what the word *rare* means. Generally, an art dealer using this qualifier in conversation means that there exist only about twenty or so examples of the etching or lithograph to which he

ROBERT REID. *Landscape—The Sea at Cameret-sur-Mer*. 1992.
Watercolor on Arches paper, 29¾ x 22½ inches. Courtesy of June Kelly Gallery, New York.

RICHARD MAYHEW. *Bayside Meadow*. 1995.
Watercolor on paper, 32 x 37 inches, signed.
Courtesy of Michael Rosenfeld Gallery, New York.

is referring. For some artists, rare can signify even fewer examples. For instance, you may discover that for work by Robert Blackburn, Georgette Seabrook Powell, Dox Thrash, James Lesesne Wells, and Wilmer Jennings, there may be only two or three impressions in existence.

Artists often make impressions for themselves without intending to distribute them publicly. Sometimes referred to as artists' proofs, these prints do find their way into the market; they, too, are rare prints, whether signed or unsigned.

ETCHING

The etching is one of the most popular forms of graphic art. It originated in northern Europe during the early sixteenth century. Essentially, this process requires that the artist cover a metal or copper plate with a coat of wax, and draw directly on the plate by cutting through the wax with an etching needle. He then submerges or dips the plate into an acid bath. The acid "bites," or eats into, the metal along the lines drawn with the etching needle, and causes furrows or

KARA WALKER. *INSURRECTION*. 1997. Gouache on paper, 60 x 42⅓ inches.
Courtesy of Wooster Gardens, New York.

grooves to appear in the metal. Successive bitings in an acid bath determine the thinness or thickness of the bitten line. Artists usually have to submerge the plate more than once to achieve the desired effects of light, shade, and accent.

After the acid baths the artist removes the wax from the plate and files the rim to a smooth finish, so as not to tear the paper during printing. To print, the artist covers the plate with ink, which runs into the etched furrows. Then, wiping the surface clean and using a simple handpress, the artist affixes a dampened piece of paper to the plate. Note that the transfer is in reverse; when you look at an etching or other form of printed graphic, you look at the reverse of the composition actually drawn on the plate.

Most etchings are black and white, but some artists work with colors, each of which requires an extra printing. In other words, if the two colors of an etching are red and blue, the artist first inks the appropriate section of the plate with red ink and prints it; he then cleans the surface, inks the section intended to be blue, and prints again in a similar fashion.

You can easily recognize original etchings by the rigid plate marks on the outermost edges of the paper. These appear as heightened and embossed edges surrounding the etching. If an etching is offered to you framed, be sure that this important characteristic is visible for your inspection. A facsimile of the plate mark is often produced photographically on reproductions. Two things will help you distinguish originals from facsimiles: first, feeling whether the plate mark is smooth and therefore photographed, or raised and therefore original; and second, noting whether the plate mark is visible from the reverse side of the paper, which is possible only on originals.

MARY LOVELACE O'NEAL. *Racism Is Like Rain*. 1991.
Mixed media on canvas, 6¾ x 11½ feet. Courtesy of Alitash Kebede Gallery, Los Angeles.

BETTY BLAYTON. *Untitled*. 1989. Monoprint, 22 x 30 inches.
Courtesy of Janet M. Harrison, New York.

The characteristic etched line does not decrease or increase in successive graduated stages. Its end is square, abrupt, and untapered. Develop a feel for its coarse texture and raised quality by gently running your fingertip over the etching. Always remember that the lines of the etcher's needle achieve all the effects of the composition, whether they are forms, or figures, or subtle tones of shadow. Henry Ossawa Tanner, Hale Woodruff, Wilmer Jennings, Claude Clarke, and Lois Mailou Jones are among the few African American artists who have made etchings.

ENGRAVING

Engraving originated in the mid-fifteenth century among the craftsmen of northern Europe as a technique for creating lines, forms, and designs by cutting the surface of wood, metal, and gold. Today, in a similar fashion, the engraver draws a composition on a metal plate by cutting lines or furrows with a burin, a small steel rod with a triangularly pointed end set at an oblique angle. This process is exceedingly slow, for the burin must scoop or cut deeply into the metal, not just scratch the surface (with etchings, the acid actually does the cutting).

The cut of the burin produces sharp, crisp lines. Whereas etched lines end abruptly, engraved lines taper gradually, as the amount of pressure placed on the burin causes the width of the line to vary. Engraved lines tend to be thinnest at the end. Moreover, the finished composition of an engraving is usually not as free flowing as that of the etching. A needle on wax can produce a line instantly, with only light scratching, and glides across the surface of the metal at the will of the artist. The engraver, however, must dig through the metal in a slower, more deliberate manner.

Engravings are printed much like etchings. The artist inks the furrows of the cut lines, then dampens a piece of paper with warm water, places it above the inked metal plate, and runs them both through a simple handpress. As with the etching, the image is in reverse, and a rigid plate mark surrounds the four edges of the engraving. The embossed edges are also visible from the reverse side.

Artists often use engravings to complete areas of an etching they have already started. In fact, the two processes are frequently combined, and it is often difficult even for experts to see which lines on a composition were etched and which were engraved. James Lesesne Wells, Charles Sallee, Wilmer Jennings, and Aaron Douglas have worked in this medium.

AQUATINT

The aquatint, an etching technique developed in the late eighteenth century, is essentially a tonal process based on the action of a resin that the artist delicately filters over the surface of an etched or engraved plate. By heating the plate and dipping it into an acid bath, the artist causes the surface on which the resin has been placed to become granulated, that is, covered with tiny holes. Then, inking the plate and printing from it, he creates a composition that combines the lines

CAMILLE BILLOPS. *I Am Black, I Am Black, I Am Dangerously Black*. 1980.
Etching, 23 x 31 inches. Courtesy of Printmaking Workshop, New York.

of the etching or engraving with the mottled tones of the aquatint. The tones vary according to the depths to which the different portions of the plate are bitten, and can reveal gradations from black to gray to white. The tones are characteristically opaque and often cause the aquatinted area of the work to resemble a flat piece of hammered antique silver. The effects of etching and engraving are created by lines; those of the aquatint, by tone, shadow, and masses. These different media are very often combined, and when we say aquatint we usually mean aquatint over engraving or etching. The aquatint rarely appears alone. When placing it over another medium, an artist is said to be "combining techniques." Eldzier Cortor, Lawrence Arthur Jones, Hayward Oubre, Aaron Douglas, and Dox Thrash are a few who have worked in this medium.

DRYPOINT

Drypoint, which resembles engraving and etching, was first executed in Germany in the late fifteenth century. Unlike the acid-bitten line of an etching, the drypoint results from the dry scratched line. To create a drypoint, the artist sketches directly on a bare piece of metal. Using a needle with a steel tip set with a diamond, ruby, or other hard precious stone, the artist scratches the surface of the metal and leaves an identifiable, irregular ridge on either side of every line. This ridged line is either saw-edged, razor-edged, or knife-edged, depending upon the direction of the drypoint and the pressure the artist applies as he works. The printing of the drypoint is similar to that of etchings and engravings. The metal plate is printed in reverse on a simple handpress.

You can recognize the drypoint line by its rich, velvety feel, by a softness that neither the etched, acid-bitten line nor the burin line of the engraving can capture. Like the aquatint, the drypoint is often an adjunct to etching. You will find that some compositions combine all three techniques—as in the etching further defined by the drypoint and heightened by the aquatint.

WOODCUTTING

The woodcut is the earliest-known printing process. Its potentials were first exploited in China during the T'ang dynasty of the eighth century and in Europe during the early fifteenth century. The woodcut remained popular among printmakers until the introduction of the daguerreotype in the nineteenth century. The color woodcuts produced in Japan and China during the latter part of the nineteenth century greatly influenced contemporary development of the technique. During the twentieth century, the linoleum, or linocut, emerged as a quicker and easier technique. However, the woodcut continues to be a major form of graphic art. Wilmer Jennings and Hale Woodruff are among its chief exponents. Elizabeth Catlett is one of many artists who make linocuts.

Original woodcuts differ markedly from lithographs, etchings, and engravings. The woodcut is a relief process, where the image is raised from the wood, while the others involve an intaglio method, which means that the drawn lines are incised or engraved. The woodcut is very simple to print, and requires only a hand-roller press. The woodcutter first draws directly on the surface of the wood block, which is usually cherry wood, seven-eighths of an inch thick. The artist uses burins, gouges, chisels, and other special tools to cut away the wood with the grain and raise the composition in relief on the block. The design areas that are left in relief are called "black," or positive, areas; those areas around the design that are cut away are the "white," or negative, areas.

After cutting, the artist inks the wood block with either black or colored ink. If the woodcut

WILMER A. JENNINGS. *DEAD TREE*. 1946.
Wood engraving, 10 x 7½ inches.
Courtesy of Kenkeleba Gallery, New York.

HAYWARD L. OUBRE. *Entanglement.* 1946.
Aquatint etching, 7 x 6 inches.
Courtesy of Sragow Gallery, New York.

is to have more than one color, he must make an additional block for each color. The pigments for colored woodcuts are ground in water and applied to the block like a paste.

Black and white woodcuts are most easily identified by the interplay of solid areas of blacks and whites. Woodcuts present form in silhouette. You can feel a variety of textures by touching them. These textures, from the grain of the wood, are an integral part of the artist's expression. The hand-printed woodcut is most often rendered on white Japanese rice paper, which you can recognize by the watermark lines approximately three-quarters of an inch apart over the entire surface. This paper retains color pigments whose penetration you can see from the reverse side of the composition. The color is not only a surface effect but also part of the paper.

The color woodcut can also be recognized by its color gradation, which is determined by the amount of pigment and water applied to the thin rice paper. Become familiar with this richness of color. When an original color woodcut is held to the light, its shading should be deepened and enhanced. You should examine a woodcut in both artificial light and daylight, since it will look different in each. See it, too, in the position in which it will be hung on your wall. Margaret Burroughs and Allan Rohan Crite were among those who worked in this medium during the Works Progress Administration (discussed further in chapter 6).

LITHOGRAPHY

The lithograph originated in Bavaria in 1796 with the unique discovery by Alois Senefelder that grease and water do not mix. *Lithograph* comes from the Greek words *lithos*, "stone," and *graphein*, "to write." To execute a lithograph, the artist draws his composition directly on a prepared slab of porous limestone with crayons,

which contain a resin or wax. He then applies ink, which adheres only to the places covered with the crayon. To print, he usually works with a professional skilled in the complicated process of "pulling," or printing, lithographs. The lithographer will clean the stone with acid and water prior to each pull.

When photography was introduced in the mid-nineteenth century, interest in lithography declined. The form, however, was revitalized by the Impressionists in the 1870s and 1880s. America's interest in lithography developed in the early decades of the twentieth century, inspired by European American artists like George Bellows, Raphael Soyer, and Thomas Hart Benton, to name a few. Early collectors favored works by members of the School of Paris—Braque, Picasso, Chagall, Léger, Rouault, Matisse, Severini, and others, who developed lithography into an art form that to this day rivals oil paintings in appeal and popularity. Many African American artists work in this medium today, including Eldzier Cortor, Charles Alston, John Thomas Biggers, Samella Lewis, Elizabeth Catlett, Robert Blackburn, John Wilson, Moe Brooker, Hilda Brown, and Louise E. Jefferson.

If you look at a lithograph stone and then see an original lithograph printed from it, you will find that the vividness and spontaneity of the drawing on the stone are always transferred to the print. This liveliness cannot be achieved by the photographic reproduction, and is thus a distinguishing trait. You will also observe the mark of the outer edge of the lithograph stone around the edge of the printed lithograph. Although it is not so easily distinguished as the plate mark of an etching, its presence can help you detect an original. Contemporary lithographs are generally rendered on Arches paper or Rives paper, heavy papers having a textured grain. By holding the paper up to the light, you can see the watermark of the printed words *Arches* or *Rives*. During the

MICHAEL KELLY WILLIAMS. *Beaubien Side*. 1989.
Woodcut, 11 x 14 inches.
Courtesy of Printmaking Workshop, New York.

printing the grain in all areas pressed by the lithograph stone is flattened. You can look for the juxtaposition of flattened and regularly grained areas on the paper. Look, too, for some slight relief, or raising of color, above the surface of the paper. This is usually good evidence of an original.

Lithographs can also be distinguished by the inklike odor almost always present, even years after printing. Also, original lithographs have subtle and widely ranged tones and textures never captured in mechanical reproductions. No method can duplicate the deep blacks and intense, rich colors of hand-printed original lithographs.

An original lithograph is an artistic creation. Instead of creating a painting with brush and oils, the artist has to master the technique and tem-perament of the plate and inks as "tools" to create his work of art. This is why original fine art lithographs should never be confused with offset lithograph reproductions, which are simply copies of something else. Newspaper or magazine printings are common examples of the offset process. The colors in hand-pulled lithographs are solid, while the colors in offset lithographs are made up of thousands of tiny dots. A quick way to tell the difference between most hand-pulled lithographs and most offset lithographs is to look at each through a magnifying glass. Dots will be evident on the offset lithograph.

Here is how a lithograph is made:

1. The artist draws directly on the plate or stone with greasy wax crayon. Wax pencils or grease-based inks (tusche) may also be used. Almost any

drawing style, from a wash tone to a fine line, can be produced in a lithograph.

2. Plates are then conditioned with gum arabic so that the nonimage area will repel ink. Here the plates rest on a slab of Bavarian limestone, mylar, aluminum, or zinc, which itself can be used as a printing surface.

3. The printer mixes each ink color to the artist's specifications. The grease-based inks naturally adhere to the waxy image but are repelled by moisture. So, the nonimage areas must be kept damp.

4. The printer carefully inks the images on the plate. Each plate is inked and sponged two or three times before each printing is made. The printer must be able to determine the optimum amount of ink needed.

5. The printer checks to see if the image is fully inked. Through a magnifying glass one can see the actual texture of the printing plate or stone, a texture that will be repeated in the lithograph.

6. Register marks on each stone are carefully aligned with register marks on the paper to assure perfect placement of the color images. If a lithograph has five colors, each print will be registered and printed five times.

7. A print with the first color applied is removed from the press. The press works by means of a sliding bed that moves under a wood-and-leather scraper. This scraper applies the pressure necessary for proper impressions.

8. The artist can make corrections directly on a plate using the greasy wax drawing materials. To

JOHN WILSON. *DELIVER US FROM EVIL*. 1943.
Graphite on paper, 21 x 19 inches, signed.
Courtesy of Sragow Gallery, New York.

correct an image, the printer must recondition the plate so that it will accept drawing material again (see step 2).

9. Throughout the proofing of a lithograph, the artist and the printer confer until the images please the artist.

10. When finished, prints are signed and numbered in pencil by the artist for distribution. When a lithograph has a white border, the signing usually is done there.

SERIGRAPHY SILK SCREEN SCREENPRINT

Serigraphy, which is basically a stencil process, has the oldest roots of any of the printmaking techniques. It is thought that some of the cave drawings of early man were done with stencils. In the Middle Ages stencils were used to enhance other prints. In seventeenth-century England flocked wallpaper was made by applying adhesive via a stencil process. In colonial America objects were decorated with stencils that had "gaps," spaces caused by the bridges of paper needed to keep delicate designs from shifting. Japanese artisans solved this problem by attaching a fine but strong network of human hairs to fragile parts of the stencil, an idea that may well have inspired the adoption of fabric stretched over bars, "silk screens."

A popular method of sign making in the United States after World War I, this art form was first promoted by the WPA during the Great Depression. Carl Zigrosser, a noted art historian, gave the art its name, serigraphy, which was derived from the Greek *sericum,* "silk," and *graphein,* "to write."

Serigraphy is a "direct" printing process in which the image is not reversed from the screen to the print. Briefly, a screen of silk, nylon, or wire mesh is tightly stretched across a frame. A design is made in stencil form on the mesh by blocking out parts of the mesh. Those areas that remain "open" allow the ink to be squeezed through to the paper below and result in the final printed image. There are numerous methods of stencil making, including tusche-and-glue, where the artist draws the image on the screen with tusche, a greasy substance. The entire area is then coated with a glue, which will dry rapidly. The tusche dissolves and the hardened glue forms the stencil, which blocks out the nonprinting area.

Paper can also be cut into any shape and attached to the underside of the screen to serve as a block-out. A popular method is to use a series of acetate overlays for each color in the serigraph. The artist draws the desired image on the overlay with a light-blocking substance. The printer exposes the image from the overlay to the screen by allowing light to pass through the acetate to the screen. This process is called "cutting" the screen. A separate screen is used for each color.

Silk-screened reproductions are prepared in the same way, but with camera-produced screens. These works are reproductions of art originally done in another medium and are usually printed without the involvement of the artist. Commercial screen printing is used on wallpaper, tote bags, ceramic mugs, greeting cards, and advertising posters, among other things.

COLLAGE

Picasso and Braque have been credited with inventing collage during their Cubist period. Fragments of newspapers and preprinted patterns are pasted into their compositions to represent a tactile reality. Collage deliberately creates spatial disharmonies and incongruities of scale that provide exciting visual dynamics within the work.

NORMAN LEWIS. *SELF PORTRAIT*. 1946. Lithograph, 12¾ x 10 inches.
Courtesy of Sragow Gallery, New York.

ROBIN HOLDER. *Don't Call Me Momi Anymore IV.* N.d. Photo silkscreen and stencil monotype, 32 x 25 inches.
Courtesy of Marilyn Mars Gallery, Tampa.

Artists Romare Bearden, Sharon Sutton, David Driskell, and James Denmark integrate collage into their work.

TECHNICAL TERMS

The terms that follow will help you to know exactly what you are purchasing from a dealer or at auction.

Artist's proofs Before an artist makes an edition, whether limited or unlimited, he first pulls trial proofs. Usually the trial, or artist proofs as they are called today, were the first states of the work. Just as the numbering of an edition is penciled on the finished etching, artist proofs are labeled "artist proof" or, in French, *"Epreuve d'Artiste"* (often abbreviated "E.A."). There are many collectors who specialize in collecting artist proofs because they are the preliminary studies of the finished product.

Canceling Before the development of steel-faced plates in the twentieth century, the metal plates from which large editions were pulled could begin to show signs of wear by the time the printing was completed. Unfortunately, these plates have sometimes been used for printing long after the death of an artist, contrary to the artist's wishes. The resulting examples are often blurred, and the lines discontinuous, but your familiarity with the graphic media should help you identify the marks from a worn plate.

To prevent further use of a metal plate or stone after an edition has been printed, many artists now will cancel their plates at the completion of an edition by boring holes in them or otherwise marking the faces, thereby preventing unauthorized use. Sometimes cancellation proofs are then pulled to show that the edition has been completed and canceled.

Chop mark An uninked, embossed stamp on the lithograph that identifies the printer, artist, workshop, or sometimes a collector. Also called a blind stamp.

Collector's marks Collector's marks are usually found either in the margins or on the reverse side of etchings, drawings, engravings, and other works. They can appear as stamped initials, signatures, crests, coats of arms, names, letters, geometric patterns, intertwined forms, numbers, crosses, and other similar objects. Several public and private collections, including those of museums and artists, use these marks. You should look for them, as well as for gallery and exhibition labels, which are sometimes affixed to the back of a picture.

Collector's marks are like diaries for a particular work of art because they identify ownership of a work from the time it leaves the artist's hand until the present. You should understand, however, that only a limited number of the prints and drawings found in the market today bear such marks. This is because only a limited number of famous collectors used them, and it in no way means that an etching or drawing lacking such a mark is necessarily of inferior quality or fraudulent. Rather, when you do come across a collector's mark, it demonstrates the work's respectable chain of ownership.

Documentation Information available on the edition of a print: the artist's name, the printer's name, the location of the workshop, number of prints in the edition, date. Although this information has some importance to print collecting, the artistic value and condition of the print are more important.

Edition The total number of prints made of a specific image.

Estate signatures A signature that looks printed or stamped is usually an estate signature and should not be confused with a collector's mark. Estate signatures are placed on the artist's unsigned works by the executors of his estate. Upon the artist's death, these signatures label

DEBRA PRIESTLY. *CADDISWORM CHRONICLES #2*. 1995.
Mixed media on birch, 33 x 32 x 3 inches.
Courtesy of June Kelly Gallery, New York.

everything within the artist's collection as authentic. At the same time, unsigned works without studio or estate stamps do not depreciate their value. Very often, in place of the estate stamp, the artist's spouse or the executor will sign the unfinished product. Norman Lewis's widow signed a great many of her husband's unsigned works and placed her initials, "OBL" (Ouida B. Lewis), after the signature.

The Print Council of America defines an original print as follows: "The artist himself has created the master image on or upon the plate, stone, woodblock or other material for the purpose of creating the print. The impression is made directly from the said material by the artist or pursuant to his directions. The finished print is approved by the artist." Notice that this definition does not mention the artist's signature. However, most original prints made in limited editions are usually signed by the artist.

Limited and unlimited editions Etchings, woodcuts, engravings, lithographs, and other graphic forms are all original art. They are the artist's method of creating more than one example of a given work. In the marketplace, you will come across original etchings and lithographs in limited or unlimited editions. With unlimited editions, you cannot tell how many impressions of a given print were produced before the plate was destroyed, if it was destroyed at all. With limited editions, however, the artist numbers the set of prints he has pulled or printed. The number of impressions is information that should be available to the consumer.

Numbered editions The numbering of limited editions did not begin until the 1920s. Before this, artists usually noted in their personal files and records the number of examples they issued from etched plates or lithograph stones. Limited editions usually numbered in the lower left-hand corner in the order of their pull. They vary in size from editions of five prints to editions of as many as four hundred prints or perhaps even more. If an etching is numbered $4/50$, this means that the edition to which it belongs is limited to fifty examples, and this particular one is the fourth made by the artist. You might wonder about the value of print number $49/50$ as compared with that of print number $1/50$. Prints of high and low numbers are equally valuable, and in many instances a print with a higher number can be superior in quality and texture to a print with a low number. The number of a print, then, should never be a deciding factor in making a purchase. Besides, considering that an edition undoubtedly has worldwide distribution, each example is even more significant than the size of the edition might at first imply.

The signature People often wonder whether or not a work of art is more valuable or better authenticated when it is signed. Although authentic old-master etchings can be unsigned, the art-collecting public still seems to consider the signature an important criterion when purchasing oils, watercolors, lithographs, etchings, drawings, and all forms of art. Of course, the signature is never an automatic sign that a work of art is genuine. In fact, for graphics in particular, signing the finished product was not a common practice until the last century. However, anyone who would forge a work of art would also forge the signature.

A graphic work can be signed in two ways: First, the artist may sign the plate or stone; second, after the edition is pulled, each print may be signed, usually in the lower right-hand margin. Signatures have become important partly because of snob appeal and partly because of the artist's desire to distinguish his own works from those done by mechanical reproduction processes. Aaron Douglas, Henry Ossawa Tanner, and Edward Bannister signed most of their works. Other important artists like William H. Johnson did not.

In general, artists take great pride in signing works of art. The majority of limited editions are signed by the artist in pencil in the lower right-hand margin. However, some Beardens bear his signature in the upper right-hand corner, running both vertically and horizontally.

The signatures of artists with permanent, career-long representation in a single gallery are usually well known by their dealers. For example, ACA Galleries in New York handles the Bearden estate, and through long familiarity with the artist's work, can authenticate any Bearden drawing or study brought to their attention. Similarly,

BARBARA E. THOMAS. *No Innocence*. 1995.
Egg tempera on paper, 22 x 30 inches.
Courtesy of Francine Seders Gallery, Seattle.

to verify a Jacob Lawrence, collectors can turn to the D. C. Moore Gallery in New York and the Francine Seders Gallery in Seattle. Any gallery that handles an artist's work exclusively is a good source of verification.

Signed and numbered At the bottom of each print in an edition, the artist pencils in his signature and numbers the print. The numbering appears as one number over another: for example, $^{15}/_{30}$, which indicates that a work was the fifteenth print to be signed and that there were thirty prints in all.

State (as in first state, second state, etc.) While an artist is pulling proofs of an etching, he may make changes or corrections that alter the plate. Each time a plate is changed, it is said to be in a state.

Tusche A greasing ink used in drawing on the lithographic plate or stone. Tusche can be applied in almost any method of drawing to produce a variety of drawing textures. Greasy wax crayons are often used as a tusche, as well as a liquid tusche, which gives the print the look of a watercolor.

CHARLES ALSTON. *LOVERS*. 1947.
Pastel and charcoal, 29 x 24½ inches.
Courtesy of Alitash Kebede Gallery, Los Angeles.

JOHN BIGGERS. *FAMILY ARK TRYPTYCH.* 1992.
Lithograph, 33 x 46 inches.
Courtesy of Lewallen Contemporary Gallery, Santa Fe.

JOHN McDANIEL. *THE WASHING*. 1995.
Charcoal on paper, 40 x 50 inches.
Courtesy of Sande Webster Gallery, Philadelphia.

ARCHIBALD J. MOTLEY, JR. *Cocktails*. Circa 1926.

Oil on canvas, 32 x 40 inches.

Courtesy of Michael Rosenfeld Gallery, New York.

3
DOLLARS AND SENSE

I learned that to merely be right analytically is not a

guarantee of success. Human factors are important. What

differentiates a man from a machine is the fact that he is

driven by passion, hopes, dreams and fears. It's the merging

of all these elements on a particular project that produces

the synthesis that's necessary for success.

REGINALD F. LEWIS

The one who asks questions doesn't lose his way.

AKAN PROVERB

ooking and learning about art does not require prior experience. However, purchasing art does, together with skill, money, research, perseverance, and common sense. Successful collectors carefully balance these variables to ensure that they spend their money wisely.

Typically, art lovers spend a great deal of time in both galleries and museums. Most gallery visiting and art buying occurs between mid-September and late May. Be aware that many galleries are closed on Mondays and during the summer. Those that do remain open for business in the summer can afford you the opportunity to browse in solitude and leisure, since patronage greatly decreases from June through August.

KERRY JAMES MARSHALL. *WATTS 1963*. 1995.
Acrylic collage on canvas, 114 x 135 inches.
Courtesy of Jack Shainman Gallery, New York.

Successful collecting depends upon where and how art treasures are bought. There are literally hundreds of sources you can utilize to begin or continue collecting.

While New York is one of the leading art capitals of the world, there are growing centers in Detroit, Chicago, Los Angeles, Philadelphia, San Francisco, Houston, San Diego, Washington, D.C., Dallas, Boston, Charleston, and Atlanta. The art market is unique in that dealers, regardless of location, know almost instantly when pictures are sold. Also, dealers who have good reputations are known among their colleagues and even among collectors, all of whom can offer you the benefit of their experience. The best way to familiarize yourself with galleries and their offerings is to spend time visiting and revisiting those that appeal to you. Use these visits to acquaint yourself with dealers with whom you are comfortable and who seem to be respected by other art sellers and by collectors. Reputable and knowledgeable gallery owners can be invaluable sources not only of art but also of information and advice.

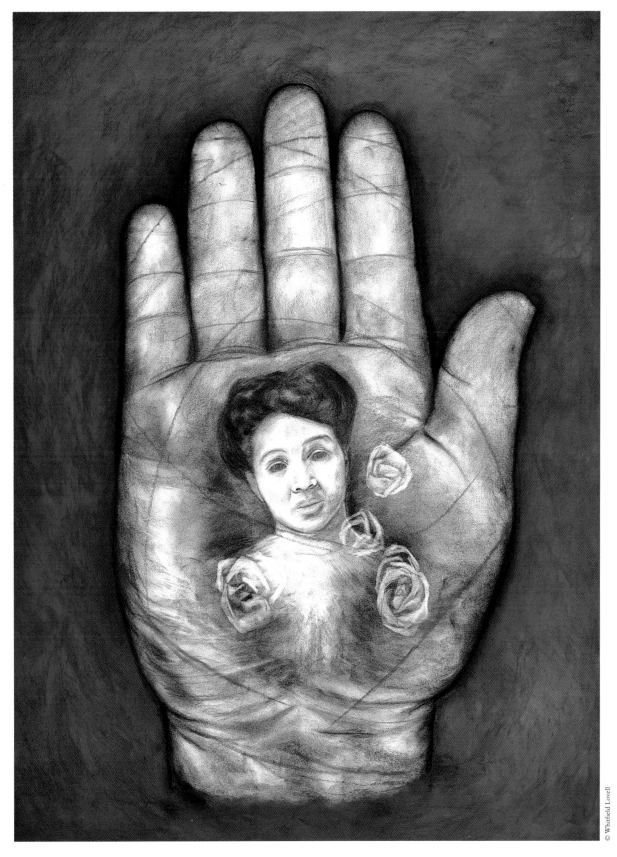

WHITFIELD LOVELL. *HAND VIII*. 1995. Oil stick and charcoal on paper, 54 x 40½ inches.
Courtesy of D. C. Moore Gallery, New York.

Some dealers stock what is referred to as general and varied inventory, which means a variety of artists, subject matter, media, and periods of art. Others carry a select or limited number of individual artists, commonly called a stable of artists, whom they sponsor and feature exclusively. You are more likely to find a greater variety of an artist's work if that artist is represented by one particular dealer. Some galleries combine both types of inventory, offering a general selection and also featuring special artists in their stable. Many black-owned galleries work with a variety of artists who are not under an exclusive contract with them. If you are looking for work by a specific artist, you should inquire at the gallery that exhibits the artist's work. Some galleries are known for their specialization in African American art; see the appendix for a comprehensive listing.

If you have never frequented art galleries before, you should start by visiting as many as possible. Galleries are public places, and unlike most museums, they do not charge admission. Some will have a greater appeal to your taste and budget than others. The more time you spend, the more familiar you become with the different types of galleries, the featured artists, and aesthetic schools of art.

HOW TO PRICE AN OBJECT

Intrinsically a work of art has no set value. It is worth whatever someone is willing to pay for it. Astute collectors and dealers have developed a way to estimate the value of a work of art before they buy or sell it. A primary determinant of the price for art revolves around the well-known law of supply and demand: There is a relationship between the scarcity of an artist's work and the rise in its price.

In addition, the artist's reputation and track record are to be considered. The work of new artists usually has lower prices than that of their better-established colleagues, who have both a reputation and a developing market. The classification of an artist as emerging, mid-career, or established is determined not by age, but rather by a set of variables that include quality, universal appeal, track record, aesthetics, the artist's developmental maturity, and the dealer's confidence in the artist's saleability. Taken together, these perspectives shape the marketplace and influence dealers' decisions about which artists they will exhibit and how they approach developing a greater market for their artists.

Prospective collectors typically ask: What is this work worth? How can I arrive at the best price? How do I protect myself from paying more than what the work is worth? Complete answers to these questions combine several variables that help determine the final price of any work of art. It is essential to know what parameters should be considered in the overall price determination process, such as:

Quality A key factor at every level of the art market, especially for the collector!

Style A particular or characteristic mode of execution that artists develop throughout their careers.

Artist If an artist is in a gallery dealer's stable, the dealer usually receives one-third to one-half of the selling price of the artist's work. The artist receives the balance. After the artist's death, his estate usually continues to receive the same percentage, but the selling prices often change markedly. If the artist was successful during his lifetime, the prices tend to rise immediately. With time, they will either level off or increase as scholars, curators, and critics write more about the artist and reevaluate his work. After Romare Bearden, Charles Alston, Norman Lewis, Bob Thompson, William H. Johnson, and Charles

White died, the prices of their work in all media increased 30 to 50 percent. When an artist can no longer produce, the prices his work commands again are subject to supply and demand. It is important to understand that generally when an artist dies, his work does not automatically fetch higher prices. In some cases the market will remain steady for a while and slowly increase, while in others the artist may be quickly forgotten. Be careful about buying speculatively right after an artist's death.

Typicality Most often a typical style emerges from an artist's later mature works, rather than early exploratory ones. For example, an artist like Romare Bearden is best known for his collages. Yet his abstract and cubistic works reflect his developmental explorations. Today these works are not considered "typical" of this artist.

Rarity A significant factor in an arena where supply and demand applies. Specific works of art tend to be expensive if they are in heavy demand or if they are hard to find. By "supply," we mean the overall quantity of an artist's work in existence.

Historical importance When illustrations in standard reference books become practically synonymous with the artist, the works acquire historical importance; examples are *Banjo Lesson* and *The Thankful Poor* by Henry Ossawa Tanner. These historically important works are considerably more valuable even than other works of comparable quality by the same artist.

LOIS MAILOU JONES. *Arreau-Hautes Pyrenees Villa.* 1951. Watercolor, 19 x 24 inches.
Courtesy of Essie Green Galleries, New York.

CHARLES ALSTON. *PALAVER*. 1948. Oil on canvas, 30 x 24 inches.
Courtesy of Bellevue Gallery, Trenton.

With a historically important work, the collector benefits from acquiring both a fine work of art and a piece of history. Although few collectors are in a position to buy historically famous paintings, most can benefit indirectly by looking for drawings that are studies for famous works, or prints based on them. These drawings and prints are worth more than other works by the same artist that lack historical cachet.

Certainty of attribution Knowing with certainty that an artist actually made a specific work gives the collector peace of mind. (See Authenticity, Provenance, and Signature and date.)

Catalogue raisonné A complete listing of an artist's work, generally by a noted scholar, with notes or commentary. Catalogues raisonnés exist for Henry Ossawa Tanner, Romare Bearden, William H. Johnson, and Ethan Alan Porter, and those for Jacob Lawrence and Richmond Barthé are currently in progress. As more and more scholars enter the field of African American art, we will see a growing number of comprehensive studies about individual careers and bodies of work. Visiting the public library is the best resource.

Authenticity Although cases of misattribution are rare in African American art, sometimes an artist intentionally produces a work in the style of a more prominent artist. The danger is that the price of the piece is based on its authenticity, and if this is questionable, the monetary value will plummet. Fakes and forgeries are every collector's nightmare, particularly if a piece has been purchased solely for investment purposes.

Fakes Fakes often begin as honest, straightforward copies. For example, a student in an artist's workshop makes a copy of the master artist's work. Later, long after it has passed from one collector to another, the piece may end up on the market as the work of the master artist.

Provenance The provenance of a work is its pedigree and lists all of the work's previous owners, ideally back to the artist. A work of known provenance is perceived as more valuable than an "orphan" work, whose origins are obscured. Scholars use provenance, along with scientific and visual data, to attribute a work to the appropriate artist.

Condition Since quality is everything in collecting art, the condition of the work is especially important. If you happen to locate both a superb impression of a print in poor condition and a poor impression of a print in superb condition, you must first decide how much you like the work itself. This is always the bottom line in collecting art. The price may be proportionately lower if the work is less than perfect. However, if the dealer has taken measures for its repair or cleaning, the price may be higher. If you decide to purchase something knowing that you will have to improve its condition, you should factor this expenditure into the dealer's price. A low price due to imperfections could be appealing, but depending on the damage, the repairs by a skilled restorer can be costly. Cleaning drawings, oils, and prints can cost from $35 to $100 an hour. Tears, stains, and water stains (also referred to as foxing marks) on paper can be patched or removed, but again the process is costly. Similarly, oil paintings can be repaired, restored, varnished, and even retouched, but only by well-paid experts. According to the American Institute for Conservation of Historic and Artistic Works, the daily rates of individual and institutional conservators can range from less than $500 to more than $2,000.

Medium The medium is simply the materials the artist used to make a given work.

Subject Preferences for the subject matter of works of art vary from collector to collector. However, art offers a range of subjects—landscapes, still lifes (especially floral pieces), portraits of ancestors and strangers, animals, religious subjects, violent subjects, political protest, or satire. If an artist is well known for portraying a particular subject, his works that depict this easily recognizable theme will command higher prices.

Size Although paintings are not sold by the square inch, the size of a work may affect its price, depending on the market value of other works by the same artist. The relative size of a work does not mean that it is more or less significant than others produced by a particular artist. Size is completely determined by the artist's preferences and/or resources. When buying pictures, your comparative pricing should be based on works by the same artist that are of equivalent or similar size. If you have two drawings of equal aesthetic appeal, there will be a relative price difference if one is significantly larger than the other.

Signature and date Collectors tend to prefer signed and dated work because they are more verifiably authentic. By signing a work of art, the artist verifies its origin. Generally, a work that is signed and dated is thought to be worth more than one that is not, assuming, of course, that the signature and date are authentic. However, you should be aware that some of the most highly prized work may not be signed. Henry Ossawa Tanner, Edward Bannister, Aaron Douglas, and Robert Scott Duncanson have all produced a few works that do not bear their signatures. Signatures tend to be more important for prints and photographs because many images can be made from the plate or the negative.

© Eldzier Cortor

ELDZIER CORTOR. *STILL-LIFE: PAST REVISITED.* 1973.
Oil on canvas, 66 x 60 inches, signed. Private collection of Mr. John P. Axelrod, Boston.
Courtesy of Michael Rosenfeld Gallery, New York.

However, here again the signature depends to some extent on the practice of the individual artist. Often the artist not only signs his work on the plate or stone but also adds his name in pen or pencil to the margins of finished prints. This extra signature may raise the price of the work but not its artistic value. Do not deprive yourself of some of the most beautiful works ever produced simply because they are unsigned. The absence of a signature does not decrease the value of the work of art, especially if the work appeals to you.

Seller As a general rule, collectors should buy works from reputable art dealers and auction houses. This minimizes any misunderstandings and unethical business practices that can result in inflated prices.

Time of sale Most collecting takes place between September and May. Activity peaks before Christmas. Auction and dealer prices are lowest during the summer and highest during the fall, depending on the artist.

Publicity The price of a work may be affected by issues other than quality or skill: Publicity—that is, whether the artist has appeared in a museum show; has been cited in books, newspapers, magazines, and reviews; has a work that's been used on the cover of a book or journal—can have an impact on price. This kind of exposure increases the value of a work and allows the market to increase the price. It is to your benefit as a collector, and to that of the artists as well, to loan select works for museum exhibitions and to allow photographic reproductions for use in catalogues and journals.

Chance When all is said and done, there are times when the price of a work of art cannot be rationally explained. Therefore research and careful analysis are the best tools for assessing the value of a work of art. In the end, however, a work of art is worth whatever someone is willing to pay for it. Like other marketable commodities, art is governed by ever-changing styles and preferences for new artists and periods of art. Some artists can be very much in demand during one decade and can then lose favor in the ensuing years. Other artists remain popular because their distinctive styles remain classic. It is not unusual for highly acclaimed artists and groups of artists to lose favor, only to be revived years later and eagerly collected once again.

One of the more unusual aspects of the art market is that merchandise can regain lost value. Books, movies, articles, scholarly study, or museum shows can draw renewed attention to an artist or group of artists. Fluctuations in demand for certain kinds and styles of art often parallel prices at auction.

Many artists work in a variety of media, and prices for one medium are closely related to those for other media. For example, an artist commanding high prices for oils will most likely command a comparatively high price for graphics and watercolors. For example, the oil paintings, watercolors, and drawings of Hughie Lee-Smith, Emma Amos, Joe Overstreet, Nanette Carter, Sam Gilliam, and Mary Lovelace O'Neal are selling for thousands of dollars, and their graphic works command prices ranging from hundreds of dollars to a few thousand. You should also keep edition sizes in mind when looking at prices. The law of supply and demand applies here as well.

A few additional expenses are a part of the overall cost of a work of art. These expenses include packing and shipping, insurance, and taxes. Proper packing is essential for safekeeping and preservation. When you buy art, make sure that you or the dealer selects an experienced and reputable packer. Packaging charges are based on size, weight, and distance. Inquire in advance about the cost of properly shipping your art. After all, you have made a sizable investment and

© Joe Overstreet

JOE OVERSTREET. *Sound in Sight.* 1991.

Oil on canvas/collage, 54 x 43 inches.

Courtesy of Kenkeleba Gallery, New York.

ROMARE BEARDEN. *PASSIONS OF CHRIST*. Circa 1947.
Oil on canvas, 30 x 24 inches, signed.
Courtesy of Michael Rosenfeld Gallery, New York.

RICHARD MAYHEW. *WOODSIDE*. 1987. Oil on canvas, 46 x 56 inches, signed.
Courtesy of Michael Rosenfeld Gallery, New York.

you want to protect that investment. Don't be surprised if packing expenses exceed transportation expenses; materials and labor are costly.

City and state taxes must also be added to your purchase price.

WHERE TO BUY AND SELL ART

GALLERY DEALERS AND PRIVATE DEALERS

Contrary to the popular belief that art dealers are elitist, a good dealer can be both accessible and extremely helpful to a novice collector. An art dealer is anyone who buys, sells, and trades art. He or she may be an individual proprietor trading in a small stock and perhaps operating from home; or a dealer may be the common one-branch commercial gallery, a gallery with numerous branches or franchised outlets, or a member of a conglomerate. All dealers are aware of the Uniform Commercial code, a statute that applies to the assurance of authenticity. A good dealer willingly helps you choose the best work of art you can afford; takes pride in helping you develop your own expertise and taste so that you can begin to buy wisely on your own; willingly refers you to catalogues, books, and other source material to enable you to research specific pictures and develop your overall knowledge; willingly recommends other well-qualified dealers, when asked; willingly guarantees in writing the authenticity of any work of art he sells; and readily takes back any work he has sold you, for exchange and occasionally for cash, at least within certain limitations. Paintings by emerging or lesser-known artists are the exception to this last point.

Some dealers do not meet these standards and should be avoided. Fortunately, many excellent art dealers throughout the nation do. New York remains the leader in the diversity and quality of paintings. A striking indication of New York's dominance can be found in the directories of the International Fine Print Dealers Association and the Art Dealers Association of America, both exclusive, by-invitation-only industry organizations founded to promote the highest standards of connoisseurship, scholarship, and ethical practice within the profession and to increase public awareness of the role and responsibilities of reputable art dealers. The current directory of the Art Dealers Association of America lists 140 members, among them June Kelly of New York, the first professional of African descent to be invited into the organization. Of the more than 400 galleries in New York alone, fewer than 5 percent represent African American artists. Detroit, however, is to contemporary African American art what it once was to Motown. Its sales volume of contemporary African American artists exceeds that of any other city in the United States.

Choosing a dealer is similar to choosing any other professional, be it a doctor, lawyer, or stockbroker. Although no precise rule governs the selection process, experience and integrity are primary criteria, as are recommendations from other dealers and friends. Equally impor-

MINNIE EVANS. *MODERN ART*. 1963. Oil on paper, 14½ x 20 inches.
Courtesy of Luise Ross Gallery, New York.

tant are your instincts about the person: Do you feel comfortable working with this person? It is also important to keep in mind that the majority of dealers trade exclusively in a particular period or style of art—such as nineteenth- and early-twentieth-century paintings, or abstract, representational, or contemporary prints. Their specialty reflects a personal sensibility and bias that can promote a particular period or style as the best or only art to collect. To maintain perspective, try to do business with at least two or three dealers with varying viewpoints.

In the art market it is appropriate to ask one dealer about another. Some dealers recommend other galleries to visit when traveling to other cities in the United States. This may seem to be above and beyond the call of duty, but you have a right to expect a lot from any dealer with whom you are *actively* doing business. Some art dealers have galleries open to the public with set hours and others work by appointment only.

Overall, dealers tend to offer a much better selection of quality pictures than auction houses. Some dealers have a large inventory of work, while others work primarily on a commission basis, selling a painting for the owner or the artist. Usually, their prices include the price that the owner wants, plus a 20 to 30 percent commission for their time and expenses. Experienced collectors usually buy from both galleries and private dealers, and an occasional auction. Beginning collectors almost always confine their art buying to galleries, largely because a good dealer can be an excellent teacher.

EDWARD MITCHELL BANNISTER. *RIVER SCENE.* 1898.
Oil on canvas, 14 x 20 inches.
Courtesy of Schwarz Gallery, Philadelphia.

GEORGE ANDREWS. *The Old One Side Clock*. 1989.
Oil on canvas board, 16 x 12 inches.
Courtesy of McIntosh Gallery, Atlanta.

JACK WHITTEN. *SUMMIT*. 1987. Mixed media, 84 x 72 inches.
Courtesy of G. R. N'Namdi Gallery, Detroit.

ARLINGTON WEITHERS. *Sperm I*. 1995.
Acrylic on canvas, 48 x 40 inches.
Courtesy of Aljira Gallery, Newark, New Jersey.

CHARLES MOSBY. *UNTITLED.* N.d.
Mixed media on board, 20 x 15 inches.
Courtesy of Phyllis Kind Gallery, New York.

Haggling over prices is a part of doing business in the art market. Many collectors don't realize that the dealer's price isn't the only price. Even if you have never before worked with a particular dealer or broker, you can try to obtain a discount simply by asking. Although such discounts are common, they are not standard. The only way you can find out is to ask. Many dealers will trim 5 to 10 percent—or more—off their stated price (depending on the terms of their agreement with the artist, or the artist's estate, or any other commitments they have made). Therefore, you need not be shy about negotiating over the price once you have made a decision on a piece of art. In all circumstances you must respect the market value, the artist's value, and

the dealer's efforts on your behalf. There are two points that you should keep in mind when buying from a dealer:

1. Unlike doctors and lawyers, art dealers are not licensed or regulated in any tangible way. Anyone is free to enter this business, which means that the art market has more than its share of less-than-reputable dealers.

2. Art dealers are free to charge whatever the market will bear. An extreme example would be a dealer attaching a $10,000 price tag to what is essentially a $1,000 painting. If you pay the $10,000 without doing any research about the dealer or the artist, you have no recourse. Therefore, you must always have a sense of the

BESSIE NICKENS. *DOUBLE DUTCH*. 1997.
Oil on canvas, 18 x 24 inches.
Courtesy of Sragow Gallery, New York.

approximate market value before agreeing to a price. You can only gain this "sense" of a work's value by learning all you can about the artist.

If you are comfortable doing so, you may try to negotiate the best possible price using any of three approaches:

- Make an offer. If the quoted price is $2,000, you may offer $1,500 on a take-it-or-leave-it basis. Your offer may not be accepted, but you figure it's worth the try.
- Try to gain a price reduction of 10 to 15 percent. Ask for the price for three or four paintings, including one you specifically want, and then probe to see whether the dealer is willing to cut prices on any of them.

- Buy several works at once; and inquire whether larger discounts are available.

Although negotiating price is a part of the business, some dealers feel that a collector can push too hard with insulting and unreasonable offers. Ultimately a collector can lose favor with the dealer, thereby missing opportunities to purchase top work. As in everything in life, it is wiser to seek the middle ground. No collector wants to overpay, but bargain hunting is not the way to approach collecting African American art. It is primarily the lesser works that can be acquired at substantial discounts. The very best ones generally cannot, yet these are the works that usually offer the greatest long-term invest-

BERRISFORD BOOTHE. *Bittersweet Concerns*.
1993. Ink and acrylic on mylar,
40¾ x 16½ inches.
Courtesy of June Kelly Gallery, New York.

ment potential. The astute collector identifies two or three dealers with top merchandise and excellent credentials, works primarily with them, seeks price discounts and extended terms where feasible, but does not press so hard as to endanger his relationship. The goal is to view these dealers as partners rather than adversaries, but you must remain alert to make sure they aren't taking advantage of you.

Many dealers will hold on to top works for a few favored customers—collectors who usually pay quickly, appreciate good art, and do not haggle too much over the price. Clearly, not every collector is in a position to achieve favored status with a gallery, but for many this is a legitimate long-term goal. In fact, most dealers of African American art will nurture collectors. If you are convinced that a work is of incomparable quality, it may be worth it to secure the work, even if you have to pay the dealer a premium price.

Most dealers are willing to allow a collector to pay over a period of time, generally one to six months at no interest. Since banks are, for the most part, unwilling to finance works of art, dealers themselves handle sales and financing through informal payment arrangements. The buyer may choose either a price discount or an extended, interest-free payment plan.

On request, and based on their relationship with the buyer, most dealers are willing to hold a picture for two or three days, without any down payment, while a prospective buyer makes a decision; send a painting to a prospective buyer's home on approval; or take back any work, for cash or a credit, within a reasonable time— usually a few weeks. Again, these terms are all subject to negotiation. Understandably, the most active customers are generally able to extract the best terms, and this is especially true for home approvals, an opportunity usually reserved for select clientele who are contemplating the purchase of very expensive works.

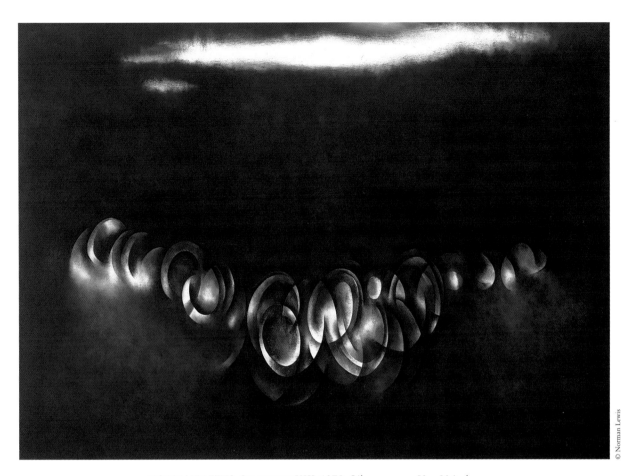

NORMAN LEWIS. *SEACHANGE XIII*. 1975. Oil on canvas, 50 x 80 inches.
Courtesy of Bill Hodges Gallery, New York.

Since the primary rule in collecting art is to select what you like, many collectors will want a trial period. Many reputable art dealers provide, and even encourage, home approval with people who have established some track record for doing business with them. The benefit of a home approval is that it allows you to live with the selection for a few days and discuss it with your family and friends.

Comparison shopping is also a part of collecting art. The conscientious collector visits many galleries and comes to understand the characteristic subject matter, medium, and sizes of an artist's work; thus he has some way of comparing a particular work to similar examples at different sources. For example, a lithograph may be offered by a number of galleries or art brokers at an identical price, but for any number of reasons, one dealer may offer the same print at a better price. The difference may be just a few dollars or a quite significant sum, so it is often worth the search. Comparison shopping will allow you to select the best piece of an artist's work, and the money saved could go toward the purchase of a better-quality frame, which must ultimately be figured into the cost of your purchase. Comparison shopping specifically applies to cities and regions with significant concentrations of galleries or dealers. Certain kinds of art are common to certain areas, and prices vary accordingly.

Buying art directly from an artist is another option that should not be overlooked. Frequently artists sell their work directly to collectors. Although many established contemporary artists have dealers through whom their work is

ROBERT COLESCOTT. *Sunset on Bayou*. 1993.
Acrylic on canvas, 90 x 114 inches.
Courtesy of Phyllis Kind Gallery, New York.

sold, many more artists represent themselves and will sell their work directly. If an artist is not represented by a gallery, by all means buy the work that you like directly from that artist. But if you have been introduced to an artist by a dealer representing the artist, respect the protocol of the market: Make your inquiries through the dealer. By not cutting the dealer out, you are supporting and strengthening the market value of an artist's work. Consequently, the work will appreciate. If you disregard this protocol, you are not supporting the artist or the gallery, nor are you protecting your future investment. If you purchase art directly from artists, unless they are self-taught, try to buy from those who have had formal

training and at least some exhibition experience, and who are represented in some well-known collections. When you purchase artwork directly from an artist, buy from one about whose background and predicted future you have gathered some information. But most important, make sure that you *like* the work.

Categorizing an artist has to do with his visibility and place in the commercial marketplace and in prestigious private and museum collections, and is valid for the active artist who is simultaneously painting, exhibiting, and selling art to public and private collectors. It is in no way an overall criterion for determining the value of an artist's work, and there are, of course, always exceptions to the rule. Bear in mind also that often many of these designations are intended to promote the intellectual prowess of art historians and the conceptual visions of ambitious curators, and to build commercial markets for the benefit of art dealers.

As in the corporate arena, a glass ceiling stunts the growth of most American artists of African descent. These artists are not allowed to mature in the marketplace past a certain point. Therefore you will discover many artists who, after twenty years, remain in the "emerging" category, and others who are in "mid-career" for thirty years, regardless of the quality of their work or the level of their aesthetic development. The pecking order as determined by the art world at large has primarily championed Romare Bearden and Jacob Lawrence, artists with extraordinary careers and distinct bodies of work. Among the more widely acclaimed artists in the mid-career category are Sam Gilliam, Richard Hunt, Howardena Pindell, Betye Saar, Martin Puryear, Robert Colescott, and Benny Andrews.

If you find that you like an artist's style, you can also commission him or her to execute, for a specific sum, a work in a medium and on a subject that you both agree upon. Here again, if this artist is working with a gallery, ask your dealer to assist you. This does not mean that you will automatically have to pay more; in fact, you can often be assured of paying a fair price. Most artists prefer not to be commissioned by individuals. An exception are portrait artists whose entire livelihood comes from private commissions. Portraits, Inc., in New York has a stable of outstanding portrait artists. Among them is Sam Adoquei, who specializes in portraiture and is on the faculty of the New York Academy of Art and Design. A commission may also refer to the sponsorship of an art project by a major private or governmental organization.

BUYING AT AUCTION

The public auction is another place to purchase art, but for the collector of African American art, it is *not* a frequent stopping place. The primary reason is that none of the auction houses have expertise in African American art history and few artists have received sufficient international acclaim to participate in the world market.

At one time the auction was the exclusive domain of art dealers who bought works of art at auction and subsequently sold them to privileged collectors. Currently the public auction is exactly what its name implies—a public event to which all are invited to participate in the competition and bidding. Newspapers and many periodicals list exhibitions and sales that may be of interest to you. Plan to attend a public auction with a friend or partner, just to get a sense of how they function. You will find that they are both educational and fun.

The main advantage of buying at auction is not larger volume or greater objectivity, rather, it is lower prices. Collectors of all means turn to auctions in search of better prices than those they find at private galleries. Auction prices are approximately 10 to 50 percent below dealer prices. After all, the most active auction goers are the dealers themselves. By bidding against dealers for the same object, the collector can avoid the dealer's markup, which ranges from 5 to 50 percent, depending on the cost of the item. However, be aware that in exceptional circumstances the structure of the auction house can reverse itself and push the price of a painting higher than what you may pay at a gallery. This is least likely to happen with African American art, because the auction market has not caught up with the rest of the marketplace for African American art.

The work that is sold at an auction house usually belongs to a private owner, a dealer, or an estate that is liquidating a given artwork or collection of art. The seller is charged a commission for the services of the auction house. In the United States commissions vary from 6 to 20 percent of the selling price, depending on whether the seller is a private collector, a museum, or a dealer. The private seller pays 20 percent on the first $2,000, 15 percent on $2,001 to $7,000, and 10 percent on sales exceeding $7,000. Dealers' fees are in increments of 15 percent, 10 percent, and 6 percent. Museums' fees are in increments of 15 percent, 10 percent, and 5 percent. All good auction houses prepare catalogues for each of their sales. These documents give information about each work, including its artist, title, medium, size, subject matter, general appearance, and former owners. Catalogues are available at the pre-auction exhibition. Attending pre-auction exhibitions is extremely important, along with consulting the sale catalogue, because buying at an auction is strictly at your own risk. There is no such thing as a return at a public auction. Read the terms of the sale, which you will find at the beginning of all auction catalogues; study their specific objectives and conditions, and especially the sections on authenticity, provenance, and history of ownership or place of origin. A work is not always guaranteed to be authentic just because it comes from a public or well-known collection. Therefore, a work whose prior ownership is noted usually sells more quickly than one that is auctioned anonymously. In essence, the auction house functions as a selling agent.

Once you have received and studied an auction catalogue, you should visit the exhibition of the works listed in it. These exhibitions precede the sale for a specified time, perhaps three to five days, and are open for your inspection. You can bring any expert whom you may want to appraise the work and also to give you estimates of the anticipated prices for the actual sale. You should record these figures in your catalogue next to each corresponding item. When the actual bids are made at auction, you can see whether the estimates were high or low and what has been the general trend in prices. As a general rule, auction prices are about 80 percent of the market prices on similar items but do not include the same assurances and guarantees. As a specific rule, auction prices for African American art do not yet have a consistent track record and are far behind the rest of the African American art market. We can expect this rule to change as this previously ignored population within the American art community is integrated into the collections of art collectors at large.

Here is a set of guidelines for buying art at an auction:

- Subscribe to catalogues for the type of art that interests you: contemporary paintings, prints, et cetera. Catalogues are mailed out to subscribers three to four weeks in advance of the auction, and they provide the best way for prospective bidders to monitor what is coming up for sale.
- Leaf through each catalogue and look at price estimates. Sotheby's and Christie's always include an item-by-item list of estimates; most other auction firms do not. If there is no formal list, you can call or write to the auction house to request estimates on specific items of interest, or you can ask in person.
- Always inspect an item carefully *before* buying, not after. If you are unable to attend the pre-auction display, you can phone and ask for details about the condition of the specific items, or you can write and ask for a written statement. The catalogue contains brief descriptions; use it as a starting point for a more thorough in-person inspection.
- Always read the terms of the sale at the front of the auction catalogue.

MOE BROOKER. *Ain't Nothing But a Maybe*. 1994.
Oil on canvas, 72 x 54 inches.
Courtesy of Malcolm Brown Gallery, Shaker Heights, Ohio.

JOE OVERSTREET. *Tension Series/Black Star Line*. 1990.
Oil on canvas, 54 x 43 inches.
Courtesy of Kenkeleba Gallery, New York.

- Never accept presale estimates as gospel.
- Determine your absolute top bid on each item in advance and then stick with it no matter how heated the action gets. If you are susceptible to "auction fever," you may be better off sending in your bids rather than attending in person. Any reputable auction house will handle the bidding on your behalf, buying your lots as inexpensively as the competition permits and in no case exceeding your maximum. Approximately a third of most bidders do not attend in person.
- If you are the winning bidder, be sure to pick up the item as soon after the auction as possible in order to minimize the chances of damage.

LEGAL CONSIDERATIONS

People often wonder when, or if, a legal case can be made if they purchase a fraudulent work of art. Legally, art is a commodity to be traded in the marketplace, and the purchase of art is a commercial transaction.

Buying art at auctions is done solely at the buyer's risk. All reputable auction galleries state in the front of their catalogues that they are making no representations as to the authenticity of the artworks offered for sale. This "no representation" language is repeated publicly by the auctioneer at the beginning of the sale. It clarifies one of the conditions of the sale, and the bidder has no cause for complaint if he or she discovers afterwards that the item bought is a fake. If you are trying to locate a bargain at an auction, be as certain as you can about the work's authenticity before you purchase it. It will be too late to do so after the sale.

You are usually on safe ground when buying from a knowledgeable dealer. Although even the most reputable dealer can, unknowingly, make mistakes, he does not make a "no representation" claim and must accept returns of purchases discovered to be fakes, or appear in court if sued. The best thing to do is to have the dealer state on the invoice, bill of sale, or receipt an exact description of the work, the artist's name, and the medium. These papers, along with other statements of ownership and exhibition, are important evidence of provenance, and are meaningful records for resale purposes. You should always save these documents and leave in place any gallery stamps or museum labels affixed to frames or elsewhere on the art. If you have anything reframed, instruct the framer to replace the stickers on the new frame.

Clearly, transactions with dealers are different from those at auctions. At the auction the guiding principle is "Let the buyer beware," but with a dealer it is usually the opposite. You rely on the dealer's representations, and in most cases, he must substantiate them. However, sometimes a dealer may not be sure of the authenticity of the artwork, particularly an unsigned piece. The reputable dealer will tell you so. Like the auctioneer, the dealer may say, "We think that this is a Bannister, but we are not sure." The work may reflect Bannister's style, stroke, or subject matter, but no one is certain that he executed it. Under these circumstances it is up to you to decide whether you want it badly enough to buy it. If you do, enjoy it and don't try to return it. You can't.

SELLING WORK FROM YOUR COLLECTION

Why would you ever want to sell a work from your collection after you have taken so much care to acquire it? One reason is money. A second reason is changing tastes. When you first began to collect, you liked landscapes, and now you prefer Color-Field abstractions. A third reason is that when you first started to collect, you were attracted to a mediocre line drawing, and now you want to sell it for a better one by the same artist. Museums also sell work from their collections for similar reasons. They call it "deacquisition." Whatever your reason may be, selling art is difficult, partly because of your emotional ties to the work and partly because of the selling process itself.

One of the first steps in selling a work is to have it appraised. It is important for you to know how much the painting or print is worth before you decide how much to accept for it. There are two types of appraisal: official and unofficial. If a work is compared with similar items, this is an unofficial appraisal, which can come from someone who knows more about the artist and work than you, like your dealer. In this case, you can send a description and a photograph to a dealer, auction official, or museum curator, or better yet, take the piece to the expert if you can. Most of them will be happy to tell you unofficially what the work is worth.

How can you locate a competent appraiser? Usually gallery dealers can provide an accurate appraisal of work that they represent or are familiar with. Dealers also can recommend official appraisers they work with. Occasionally the auction houses can offer some assistance, but in the case of African American art, most auction houses do not possess the necessary expertise. Often they confer with dealers who are more familiar with the artists. Museum curators are another good source. You can also contact the Art Dealers Association of America or one of the two appraisers' associations: the American Society of Appraisers and the Appraiser's Association of America. ASA is the more respected group because it has an elaborate entrance examination and a required program of continuing professional education. Once you have a list of candidates, you should interview them. The American Society of Appraisers emphasizes the importance of checking an appraiser's credentials: special expertise, membership in professional associations, and prior experience.

An appraisal should be recorded in writing and should include the following items:

1. Date of the appraisal
2. Client's name and address
3. Purpose of the appraisal
4. Statement of disinterest
5. Artist's name
6. Title of work
7. Exact size
8. Medium
9. Support
10. Signature and/or date
11. Condition
12. Complete description
13. Provenance
14. Exhibition history
15. Bibliography
16. Special conditions affecting valuation
17. Statement of corollary opinions
18. Sales record
19. Value
20. Photograph, preferably color
21. Appraiser's qualifications
22. Appraiser's signature

It is best to prepare for an appraisal well in advance. Assemble as much of the information listed above as possible, including a photograph of the object. Be aware that an appraiser can sometimes overstate the value of an object to account for inflation; therefore, you should periodically update your appraisals every three to

DAVID DRISKELL. *IMAGES OF ANCIENT MASKS.* 1995.
Collage and mixed media on paper, 11½ x 8½ inches.
Courtesy of D. C. Moore Gallery, New York.

TODD WILLIAMS. *Untitled.* 1994.
Mixed-media construction on paper, 22¼ x 30 x 2¼ inches.
Courtesy of Peg Alston Fine Arts, New York.

four years or so, depending on the inflation rate.

Besides becoming the basis for proper and responsive insurance policies, appraisals can be invaluable in other ways. An appraisal can help someone writing a will to make equitable distributions. An appraisal can also result in a joyful discovery—for example, a family heirloom that turns out to be quite valuable. Unfortunately, the opposite can happen as well. Those requesting appraisals should be prepared to learn that an object treasured within a family for generations can turn out to be virtually worthless (except for its sentimental value). For many practical reasons it is good to know what a collection is really worth. This is particularly important with regard to taxes.

If you ever doubt an appraisal, get a second opinion, and always do so for works that exceed $10,000. For works valued at less than $10,000, a verbal appraisal is fine. Also, if you discover a significant discrepancy between the two appraisals, by all means seek another written appraisal.

Once you have a good idea about the market value of the work you are trying to sell, you can consider four options for selling your work: to a dealer for immediate cash; through a dealer on consignment; directly to another collector; and at auction. If you decide to sell a work through a dealer, go first to the gallery where you bought it. The dealer who sold you the work may want to buy it back for any number of reasons. Do shop around before you commit yourself, though.

Another dealer may offer you a better price. At the very least, other bids will strengthen your position for negotiation with the original dealer.

If you choose to sell directly to a dealer who is in the market to buy your art, you should expect to receive 50 to 75 percent of the work's current market value. If, for example, you bought the work a decade ago for $10,000 and its current appraised value is $25,000, then the dealer should give you between $12,500 and $18,750 for it. If the painting can be sold easily, you may be able to get as much as $20,000. Bear in mind that a dealer is under no obligation, legal or moral, to pay anything even remotely close to market value. Also, the easiest way to be taken advantage of is to be ignorant of the market value. In other words, don't rely totally on a dealer's sense of fair play. Use your common sense.

If the dealer is not in the market to buy, you might decide to sell the work through the dealer in a consignment arrangement. In such cases, the dealer sells the work for you in what is referred to as a secondary market, where the dealer earns a 10 to 30 percent commission on the sale price. For example, if a painting is valued at $25,000, you could get $17,500. The only disadvantage of selling on consignment is that you do not get paid until the work is sold. The primary advantage of selling on consignment is that there is less likelihood that you will be taken advantage of on the price, because it is in the dealer's best interest —and in yours as well—to get as much as possible. Also, be sure to consider these issues: Will the work be insured while on the dealer's premises? What is the amount of the dealer's fee? Will there be any charges beyond this fee? When will the consignment arrangement terminate in the event that the work remains unsold? To avoid any misunderstanding, have some sort of written contract specifying these points.

Few collectors of African American art choose to sell at auction houses—auctioneers have such limited knowledge about this genre of American art, and the likelihood of getting the best possible price is unpredictable. However, collectors who consider selling at auction do so because of the relatively low commission. Once again, this option is for people who truly know what they are doing. If this is your choice, do your research, as you want to be sure that your artwork will bring in a competitive price at auction. Otherwise, you are better off working with a dealer.

Auction sales provide public exposure for the artwork and the seller; dealer sales are more private and discreet. One advantage of an auction is that its openness is likely to attract a larger number of potential buyers. But this very advantage can turn into a disadvantage at times, particularly for work that does not sell.

One of the first steps in selling at auction is to send a good photograph of the work and a complete description to several houses for a preliminary appraisal. Often saleability can be determined by mail. This informal appraisal is usually done at no charge. If you want to sell an entire collection, the houses will send a representative to appraise your works in person. This personal visit is not free. Once you have decided on a house, a number of issues need to be resolved: What are the commission rates? Are these rates calculated per lot or on the basis of gross proceeds? Are there any insurance fees? Who is responsible for the cost of shipping the art from your home to the auction? Will there be a catalogue? Will it contain photographs, and if so, who will pay for them? How will the sale be publicized? Who will pay for advertising? Who is responsible for absorbing the cost of any damage to the works while they are in the auctioneer's possession? When will the sale take place? How

NORMAN LEWIS. *JOHNNY THE WANDERER*. 1933.
Oil on canvas, 37 x 24¾ inches. Private collection.
Courtesy of Bill Hodges Gallery, New York.

soon after the sale will you receive your money? All these details must be negotiated and specified in a written contract. If the work sells, you will receive a check at least a month after the auction for the final sale price minus the 10 percent seller's fee and any applicable service charges.

TAX CONSIDERATIONS AND ART

Buying and selling a work of art is a financial transaction. You may earn a profit or you may incur a loss. Either way, you will incur some expenses that have specific tax consequences determined by your status as a collector. Many collectors have found significant tax advantages in assuming the status of art investor rather than that of simple collector. On the other hand, the Internal Revenue Service occasionally classifies active collectors as dealers, whether or not they own established galleries. Dealer status entails many disadvantages, which explains why most dealers become annoyed when collectors approach them with unreasonable requests for discounts.

The most basic tax considerations are ways to minimize your current tax bill by donating works of art to museums and/or other nonprofit institutions; ways to plan ahead and minimize estate taxes on your art holdings when you die; tax treatment of cash proceeds from the sale of art; and deductibility of such out-of-pocket expenses as insurance and maintenance costs. Contrary to popular opinion, art "investing" does not provide special tax advantages. The new and complex provisions of the various tax reform acts can be extremely confusing for collectors, if only because of the unique difficulty in ascertaining the value of collectible tangible property.

If you choose to persuade the IRS that you are an art investor, you are responsible for demonstrating that you buy art primarily as an investment—in other words, strictly for profit and not for pleasure. There are several ways to do this. You can employ professional investment counselors, keep your works of art in storage instead of displaying them, maintain careful records of the rates at which your objects appreciate, and sell works frequently, instead of holding them for many years. In addition, it is helpful if your collection represents a major portion of your assets. With art-investor status, you may deduct the costs of collecting: investment advice, appraisals, buying trips, conservation, storage, and insurance. You can also deduct any losses you may incur in selling a work. Dealer status allows you to deduct all expenses and losses, but you may not be able to declare profits derived from the sale of works as capital gains. Conversely, if you are a collector or an art investor, but not a dealer, you can declare as capital gains all profits on the works you sell. Works held for less than one year will be treated as short-term capital gains; works held for more than a year will be treated as superior long-term capital gains.

Tax benefits are available primarily for those collectors in the higher tax brackets. The basic rule is that in any given year you can claim tax deductions for up to 30 percent of your adjusted gross income for donations of paintings to museums. For example, if you earn $50,000, you can donate up to $20,000 worth of paintings per year and claim full deductions. Of course, there are variations on this basic theme, including five-year carryforwards for donations that exceed the 30 percent limit and special "fractional" contributions that involve donating part ownership of a work of art.

Three factors determine the size of the tax deduction you can claim for a donation: the status of the charitable organization; whether the work of art is a "capital-gain property," in other words, whether the sale of the art would result in a long-term capital gain; and whether the donation meets the "related use" rule.

Tax law categorizes charitable organizations in two ways: the 50 percent organization, like museums, churches, schools, and hospitals, and the 20 percent organization, like the various types of private foundations. Donations to 50 percent organizations provide the greater tax benefits. To qualify as a 50 percent organization, an organization must be supported in part by taxes or by public admission charges or donations. In most cases, donations to 50 percent organizations are deductible in an amount of up to 50 percent of the donor's adjusted gross income—although when it comes to works of art, the limit is usually 30 percent.

For 20 percent organizations, the annual limit is 20 percent of adjusted gross income. Also, the size of your tax deduction must be reduced by an amount equal to 50 percent of the appreciated market value of the work. These and other restrictions limit the viability of this approach to saving on taxes.

Another variable influencing the size of your deduction is whether the work of art has appreciated in value since you bought it. The greater the appreciation, the more attractive it becomes to give the work away. As previously mentioned, you may be able to make more money donating a painting to a museum than by selling it and keeping the cash proceeds for yourself. The financial benefit of donating to a nonprofit institution like a museum is that you are exempted from all capital gains taxes on the appreciated value. The personal benefit is that you are giving a work of art to an institution that will appreciate it and take care of it. In addition, you are helping an institution that has made a long-term commitment to preserving and exhibiting African American art, yet has a restricted acquisitions budget. The following institutions have been collecting African American art long before it became valuable to mainstream collectors: the Museum of North Carolina Central University, the James E. Lewis Museum at Morgan State University, the I. P. Stanback Museum and Planetarium at South Carolina State University, Spelman College, Howard University Gallery of Art, Atlanta University, Fisk University, Hampton University Museum, the African American Museum in Dallas, the National Center for Afro-American Artists in Massachusetts, and the Studio Museum in Harlem.

As a basic rule, it is better to donate a painting with an appreciated market value than to sell the work and donate the cash proceeds. For instance, say you purchased a painting for $2,000 several years ago and now it is worth $10,000. By giving this painting to a museum, you would be able to claim a full $10,000 tax deduction, not just the original $2,000 cost. If you were to sell the work, you would end up having to pay capital gains tax on the $8,000 profit.

If the work has not appreciated in value, it is not subject to the 30 percent limitation on tax deductions in any given year; instead it will fall under a higher, 50 percent, rule. If you are earning $50,000 a year, you may be able to deduct up to $25,000 for donations of nonappreciated paintings in any given year, as opposed to $15,000 for paintings that carry market values above original cost. This is a benefit to those who invest and collect contemporary art and who systematically unload select works to a willing museum. In essence, it makes little difference whether you sell a nonappreciated painting and donate the proceeds or donate the painting itself; the tax consequences usually are the same.

Bear in mind that the government does have a way to prevent art collectors from claiming large tax deductions for donations of paintings to institutions that have no related use for the works. This is the "related use rule." In order to claim a full deduction, you must donate the work to an institution that can reasonably be expected to make use of it—for example, a museum that is likely to exhibit the work, use it for research or educational purposes, or store it in anticipation of future exhibitions, or a college or university that is likely to use the work in an art history course. It is best to restrict your donations of paintings to museums; always ask the museums to sign a statement that they intend to make use of the work, whether for public exhibition or for scholarly research.

There is another possible approach to saving taxes. You may combine a partial sale with a partial donation. For instance, say several years ago you acquired a painting for $1,000 and it is currently worth $10,000. You may be able to sell the work to a museum for less than the current market value, say, $2,000. You then can claim as a tax deduction the $8,000 difference between the sale price and the market value. However, you are required to pay capital gains tax. This means that if the painting originally cost $1,000, the 20 percent portion that you sold for $2,000 would be considered to have cost $200, or 20 percent of the original cost, resulting in a taxable capital gain of $1,800. The primary benefit here is that the collector recovers all or part of the initial purchase price. Generally, the after-tax financial results of a bargain sale are somewhat more favorable for the collector than an outright donation. For a museum, this approach is less favorable because cash outlay is required. This kind of "bargain sale" usually occurs when the donor has exceptional works that are of great interest to the acquiring museum. Be aware, though, that there is always a lengthy period of negotiation.

The key to all charitable donation of works of art is to obtain an independent appraisal of market value that will stand up to the scrutiny of the Internal Revenue Service. A panel of dealers, scholars, and museum curators assists the IRS in reviewing claimed deductions. They review appraisals and photographs of works and provide their opinions on authenticity and valuation.

The best way to avoid a federal tax audit is to submit a detailed, independent appraisal. This can be arranged through the Art Dealers Association of America, which claims to offer the "most competent, effective and independent" appraisal service available for works being donated to museums. The other option is to obtain an expert appraisal that avoids all conflict of interest; in other words, do not obtain an appraisal from the dealer who originally sold you the art, or from an appraiser whose fee is based on a percentage of the appraised value. A final caution: A donation to a museum is disallowed if you originally acquired the work as a gift from the artist. Your deduction in this instance is limited to the artist's costs in producing the work. So, be careful: If your intention is to sell or donate a work, do not accept it as an outright gift from the artist. If you pay as little as one dollar, the work is automatically transformed into a "capital gain property," subject to more liberal tax provisions. Please seek the advice of your accountant.

With regard to estate and gift taxes, any implementation of specific strategy should be planned with a competent lawyer. The most difficult problem in planning the collector's estate is knowing what he or she really wants. Generally, the federal estate tax is levied on all estates in excess of $650,000. The following assets must be included in the estate for tax purposes, regardless of whether they are processed through probate court or not: real estate, cash, stocks and bonds, annuities, life insurance proceeds, business interests, and personal possessions (including art). Works of art must generally be included at current retail market value, not at resale value or cost. Deductions are allowed for the following items: funeral expenses, executor's and lawyer's fees, certain other mandatory administrative costs, state inheritance taxes, and debts. There is also a marital deduction permitting a spouse to leave the surviving partner an unlimited amount of his or her assets free of any estate taxes; taxation begins on amounts in excess of $625,000 and is calculated on a sliding scale, ranging from 37 percent to 55 percent. There is an additional surcharge on estates exceeding $10 million.

Estate taxes present a major problem for large art collections. Often it is difficult to convert these collections into enough cash to pay estate taxes, which is why they are left to charity.

A large collection may be passed directly to heirs through the judicious use of trusts and the judicious use of tax-free gifts. Careful planning of your financial affairs during your lifetime can reduce estate taxes on your property when you die.

Trusts are set up to prohibit an estate from immediately being inherited by the heirs. This can sometimes be a tax-saving device, though at other times it is arranged this way simply because the legator does not consider his heirs capable of managing the property on their own. A trust provides title to property that passes tax-free to a trustee, often a professional, who then administers the assets for the designated beneficiary. In its simplest form a trust might be established by a husband for the benefit of his wife for the remainder of her lifetime. She would receive an income from the trust; on her death the trust would be dissolved and the assets passed on to the children for use as they see fit. This is a common device for combining two taxable transfers of an estate, from husband to wife and then from wife to children.

It is important to specify who is responsible for paying insurance, storage, and maintenance expenses for artwork when ownership is transferred through the use of a trust. The trustee should be given limited but clear power to sell works of art from the trust as necessary, and the terms of the trust should specify how the proceeds from such sales are to be held and used. If you neglect to include these provisions, the surviving spouse may find it legally impossible to sell the art and raise cash in an unforeseen emergency.

You can also reduce or eliminate estate taxes on your art collection by making gifts of art during your lifetime. Gift taxes are at least 25 percent lower than estate taxes. With certain limitations, gifts are free from all tax. Please seek the advice of a seasoned estate planner.

A primary drawback of giving away works of art is loss of both ownership and the illusion of control. Also, for extremely valuable works of art, the gift tax may be so high as to make such transfers impractical. The IRS may also declare that any gift made within the three years preceding your death is a last-minute attempt to dodge estate taxes. Establish a pattern of gift giving early in your life, which will show that your gifts represent a consistent practice. In this instance you may want to tie all gifts to occasions like birthdays, holidays, and benefits to reinforce the notion that you are motivated primarily by nonfinancial considerations.

To avoid heavy taxation of your art holdings when you die, it is important to carefully word your will so that any art sales from your estate qualify as "necessary" within the law.

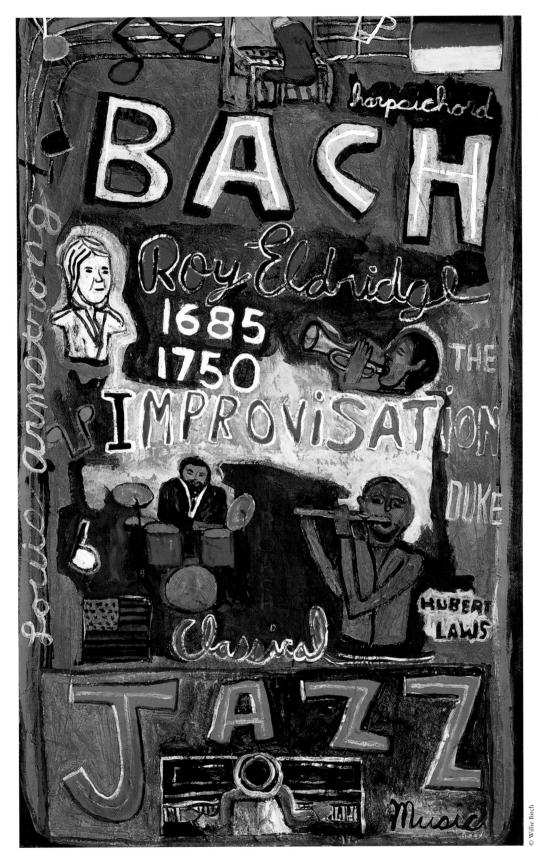

WILLIE BIRCH. *What's the Relationship Between Bach and Jazz?* 1994.
Acrylic on paper, 52½ x 33 inches.
Courtesy of Luise Ross Gallery, New York.

WOSENE W. KOSROF. *She Ethiopia #III*. 1994. Acrylic on goat skin, 14 x 18½ inches.
Courtesy of Parrish Gallery, Washington, D.C.

4
DISPLAYING
AND TAKING CARE
OF YOUR
COLLECTION

Responsibility is the first step in responsibility.

W. E. B. DU BOIS

Art collectors are better at wanting than at having. They often exert tremendous energy in a diligent search for the best piece of art they can afford. Then, having acquired their treasures, they ignore the value of caring for them. Collectors have duties as well as rights, and prime among these duties is the obligation to take proper care of their collection.

As a collector, you are just a trustee of the art you acquire. It is yours to keep and enjoy for a short time, then pass on for others to enjoy. Taking responsibility for your art involves physical care, including framing, restoration, and maintaining the proper atmospheric conditions, and protection from theft, including securing insurance and appraisals, which are discussed in chapter 3.

PHYSICAL CARE

Because paintings, drawings, and prints are made of materials that are subject to processes of deterioration, they tend to be fragile. From the moment of completion, art begins to change through exposure to varying cycles of sunlight and temperature and fluctuations in condensation and evaporation. Artwork is also subject to damage from improper handling by collectors and those with whom they share the pleasure of viewing it.

The ideal atmospheric conditions for paintings and prints are a steady temperature range of 68 to 74 degrees Fahrenheit and a steady humidity of 50 percent. Of the two, being concerned about humidity is more important because humidity above 70 percent can foster the growth of fungus and mold. Unusually low humidity combined with excessive heat can draw the oil out of a painting and eventually cause the work to chip and flake. Although 50 percent humidity is optimum, 30 to 70 percent represents an acceptable range. An air conditioner, humidifier, or dehumidifier can be an asset for the well-being of your collection.

Avoid displaying paintings in bathrooms and kitchens, near swimming pools and radiators, or over working fireplaces. Sharp fluctuations in temperature or humidity should definitely be avoided. In addition, avoid placing them in smoke-filled rooms and extremely narrow halls where people may rub against the art.

Do not wipe paintings with a cloth, dry or damp, or with a feather duster (feathers tend to catch and shift paint particles). Do not use any kind of wax or solvent. If you want to remove dust or loose dirt, use a long, extra-soft brush like a camel's hair brush or a quality shaving brush.

Heavy dirt or major physical damage may require the services of a restorer or conservator.

One way to check for heavy dirt on your piece is to gently rub some saliva, with the tip of your finger, onto a small surface section of the work. This is harmless to the painting itself, but it should remove enough grime to give you an indication of just how bright the colors are beneath the overlay of dirt. Your assessment will tell you whether you need the help of a professional restorer. Consult restorers recommended by the dealers you work with, or ones used by local museums.

Works of art on paper—prints, drawings, and photography—present their own special problems. Paper tends to react chemically to the elements surrounding it, including the frame, the backing, and the mat. Framing is supposed to provide protection, but for prints and drawings, bad framing is more destructive than no framing at all. Make sure that the framer attaches the print or drawing to acid-free board with rice paper hinges. The only safe board is made of 100 percent rag stock, otherwise referred to as museum rag board. Be aware that some framers use cardboard sheets with a core of ground wood. The ground wood is acidic and will eventually deteriorate or stain any paper with which it comes into contact. Therefore, you must insist that the framer use 100 percent rag stock for the backing and window mat. The work should be attached to the mount. Under no circumstances should the print be glued. The adhesive on the hinges should be a vegetable-based paste, never an animal glue or synthetic adhesive like rubber cement. Gummed linen tape, which is used by some framers, will also stain with time and therefore is unacceptable in archival framing.

The only way to protect a work on paper from dirt and pollutants is to have it framed behind a sheet of glass or acrylic. Although the surface of an oil painting can be protected with varnish, any such film applied to a work on paper will change its appearance and value. The

BETYE SAAR. *Letters from Home . . . Wish You Were Here*. 1976.
Oil on paper with collage, 19¼ x 14 inches, signed.
Courtesy of Michael Rosenfeld Gallery, New York.

print or drawing should not touch the protective glass because any condensation that forms on the glass could transfer to the paper and stain it. The work should be set back from the glass by at least an eighth of an inch. When you handle unframed prints and drawings, always use both hands to reduce the risk of bending, creasing, or tearing. Unframed prints should not be stacked directly on top of one another but should be separated by sheets of smooth, nonacidic tissue.

Keep in mind that prints and drawings are extremely vulnerable to the effects of bright light, particularly sunlight and fluorescent lighting. Incandescent lighting is relatively harmless. Under no circumstances should prints or drawings be hung in direct sunlight. Even bright indirect light should be avoided. You can purchase ultraviolet filtered (UV3) glass, which costs more than regular glass and lasts for only a few years. Acrylic glazing should not be used with charcoal drawings or pastels because it causes static electricity, which can pull the pastel particles from the paper.

Mold growth in paper, or foxing, is another common problem. Foxing, which shows up as dull rusty patches, weakens the sheet by feeding on paper fibers and is usually the result of prolonged exposure to high humidity. If water itself seeps into the frame, mold may proliferate rapidly and envelop an entire sheet of paper. When this happens, open the frame and remove the work to a dry environment. *Then seek the advice of a conservator.* All this may seem a great deal of fuss over an inanimate object, but it is

WILLIAM CARTER. *L.A. INCIDENT.* 1993.
Gouache, 11 x 15 inches.
Courtesy of Essie Green Galleries, New York.

CHARLES WHITE. *I Accuse.* Circa 1950.
Oil on canvas, 25 x 30 inches.
Courtesy of D. C. Moore Gallery, New York.

important to take care of things that hard-earned money allows you to enjoy. Otherwise you are wasting your time and money. It is important that you know the principles of print preservation because too many framers are notoriously ignorant and/or indifferent.

FRAMES

Frames can be traced back to the early 1800s B.C. when the Egyptians surrounded their tomb monuments and religious artifacts with gold borders. The Romans devised elaborate wall decorations for their villas and city dwellings around 50 B.C. to A.D. 100. In the twelfth century, during the early Gothic period, artists placed wooden frames around panel paintings to make them fit into the architectural plans of chapels and churches. It was not until paintings were regarded as works of art unto themselves that frames became noticed as an independent art form. In fact, trained craftsmen in Florence and Venice are credited with the earliest examples of frames designed as aesthetic and self-expressive entities. Other artisans from Italy, Spain, and Flanders were encouraged to follow suit. France also developed a more refined, graceful frame aesthetic consistent with its national character.

The majority of frames used today are not the traditional elaborate heavy forms. The collector

DANNY SIMMONS. *URBANCITY*. 1997.
Oil on canvas, 5 x 6 inches.
Courtesy Peter Findley Gallery, New York.

can choose from a variety of periods and styles of frames. Framers focus on the canvas and the size and shape of the painting. An effective frame sensitively complements the painted field it surrounds, and relates to and enhances the image.

Tasteful framing is essential to any pictorial image, and the right frame can enhance the artist's expression. In a sense, the picture lives in the frame, and with it the viewer is led to full enjoyment of the work. The first question to ask when selecting a frame is "What am I framing?" The answer has to do with a pagan concept, what frame makers call the "spirit" of a work of art—a particular school or era of painting, which suggests a certain type of framing. Cultural period is the best guide for selecting a frame. For example, paintings that are baroque in feeling require a baroque frame; paintings that are simple, linear, and contemporary in design require clean, unobtrusive modern frames.

Harmonizing a frame with your work of art is less desirable than providing a contrast. A frame is improper only if it overpowers artistic expression, competes with a picture, distracts the viewer from the drawn image, or actively clashes with it. Guide yourself by the fact that, whether contrasted or matched with a work of art, a frame is acceptable and effective if it is not inordinately creative. A word of caution about using color: Do not select a frame that matches a color from the picture, a common mistake. The frame will then compete with the artwork for the viewer's attention. Cautions aside, there really is no infallible theory of frame selection; you can only tell whether a frame is right for a work of art when you come face-to-face with it. The best guide is the picture itself, for although there are traditional framing practices, there are certainly no set formulas. Some art seems to frame itself, while other art requires much trial and error. A curious thing about selecting frames is that the works of art you like the best often prove to be the hardest to frame.

One of the more distressing tendencies in art is the decorator approach to picture buying and framing. In the same way that there is nothing more tragic than buying an inferior work of art simply because it matches the rug or sofa pillows, there is nothing more absurd than mis-framing a fine work of art merely to match a coffee table. The first duty of the frame is to the picture. Its job is to enhance the picture by making it a pleasing focal point of the room, not to debase it by making the picture a mere wall decoration. The picture and its frame should stand on their own merits.

You ask, "How do I select a framer?" Practically every community has frame makers or someone qualified to assist you in finding a good one. Some stores will only provide a few standard frames, while others have a more varied selection. Shops differ, both in quality and the price range of their offerings. All, however, should quote you a price that includes the molding, the matting, the glass (if needed), and the proper fitting of these components, and provide an itemized invoice. If possible, purchase your frames from a shop that employs a certified picture framer. The CPF is qualified to give advice on conservation and archival framing.

Every dealer works with framers, so ask yours to recommend one. A good framer is one who is dependable, has the respect of his colleagues, and handles your artwork with caution and care. A good framer sees that the edge of a drawing or a print is never cut or trimmed, for this ultimately reduces its resale value. He uses pure wheat or library paste on the rice paper hinges holding the art to the mat—never non-archival glues, which eventually rot and discolor the paper. He backs the framed picture with boards made of good, nonacidic 100 percent rag,

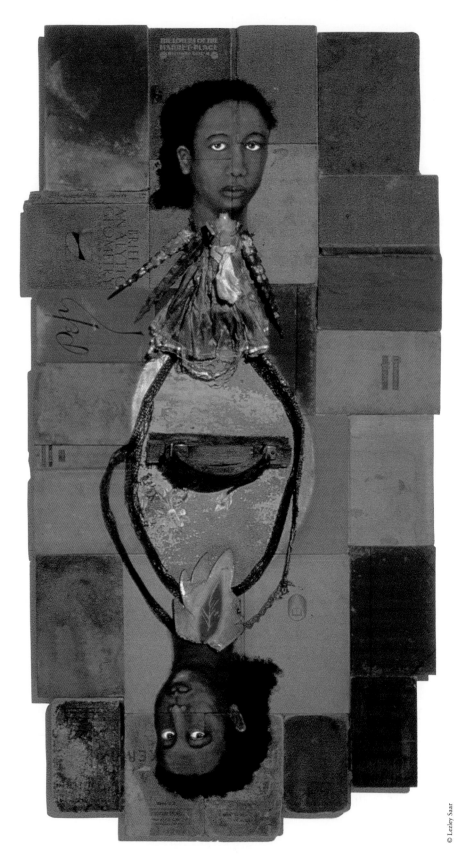

LEZLEY SAAR. *THE SILENT TWINS.* 1996.
Mixed media, 48 x 26½ inches.
Courtesy of David Beitzel Gallery, New York.

CHARLES BURWELL. *Untitled #80.* 1983.
Oil stick/mixed media on paper, 56 x 40¼ inches.
Courtesy of Sherry Washington Gallery, Detroit.

not wood pulp. Finally, the framer carefully fits and joins the corners of the frame.

An excellent framer can offer a variety of framing solutions that meet your taste and are within your budget. See what the prices of his frames are, the least expensive and the most expensive. A work of art by any artist can be as eye-catching in a twenty-dollar frame as in one costing a hundred dollars. Don't be afraid to rely

on your own taste. In the final analysis, follow the cardinal rule of collecting: Buy what you like.

Sometimes visits to a museum or art gallery will help you develop your eye for the most appropriate frames for different types of work. Museums change their exhibits regularly, thus providing a great opportunity to see a variety of art and frames. Often museums borrow works from private collectors, who tend to purchase

TOYCE ANDERSON. *House of Spirits*. 1994.
Mixed media on canvas, 18½ x 20 x 2½ inches.
Courtesy of June Kelly Gallery, New York.

OLIVER JACKSON. *Untitled (12.10.86)*. 1986.
Oil pastel on gessoed paper, 48 x 42¼ inches.
Courtesy of Porter Troupe Gallery, New York.

KEITH MORRISON. *A Night in Tunisia.* 1991.
Oil on canvas, 60 x 68 inches.
Courtesy of Bomani Gallery, San Francisco.

more elaborate frames. Pay particular attention to these works, as they may suggest additional possibilities. It's also helpful to ask yourself why certain frames were chosen and what alternatives might have been just as good or better.

There are many types of frames constructed on bases of wood, brass, aluminum, and plastic. Some of them are hand carved and machine molded. Typically, a gold frame is made with a layer of gesso and sometimes a layer of red clay placed over the raw wood. The clay provides a protective layer that allows the leaf finish to

adhere. Finishes include gold, silver, and metal leaf; and paint, stain, or natural wood with a wax or lacquered finish.

There are also innumerable styles of frames. Some are elaborate and antique in feeling; others are extremely linear in keeping with the modern tradition. Historically, one of the oldest styles is the Gothic, or medieval, frame, a four-cornered frame shaped like an ornamental container used for sacramental offerings. Frames in this style are intended to be an integral part of the work of art; they complement icons and woodcuts, and work with a medieval aesthetic. Gothic frames are not found in most frame shops and are generally made to order.

Italian Renaissance frames are bolder than those in the Gothic style; they are heavier in feeling and often have little decoration. They can be found painted with dark colors and are well suited for religious subjects and surrealistic compositions. Similar to the Italian frame is the Spanish frame, a period frame that dates back to the sixteenth century. Spanish frames have a strong, bold, chainlike appearance and work well with twentieth-century graphics. Spanish frames are hand carved. Machine reproductions can be found for a fraction of the cost of originals.

Dutch frames are plain and austere in the unornamented style typical of northern Europe. This style is most successful with art that is enhanced by simplicity—still lifes, genre paintings, and landscapes.

Another group of frames are the French Louis XIII, XIV, XV, and XVI models. Louis XIII frames are straight panels that usually have some sort of floral decoration carved within them. Louis XIV frames have ornate corners that are delicately carved often with scroll design. Louis XV and XVI frames have large corners with extremely elaborate hand-carved sweeps, and there is little emphasis on decoration within the panels. These frames work best if you want something tasteful but more elaborate than the band or stripping frame. All the French frames work well with the Impressionist, Post-Impressionist, and Fauvist paintings of the late-nineteenth and early-twentieth-century styles of painting. Framers recommend Louis XVI frames for American landscapes and scenes of the nineteenth century.

For those on limited budgets who desire tasteful frames for any medium of art, the popular and successful stripping and band frames are best. They are clean, linear, and have no defined pattern. Made of wood, these frames have front edges that are often leafed with gold or silver trim. They go well with abstractions and black and white images, and never conflict with busy painted forms. Sometimes plain moldings are even more desirable than the more elaborate ones. These frames enhance works on paper and are moderate in price. There is also the shadow-box frame, a narrow wooden frame with a space between the frame and the art, which is usually three-dimensional.

GLASS

Glass is used in picture frames to protect works of art on paper: drawings, watercolors, pastels, gouaches, and graphics. Over the years more and more people have begun to use nonreflective glass, which has an etched surface that refracts light and provides a nonglossy, varnished finish. Unfortunately, this effect has a tendency to dim and distort the true quality of a work of art. In fact, in many instances it can make originals look like reproductions. Moreover, since it requires that the work of art be flush with the glass, it is impossible to use for drawings and pastels; rubbing the glass against these surfaces would destroy them. This etched surface also collects condensation, which can damage the art and is unacceptable either for conservation or archival framing. Denglas, a recently developed nonreflective glass, has both a smooth surface and is 90 percent UV filtered.

MATS

Prior to the nineteenth century mats were not extensively used. Today they seem to be an integral part of the entire frame composition. A mat has many functions. It can be used to enclose or provide a background for the picture. A primary

WADSWORTH JARRELL. *HIT MAN.* 1991.
Acrylic on canvas, 69 x 48 inches.
Courtesy of Parrish Gallery, Washington, D.C.

function is to separate the art from the glass. If your work of art is damaged along the outer edges by an indelible stain or tear, you can "mat out" these flaws. It is important to consider the area a mat could or should cover. Generally, you will want the signature to be visible and also at least one inch around the entire composition. With graphics, this will allow you to see the plate or stone mark.

Mats are available in almost all colors imaginable, and they can be cardboard, silk, linen, or other fabrics. The colorful paper mats offered by many framers are not archival and should never be used with valuable artwork. Museums use 100 percent rag mats usually in white, off-white, creams, pale grays, and tans. A properly cut mat has an inner beveled edge. This bevel forms a frame within the frame. An additional accent in framing is a colored bevel, which is usually hand painted by experienced framers.

Antique prints are frequently framed with French mats, which have beveled edges, drawn lines, and watercolor panels. The lines can be gold, silver, or other colors, which further define the mat and enhance the image. Since these lines are drawn by hand, French mats tend to be more expensive than plain rag mats.

Occasionally works of art are executed on both sides of a piece of paper as in a sketchbook. Some collectors choose to display only the picture they like best, but it is possible to exhibit both. Use a mat on each side of a frame that has glass on each side. Such mats and frames have two faces and are usually placed on small stands on coffee tables as conversation pieces.

Floating is a method of matting in which an entire picture is placed in front of an uncut mat. This is ideal if the art is executed on paper that has deckled edges or if the image bleeds to the end of the paper.

ALONZO DAVIS. *OREGON PLATEAU IV.* 1994.
Acrylic on paper, 30 x 22 inches.
Courtesy of Cheryl Sutton and Associates, Carey, N.C.

MAREN HASSINGER. *FLOATING*. 1994.
Offset lithograph, 21½ x 30 inches.
Courtesy of Brandywine Workshop, Philadelphia.

INSERTS

Inserts, unlike mats, are used only with oil paintings. They are wood or fabric liners that set off a composition from its enclosing frame. Generally, linen inserts are used when a painting has a heavy texture that calls for "room to breathe" before the frame is affixed. Liners are not as popular as they used to be.

INSURANCE

Serious collectors acquire art not only because it is a good investment but also because they enjoy doing it. The best collections have been assembled with good eyes and great passion. Yet we cannot overlook the economic reality of art and how it affects our lives. Please insure your collection. You may not be able to replace lost objects (nothing can do that), but adequate insurance does allow you to minimize your financial loss.

If you have a homeowner's policy or a renter's policy, your collection is already insured against fire, theft, smoke, vandalism, hail, ice, sleet, falling trees, falling airplanes, and a host of other occurrences. Although most people who own art are careful by nature, art can be defaced, broken, damaged by water, or destroyed by fire. In fact, statistics show that insurance companies pay out more money for damage claims than they do for theft claims. There are usually two parts to a damage claim: the cost of restoring the

ASSANE N'DOYE. *UNTITLED.* 1996.
Mixed media, 30 x 40 inches.
Courtesy of Third World Art Exchange, Los Angeles.

RICHARD YARDE. *PALM WITH DOTS II.* 1993.
Opaque watercolor, 37¾ x 66¼ inches.
Courtesy of June Kelly Gallery, New York.

object to the best of a conservator's ability and the loss of value suffered as a result of the damage. Your policy protects both your dwelling and the personal property in it. Personal property is protected only to a certain point, generally 50 percent. This form of insurance is generally sufficient for new collectors and those whose work is valued at less than $100,000. Have an expert appraise your collection, and obtain any other documentation that can substantiate the value of a claim.

The best way to insure more expensive art collections is to purchase a special fine arts policy, which can be either a "personal articles floater" or a "scheduled personal property endorsement" attached to your primary policy. The policy is scheduled because the protected items are listed individually. With a fine arts floater, you can be insured for accidental loss at the full appraised value of the art. Collections worth more than $100,000 and protected by

central alarm systems are the ones that usually secure fine arts floaters. Under no circumstances will an insurance company issue a fine arts floater without a recent bill of sale or a professional appraisal. In order to maintain the policy, you must periodically update your appraisal, usually every three years.

Some collectors choose to leave their collections uninsured, which means that they themselves assume the risk of loss. Part of that risk, however, is shared by the United States government in the form of a tax deduction. You cannot take a tax deduction if you lose money when a work is sold unless the IRS considers you a dealer or an art investor instead of a simple collector. However, with adequate documentation and regardless of your status, you can take a full deduction when a work is either lost or destroyed.

How do collectors cope with the problem of knowing what their possessions are really worth

EMMA AMOS. *NEVER: FOR VIVIAN (BROWNE)*. 1993. Acrylic on linen canvas, laser transfer collage with African fabric and borders, 45 x 34 inches. Courtesy of Sherry Washington Gallery, Detroit. Photo by Becket Logan.

BOB THOMPSON. *Jan Mullers Funeral.* 1958.
Oil on canvas, 36 x 42 inches.
Courtesy of Martha Henry, Inc., New York.

and seeing to it that they are properly insured? As discussed in chapter 3, an appraisal is an important document. Not only will it provide the collector with a professional description of each object he owns, it also tells the collector what each item is worth. It is not unusual for appraisals to include photographs of each object or a videotape record of the entire collection.

There was a time when appraisers charged a percentage of the value of the objects they appraised as a fee for their services. For obvious reasons this led to many allegations of impropriety, and the practice has largely been abandoned. Today appraisers charge by the hour, plus transportation expenses. It is extremely important to specify why an appraisal is being requested. An appraisal for estate-tax purposes is different from an appraisal for insurance purposes.

Insurance has become an ever more significant factor in asset protection. Typically, a collector obtains an appraisal, hands it to an insurer, and the appraisal becomes the basis of the resulting insurance policy. Most art policies will pay losses on the basis of the values assigned to each object on the schedule that appears on the policy. Insurance policies that cover art are considered "valued" policies, different from those that cover furs and jewelry, where insurers usually reserve the option to either replace the lost object themselves or pay out its real value at the time of loss, which with a fur coat can be a good deal less than the value stated on the policy. Valued policies

BENNY ANDREWS. *REPENTER*. 1994.
Oil/collage on paper, 39 x 27¼ inches.
Courtesy of McIntosh Gallery, Atlanta.

MICHAEL RAY CHARLES. *(F'Ver Free) Before Black (To See or Not to See).* 1997.
Acrylic latex, stain, and copper penny on paper, 60 x 37½ inches.
Courtesy of Tony Shafrazi Gallery, New York.

MICHAEL RAY CHARLES. *(F'Ver Free) After Black (To See or Not to See)*. 1997.
Acrylic latex, stain, and copper penny on paper, 60 x 37½ inches.
Courtesy of Tony Shafrazi Gallery, New York.

EMILIO CRUZ. *HOMOSAPIEN SERIES.* 1996.
Oil, beeswax, and sand on panel.
Six panels, 96 x 18 inches each.
Courtesy of Steinbaum Krauss Gallery, New York.

include words like "insured for and valued at," which guarantee that the insurer will pay the stated value. Insurers recognize that many collectors maintain sufficient security, so that the maximum loss a collection might suffer is probably something less than its total value. It is not unusual for a collection to be dispersed between a principal home, a second home, and an office, which is a form of insurance in itself. Insurers are willing to offer blanket-limit policies, or art insurance at a level below the total value. These policies will cover every object in a collection up to the blanket limit selected, and will pay losses on the basis of the current market value. This is exactly how museums have been buying their insurance for years, and it is very similar to the kind of policies commercial art dealers choose for their insurance. Blanket-limit insurance has only recently become available to private collectors.

There are several features in insurance policies for art that should be understood. For example, if a lost object is one of a pair or a set, traditional insurance policies will pay the value of the lost piece and will not recognize that the loss of one piece may render the pair or the set virtually worthless. A properly written insurance policy will afford the collector the option to surrender the remaining piece or pieces to the insurance company and to be paid for the entire pair or set. In addition, art insurers recognize that if a picture is stolen today and recovered ten years from now, it could be worth more than its current value. Accordingly, it is possible for a claimant to buy back a recovered object at the price paid at the time of loss, as stipulated in what is referred to as the loss buy-back clause.

It is not unusual for a collector eventually to be asked to loan a work of art to a special exhibition, perhaps one that will travel to more than one museum and even to museums in other countries. The borrowing institution asks the lender to sign a loan agreement form. These forms ask the lender to stipulate the value of the objects being loaned. It is important to understand that these values immediately become agreed values, especially if the lender also agrees to allow the borrowing institution to provide the insurance. The lender also has the option to provide his own insurance and to bill the borrower for it, but if the borrower is allowed to insure, the lender should know that the value placed on the loan agreement is sacrosanct. In essence, if there is a loss, the borrower's insurer will pay the claim on the basis of what the loan agreement says, no more, no less. It is important not to understate or overstate the value of a loaned object.

The fine arts insurance policy is somewhat inaccurately described as an "all risks" policy. A standard clause reads, "The policy insures against all risks of physical loss or damage for any exter-

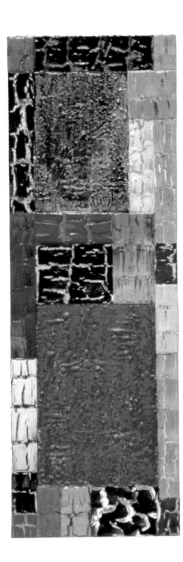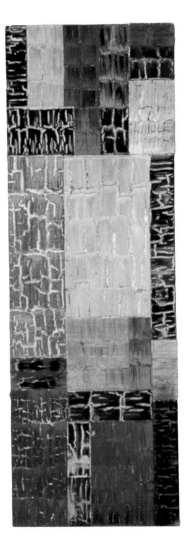

WILLIAM T. WILLIAMS. *Catherine's View.* 1993.
Acrylic on canvas, 76 x 24½ inches.
Courtesy of Peg Alston Fine Arts, New York.

nal cause, except as hereinafter excluded." The key word is "except." Fortunately, the exclusions and exceptions are relatively few. For example, wear and tear and gradual discolorations are not included, nor is damage by moths and vermin.

Damage due to or resulting from any repairing, restoration, or retouching process is a standard exclusion; therefore, it is of paramount importance that you select a top-rated conservator to clean or repair the objects in your collection. If you can prove that the conservator's negligence caused the damage, the conservator could be held personally liable. There have been very few instances, though, where mistakes in the conservation process have actually caused damage to a work of art.

RADCLIFFE BAILY. *A Love Supreme*. 1996.
Mixed media, 80 x 80 x 4 inches.
Courtesy of David Beitzel Gallery, New York.

GREGORY COATES. *Cleo*. 1994.
Mixed media, 18 x 20 inches.
Courtesy of Christiane Nienaber Contemporary Art, New York.

In addition, there are exclusions that have to do with war and nuclear reaction, radiation, or contamination. The war exclusion includes "insurrection, rebellion, revolutions, civil war, usurped power . . . and confiscation by any government authority, risks of contraband or illegal transportation or trade." The war exclusion should not include the risks of "strike, riot, or civil commotion," since these are covered under a fine arts insurance policy. Some insurers exclude breakage, mysterious disappearance, and the dishonesty of employees. For obvious reasons, these three exclusions are to be avoided if at all possible.

Be aware that there is a standard clause warning that if there exists "any other valid and collectible insurance covering the property insured,"

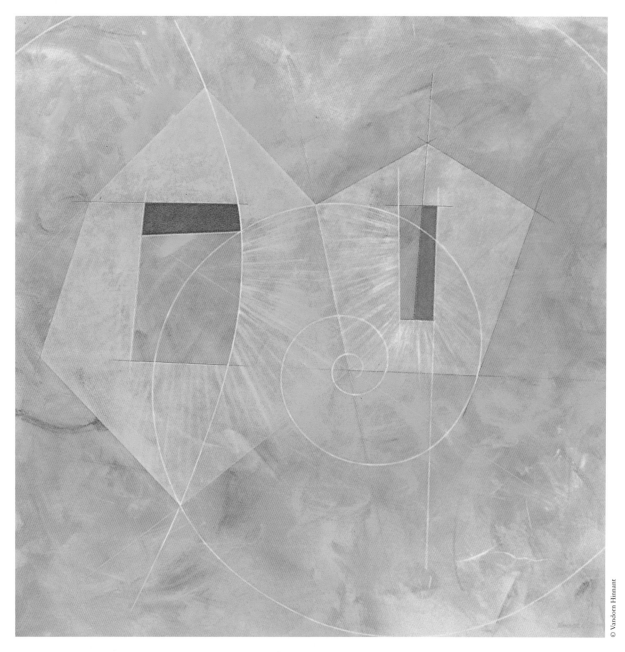

VANDORN HINNANT. *Marriage*. 1990.
Acrylic on paper, 61 x 61 inches.
Courtesy of Aljira Gallery, Newark, New Jersey.

then such other insurance is to be considered primary. In fact, every insurance policy carries such a warning, and in those rare instances when two or three policies cover the loss of the same object, each of them contributes its proportionate share. It is not unusual for a collector to lend several objects to a museum exhibition and to request that the museum insure them, even though his personal insurance remains in force. In this situation, the museum's insurer is considered the primary insurer and therefore pays first. If two sisters own a collection, and each, unbeknownst to the other, obtains insurance on the collection, then each sister's policy would pay its proportionate share of any claim. Insurers see to it that they are never in the position of paying for a loss twice.

Art insurance policies have a subrogation clause, which reads, in part, "The Company shall

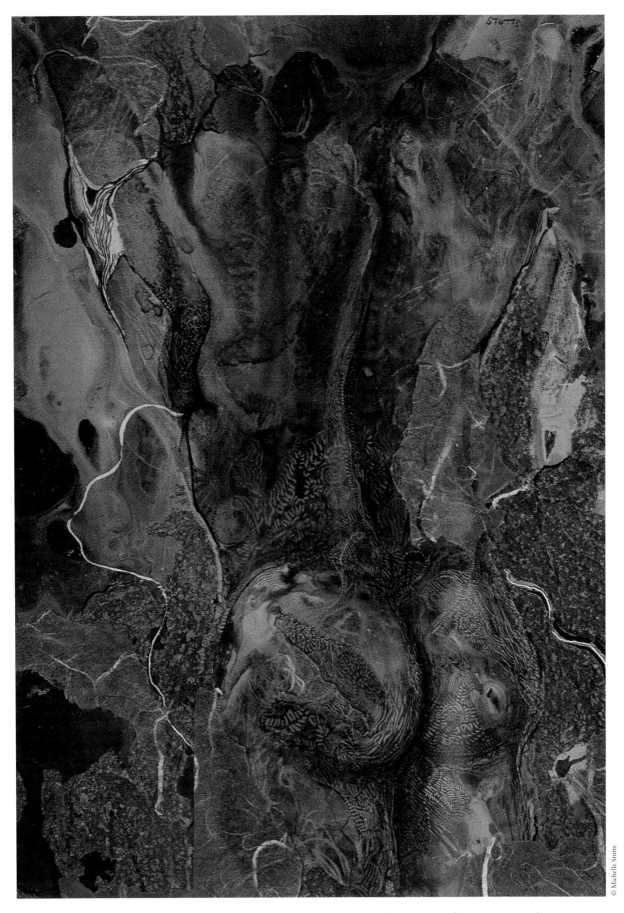

MICHELLE STUTTS. *STILL MOVEMENT.* 1994. Mixed media, 15 x 23 inches. Courtesy of Satori Fine Art, Chicago.

GILDA SNOWDEN. *Sorcerer*. 1993.
Oil on canvas, 72 x 68 inches.
Courtesy of Sherry Washington Gallery, Detroit.

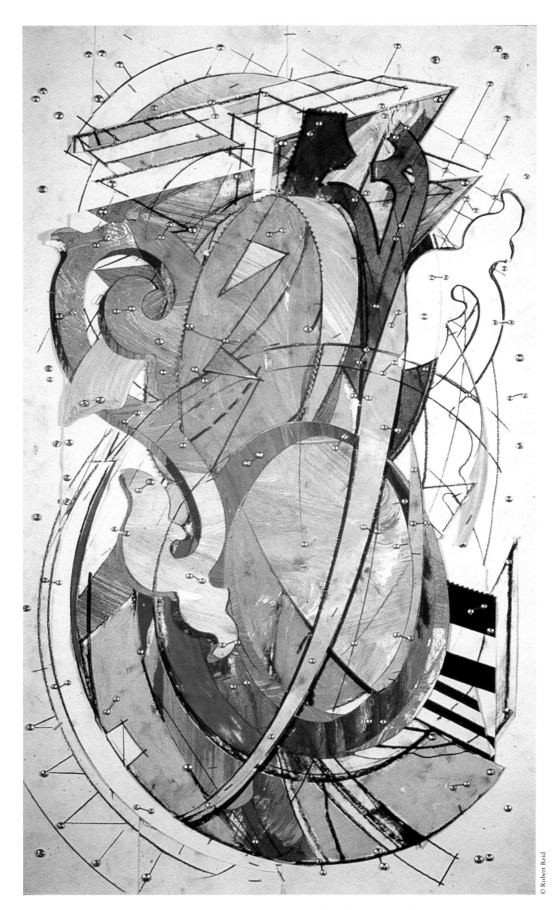

ROBERT REID. *PEW VISION*. 1994. Mixed media, 36 x 24 inches.
Courtesy of McIntosh Gallery, Atlanta.

be subrogate to all the Insured's rights of recovery . . . against any person or organization." This means that if a collector lends a work to a museum and elects to insure it personally, in case of loss or damage that is clearly the fault of the museum, the insurer can pay its customer in full and then simply turn around and sue the museum to recover that payment. Most museums will not accept an insured loan unless the lender submits in advance a certificate of insurance waiving this right of subrogation.

At this point you may be wondering if this is more involved than you want to become with caring for your collection. Remember, the majority of claims involving art are settled quickly and judiciously. And when disagreements occur, the prescribed remedy is the appraisal or arbitration clause, which stipulates that in the event of a disagreement about the amount of the loss, the customer and the insurance company must each elect an appraiser of choice, and the two appraisers must then select an umpire satisfactory to both.

An insurance policy can usually be canceled at any time, at the request of either the insured or the insurance company. If the policy is canceled by the insurer, notice must be provided thirty days in advance, and the premium credit issued on a straight pro-rata basis.

In tandem with the heightened interest in art that we've seen in the last few decades, an increasing number of agents who specialize in conservation issues have emerged. Collectors tend to be better served by specialists who understand art and what can happen to art. A claims adjuster without an art background has a difficult time understanding depreciation; an insurance broker who serves construction contracts will not necessarily have much knowledge about a nineteenth-century painting by Joshua Johnston; and a paper conservator would shy away from working on a statue. There are varying degrees of specialization, and you should discuss them with reputable commercial art dealers, the registrar at your local museum, or another collector.

BILL TRAYLOR. *UNTITLED*. 1939–42. Showcard color and pencil on cardboard, 13¼ x 7¼ inches.
Courtesy of Luise Ross Gallery, New York.

WILLIAM H. JOHNSON. *FLOWERS IN A VASE*. Circa 1931.
Oil on burlap, 23½ x 20 inches, signed.
Courtesy of Michael Rosenfeld Gallery, New York.

5

HISTORICAL
OVERVIEW

Art is the material evidence that reminds us

of the wealth of our culture—of who we are.

MARY SCHMIDT CAMPBELL

The art and science of ancient cultures, like those of the Egyptians, Aztecs, Mayans, Greeks, and Romans, tell us how those people perceived themselves and what they saw as their culture's purpose. It is the nature of human beings to be affected by the people, the circumstances, and the environment that surround them. Artists combine these experiences with imagination and talent, thus becoming the visual "conscience" of a society.

Responses within the art community continue to vary on whether the aesthetic value of African American art can be isolated from its history. You are encouraged to explore this issue as you familiarize yourself with the full range of African American art. The overview here is intended as an introduction; for a more detailed treatment of the topics discussed, please refer to the Selected Bibliography.

EMANCIPATION AND ART

The earliest artistic contributions by Americans of African descent date back to the arrival of the first Africans at Jamestown in 1619. Between 1619 and 1880 African Americans produced craft art, a continuation of the African artistic tradition. Many of the enslaved Africans were already skilled in one or more of the trades needed by a rapidly developing colonial society. Among them were carpenters, metalworkers, potters, sculptors, weavers, and designers of various wares. During the late eighteenth century, a system of renting and apprenticing talented African Americans to European American craftsmen developed in the colonies. Remnants of pre-enslavement African influences are evident in Southern architecture, American food, fashion, dance, and American popular music and jazz.

How, then, was it possible for people brought to America as slaves to become successful portraitists and landscapists? One answer is that before the Revolution, in the North and the South, increasing numbers of African Americans attained freedmen status. This group exchanged indigenous and learned skills, and over time a successful community of African American artists developed. Most artisans of the colonial period used traditional European patterns that required a high degree of technical skill rather than innovative design.

Patterns for creative development were nurtured by apprenticeships with skilled artisans, which served to prime talent in painting, drawing, and sculpture. An artist could move from journeyman to master craftsman and then into the fine arts.

One of the most celebrated African American painters of the time was Joshua Johnston (1765–1830), who was primarily active in Balti-more. More than fifty of his works survive, and they are typical of the popular Federalist style of portraiture, with their flat background and special attention to the painting of hair and lace. In the European tradition, his subjects hold objects indicating status and social standing. Johnston's work bears characteristics similar to those of his Baltimore contemporaries Charles Wilson Peale and Charles Peale Polk. His subjects were members of wealthy slaveholding families.

Following the Civil War African American artists experienced the broadened opportunities afforded by emancipation. However, while they often had the advantage of studying in leading American fine arts centers, their limited access to patronage and the broader cultural milieu frequently made it impossible for them to parallel the status of their white contemporaries. The post–Civil War migration of African Americans from the rural South to the urban North resulted in the concentration of African Americans in major cities like Baltimore, Philadelphia, Boston, New York, Washington, Atlanta, and San Francisco. It was in these cities that African American artists found endorsement and support from a small number of the enlightened European American middle class, many of whom had been involved in abolitionist activities.

Until the mid-nineteenth century, survival was the single primary concern for African Americans. After the Civil War, finding employment was one of the greatest challenges. Because of this lack of opportunities, few African Americans became trained artists. However, artistic expression did not die during this period. Those who continued to make paintings and lithographs approached this period from two distinct perspectives. One group consciously integrated their environment and experiences into their work, and the other abandoned African American values for European aesthetics and tastes. This latter

ROBERT SCOTT DUNCANSON. *Vale of Kashmir.* 1864.
Oil on canvas, 49 x 26 inches.
Courtesy of George and Joyce Wein Collection, New York.

group prevailed because the criteria for measuring work were based on European cultural traditions. While avoidance of Afrocentric themes was common among black artists, in nineteenth-century paintings by white Americans, African Americans were frequently depicted as clowns, simpletons, and inhuman creatures.

The first significant African American landscape painter to enter the mainstream of American art was Robert Scott Duncanson (1821–72). Duncanson gained recognition for his romantic compositions and fresh nature studies. Contemporary critics compared him favorably with other artists working in the style of the Hudson River school. Examples of his work include *Vale of Kashmir* (1864). His work exemplifies the beauty and poetry of both subject and style in a rich harmony of tone and color.

Edward Mitchell Bannister (1828–1901) worked as an unskilled laborer, sailor, barber, and daguerreotypist. In the 1850s and early 1860s Bannister focused on portraits, landscapes, seascapes, and religious and genre scenes.

By the 1870s he had begun to concentrate on landscapes, which showed the increasing influence of the Barbizon school, and was promoted by William Morris Hunt, one of the most important European American exponents of this lyrical style. Bannister won a gold medal for his *Under the Oaks* (lost for almost one hundred years) at the 1876 Centennial Exposition in Philadelphia. He became a respected and active member of the arts communities in Boston, Massachusetts, and Providence, Rhode Island. His works *Fishing* (1881) and *Oak Trees* (1870) exemplify his interest in the picturesque; here simple intimacy is captured in the composition, suggesting calm and tranquillity.

Nelson Primus (1842–1916), a contemporary of Bannister, worked in Boston and was a painter of portraits and religious subjects. Though Primus was well received in Boston, he did not enjoy a great deal of financial success. His careful style seemed to rely on photography. Unfortunately, much of Primus's work has been lost.

HENRY OSSAWA TANNER.

The Poor Ye Have with You Always. Circa 1920.

Oil on panel with tabernacle frame, 36 x 27¾ inches, signed.

Courtesy of Michael Rosenfeld Gallery, New York.

© Edward Mitchell Bannister

EDWARD MITCHELL BANNISTER. *UNTITLED*. 1888.
Oil on canvas, 15¼ x 23¾ inches.
Courtesy of Kenkeleba Gallery, New York.

Grafton Tyler Brown (1841–1918) worked as a painter and lithographer in the West. His style emphasizes flatness and invites comparison with folk art and early lithography.

Henry Ossawa Tanner's (1859–1937) life spanned the Civil War, Reconstruction, post-Reconstruction, and the New Negro movement (also referred to as the Harlem Renaissance), which followed World War I. Tanner became an expatriate and lived in France, where, beginning in the early 1890s, he exhibited regularly at the Paris Salon. By 1910 word of Tanner's fame had spread back to the United States. He won the

Harris Prize at the Art Institute of Chicago and a gold medal at the 1915 Panama-Pacific Exposition in San Francisco. Tanner traveled and painted throughout the Holy Land, and served with the American Red Cross during World War I. The French government made him a chevalier of the Legion of Honor in 1923, and he became a full member of the National Academy of Design in 1937. No other expatriate artist since the European American Benjamin West participated in so many reputable exhibitions and received so many honors for his work, at home and abroad. Typical of Tanner's painting are his expressive use of light and color, a selective simplicity of setting, and subject matter rendered in textured, naturalistic forms, as is evident in *The Three Marys* (1910), *Banjo Lesson* (1893), and *The Thankful Poor* (1894).

Two of Tanner's students in Paris were William A. Harper (1873–1910) and William E. Scott (1884–1964). Harper worked in a style influenced by Claude Lorrain and the Barbizon school. Scott was a painter, illustrator, and muralist, and focused on scenes from everyday life. Unlike their teacher, they painted with the more brilliant palette favored in French painting of the period. Scott, the younger artist, was later influenced by the French Fauves. He also developed an interest in depicting African American subjects, which later became the focus of the Harlem Renaissance (1919–29). Typical of many African American artists after Tanner, Scott pursued his initial studies in the United States, then relocated to Europe for further study and greater artistic freedom.

It was not until the late nineteenth century that African American women artists began to make their mark. Their chosen medium was sculpture, not painting. Mary Edmonia Lewis was born between 1843 and 1845 and died sometime after 1911. She had a colorful career and was an extraordinary sculptor favoring Classical and Romantic subjects. Meta Vaux Warrick Fuller (1877–1968) became a significant figure in the transitional period between Reconstruction and post-Reconstruction, as well as in the Harlem Renaissance of the 1920s and the New Deal programs of the 1930s and early 1940s. A great deal has been written about these pivotal women artists and their work.

At the turn of the century, as the United States shifted from a predominantly rural society to one dominated more by urban centers, the art of African Americans underwent radical changes as well. Changes in aesthetic, racial, and cultural consciousness were due primarily to ideological shifts within black America. It was in the 1920–50 period that African Americans, now concentrated in the urban North—in New York, Chicago, Washington, and Baltimore—experienced heightened self-awareness, optimism, and a sense of social, political, and economic security.

The intellectual and artistic movement called the Harlem Renaissance was an expression of a new and buoyant self-esteem among African Americans. Fifty-six years had passed since President Abraham Lincoln's Emancipation Proclamation abolished slavery. Across the country African Americans met to define strategies for improving their conditions and to counteract the effects of violent racial conflicts. The National Association for the Advancement of Colored People was organized in 1910. Marcus Garvey's United Negro Improvement Association, founded in 1914, encouraged African American pride, especially among the working class. Interest in Afrocentric music, literature, dance, and visual arts grew along with an enlightened and sophisticated middle class. The phenomenon of African Americans pursuing a new life in the North gave rise to the concept of the New Negro, who embodied heightened ethnic and cultural awareness.

In New York City, African Americans began to gather in upper Manhattan, where real estate was cheaper, partly because of its distance from the business and culture of downtown Manhattan. The African American population in this area grew rapidly. For the first time New York City had a politically important African American center—Harlem. By 1923 New York's Harlem had the largest African American population of any city in the United States. The environment allowed an outpouring of creativity to emerge. African

JOSEPH DELANEY. *Street Festival, NYC.* 1940.
Oil on canvas, 30 x 24 inches, signed. Private collection, Indianapolis.
Courtesy of Michael Rosenfeld Gallery, New York.

HALE WOODRUFF. *AFRICAN MEMORY*. Circa 1967–68.
Oil on canvas, 52 x 27 inches. Courtesy of Kenkeleba Gallery, New York.

BOB THOMPSON. *The Accusation*. N.d.
Oil on canvas, 24 x 30 inches.
Courtesy of Sacks Fine Art, New York.

American artists decided to portray themselves in the fine arts in a manner that was contrary to the derogatory representations of the nineteenth century. In addition, still influenced by European American aesthetics, many were encouraged by the more positive representations of established white artists like Thomas Eakins, Robert Henri, and George Luks, who included African American people as a part of serious studies, not as trivial or sentimental stereotypes.

African American intellectuals took advantage of the opportunities offered by Harlem and generated an artistic revolution that would stim-ulate and advance social and cultural interests of Americans of African descent. They included W. E. B. Du Bois, a Harvard-trained sociologist and editor of the NAACP publication *Crisis;* Charles Spurgeon Johnson, a University of Chicago sociologist and director of research and investigation for the National Urban League; and Alain L. Locke, a Harvard-trained professor of philosophy at Howard University and an avid champion of the visual arts.

Du Bois called for an emphasis on Afrocentric art as early as 1910, which, in turn, motivated a number of editors to publish the works

ARCHIBALD J. MOTLEY, JR. *SELF PORTRAIT.* 1920.
Oil on canvas, 30 x 22 inches.
Courtesy of Robert Henry Adams Fine Art, Chicago.

of African American writers like Claude McKay, Jean Toomer, Jessie Fauset, Countee Cullen, Langston Hughes, James Weldon Johnson, and Zora Neale Hurston.

This core group of brilliant and dedicated intellectuals gave life to the Harlem Renaissance. Together they functioned as a kind of public relations team. Their goal was to make every aspect of African American and African life, art, literature, music, and dance understood and appreciated by the entire country. Through their efforts white interest in an American minority culture grew.

The Harlem Renaissance was an essential system of support for African American artists. For example, the staff of *Crisis* awarded Amy Springard Prizes to visual and literary artists. From 1927 to 1933 the Harmon Foundation exhibits served as an important stimulus to artists. During these years African American artists received encouragement and support from people who saw themselves as patrons of the Harlem Renaissance. Both Du Bois and Locke urged African American artists to consciously celebrate the African American lifestyle. Locke emphasized the importance of African art to the development of African American artists. In this newly supportive climate, African American artists were increasingly in a position to make significant visual statements in both the conservative styles still prevalent in the United States and the styles promoted by the New Negro movement.

The artists involved in the early stages of the Harlem Renaissance included Aaron Douglas, Archibald Motley, Jr., Palmer Hayden, and Malvin Gray Johnson. They all began their careers painting in the Academic or Impressionistic styles of the time, but during the Harlem Renaissance they integrated a renewed perspective on the role of the African American artist into their work.

Aaron Douglas (1899–1979) developed a style that combined the linear rhythms of Art Nouveau and Art Deco with angular Cubist elements. He used flat tones to convey African music and dance. An example is *Aspects of Negro Life* (panels 1–4). For his portraits he used Impressionist techniques to produce brilliant character studies. He also painted landscapes. Inspired by the theories of Du Bois and Locke, he developed a unique style, combining African elements and modernist aesthetics of the 1920s. *Noah's Ark* and *Go Down Death* are examples. For his use of African themes he has affectionately been called the Father of the Harlem Renaissance among painters.

Ellis Wilson (1899–1977), less well known than Douglas, was also an early painter of African American subjects. His works include studies of ordinary people of Caribbean descent and southern field hands, and exotic color compositions of regional flora and fauna.

Archibald Motley, Jr. (1891–1980), born in New Orleans, worked in two distinct styles simultaneously. In one he painted fascinating realist studies of African American people, as in *Mending Socks*. In his second style he did brilliantly colored, fantastic compositions that depicted Afrocentric rituals and rites. Later on he painted sophisticated scenes of African Americans in Harlem and Paris, as in *The Jazz Singers*. He was the first African American to receive a Guggenheim Fellowship in painting.

Palmer Hayden's (1890–1973) focus on African American subjects came later in his career. In 1927 he moved to Paris. Like other African American artists before him, he was strongly influenced by the forties Impressionist palette. In the years that followed he began to use themes that derived from African American folklore and mythology, as exemplified in his John Henry series (1944–54). Hayden's interest in these subjects paralleled the nation's interest in folk and regional art of the 1930s. He ultimately became known for his genre paintings of urban and rural people. He adopted a style that seemed to integrate a sense of humor with an expressive technique that conveyed an earthy, theoretical, and somewhat absurd comment about African American culture.

In sharp contrast to Hayden, Laura Wheeler Waring (1887–1948) viewed her environment and humanity from a more refined and stately perspective. Her portraits from the 1920s extend the bravura brush strokes and haughty poses of American painter John Singer Sargent using African American subjects. Waring, like countless other artists, made the trek to France to study the great masters and to have direct contact with a living artistic tradition.

Malvin Gray Johnson (1896–1934) had a more modernistic style, which was influenced by his studies at the National Academy of Design. His later works of the 1920s and 1930s show the influence of Impressionism and Cubism, as Johnson emphasized flat planes and bright colors. Toward the end of his career, Johnson focused on scenes from everyday African American life.

Like Aaron Douglas, James Lesesne Wells (1902–93) balanced an art of inspirational propaganda with conceptual intrigue during the late 1920s and early 1930s. He studied at the National Academy of Design and Columbia University Teachers College and emerged as a major printmaker and painter. Douglas focused on religious subjects.

While Douglas, Motley, Hayden, and Johnson adopted neoprimitive styles in response to the Harlem Renaissance, Horace Pippin (1888–1946) was entirely self-taught. Pippin returned to the United States from France in 1920 after fighting in the Great War as a member of a black regiment. Because his right arm was incapaci-

tated during the war, Pippin developed his own method of handling a paintbrush. By 1929 he had perfected a technique and had begun to gain attention and acclaim. His paintings, rendered in a neoprimitive style, focused on religious, military, domestic, and everyday themes. Some of the unique characteristics of Pippin's work are his simplified flat forms, unusual juxtapositions of color, and lack of modeling and perspective, qualities praised by contemporary modernists.

After the crash of 1929 much of the support that had been available to African American artists ceased to exist, with the exception of the Harmon Foundation and President Roosevelt's Works Progress Administration. As a result of the WPA's Federal Arts Project, African American artists received government support for their creative output. *The Blue Jacket,* for instance, was painted by Charles Sebree (1914–58) in 1938 while he was employed by the Easel Division of the Illinois Federal Art Project. Art centers began to emerge in Harlem, Chicago, and other cities. Painters who found outlets for their art through the WPA included Charles Alston (1907–77) and Norman Lewis (1909–79). Alston's work oscillated between figuration and abstraction throughout his career. *Farm Boy* is characteristic of Alston's figurative style and shows his interest in black subjects. Although Lewis's paintings were explicitly social and political in content during the early and mid 1930s, his works in the late 1930s and 1940s, like *Jazz Musicians,* became increasingly abstract.

Unusual among artists of the period, Hale Woodruff (1901–80) was able to support himself outside the framework of the New Deal social programs. He found a position as a professor at New York University. In 1926 he received a Harmon Foundation Award and traveled to Europe to study with Henry Ossawa Tanner at the Académie Scandinave and the Académie Mod-

AARON DOUGLAS. *Corporal Horace Marshall*. 1942. Oil on canvas, 24 x 20 inches, signed.
Private collection, California.
Courtesy of Michael Rosenfeld Gallery, New York.

erne, where like others he was attracted to Impressionism. *The Card Players* is an example of Woodruff's interest in European modernism and its integration of Cubism and references to African sculpture.

Among his best-known work are the Amistad murals at Talladega College in Alabama. Completed in 1939, they depict the 1839 revolt of African slaves aboard the Spanish slave ship *Amistad*. With their vigorous composition and strong color, they owe much to the Mexican muralists Diego Rivera and José Clemente Orozco. Later in his career Woodruff shifted his style to Abstract Expressionism.

James Lesesne Wells worked as a teacher at the Harlem Library Project for Adult Education. During the 1930s he painted religious works based on biblical themes, and favored a two-dimensional Expressionist style. For the remainder of his career he devoted himself to printmaking. He was a virtuoso whose images are simple and powerful in their integration of African and religious themes, and show a debt to German Expressionism and Cubism.

William Henry Johnson (1901–70) was also attracted to simplified forms and brilliant colors. Originally from Florence, South Carolina, he arrived in New York in 1921 to study at the National Academy of Design with Charles L. Hinton. He traveled to Paris in 1926 and there came under the influence of the rigorous structuralism of Cézanne, the painterly emotionalism of Van Gogh, and the bright colors and Expressionist style of Chaim Soutine. Within two years he was painting exaggerated, twisted forms that imbued his subjects with vibrant emotion. In 1930 he won a Harmon Foundation gold medal in an exhibition at the International House.

In 1938 his style underwent a radical transformation—he adopted a naive approach based on broad areas of flat, brilliant color and primitive, childlike forms. His themes ranged from scenes of everyday rural and urban life to folk-inspired portrayals of religious subjects.

JAMES B. NEEDHAM. *At Forks.* 1821.
Oil on board, 8 x 15 inches.
Courtesy of Robert Henry Adams Fine Art, Chicago.

ROBERT SCOTT DUNCANSON. *The Upper Mississippi.* 1852.
Oil on canvas, 16 x 26½ inches.
Courtesy of Schwarz Gallery, Philadelphia.

African American artists have a strong tradition of intentionally cultivating a naive or raw style in the interest of expressionistic directness. This can be seen in a variety of forms, beginning in the 1920s and continuing to the present day. With the advent of Neo-Expressionism, this kind of cultivated rawness has become fashionable within the art establishment.

In the 1930s, however, it was the first time a cultivated naiveté appeared in the work of African American artists. Working independently of the theories espoused by Alain Locke and Langston Hughes, artists like Palmer Hayden, William H. Johnson, Sargent Johnson (1888–1967), and Jacob Lawrence (b. 1917) produced work that looked like it had been made by self-taught artists. By stripping style to an expressionistic core, these artists were able to remove from their work the baggage of Western culture.

An interest in the primitive, championed by the Surrealists in the 1930s, brought the genuine black folk artists into vogue for the first time. In 1937 and 1938, at the height of the black Neo-Folk movement, the Museum of Modern Art showed William Edmondson (ca. 1870–1951) and Horace Pippin.

The federal government played a special role in providing patronage for these "naive" African American artists who had otherwise been removed from the closed world of art museums and commercial galleries. Self-taught, and residents of small rural communities in the South, they were considered intuitive talents. Frequently described as either "primitives" or "folk artists," these painters received recognition that often surpassed that of their more sophisticated peers.

Bill Traylor (1854–1947) and Clementine Hunter (1885–1988) were two such "outsiders"

HALE WOODRUFF. *Mural Panel*. 1941.
Oil on canvas, 21 x 33 inches.
Courtesy of Bellevue Gallery, Trenton.

whose unpretentious formats and charming scenarios triggered a great deal of critical notice at the time their works were unveiled. Both artists had the ability to make provocative images using simple drawing techniques. Clementine Hunter's *The Pole Watchers* (ca. 1948) is an elegant and naive composition using surreal shapes of the flanking trees and spots of color that represent three pole watchers.

Other African American folk artists include Jesse Aaron (1887–1979), Steve Ashby (1904–80), David Butler (b. 1898), Ulysses Davis (b. 1914), William Dawson (b. 1901), Sam Doyle (b. 1906), James Hampton (1909–64), Sister Gertrude Morgan (1900–80), Inez Nathaniel Walker (b. 1911), Leslie Payne (1901–81), Elijah Pierce (1892–1984), Nellie Mae Rowe (b. 1900), James "Son Ford" Thomas (b. 1926), Mose Tolliver (b. 1915), Charles Mosby (b. 1949), George White (b. 1911), Thornton Dial (b. 1942), Luster Willis (b. 1913), and Joseph Yoakum (1886–1972).

This tradition of cultivated naiveté, so strong among African American artists, can be seen in the works of contemporary artists such as Bob Thompson (1937–66). His figurative compositions recycled and reinterpreted the European masters Gauguin, Matisse, and Goya, and the Italian Renaissance painters Masaccio, Titian, and Piero della Francesca. *Music Lesson* (1962) shares the serenity of the pastoral landscapes of Giorgione and Titian. His later work was sym-

JAMES L. WELLS. *HARRIET TUBMAN AND THE UNDERGROUND RAILROAD.* 1943.
Woodcut print, 11 x 14 inches.
Courtesy of Julliette Bethea Collection, Washington, D.C.

SISTER GERTRUDE MORGAN. *ANGEL CALLED JOSEPH.*
Mixed media on paper, 11½ x 12 inches.
Courtesy of Phyllis Kind Gallery, New York.

bolically dark and overtly sexual, reflecting the influence of Goya's paintings.

Other African American painters widely recognized during the 1930s and 1940s include Richmond Barthé (1901–89), Beauford Delaney (1901–78), and his brother, Joseph Delaney (b. 1904). Barthé studied at the Art Institute of Chicago and won the prestigious Julius Rosenwald Fellowship. When he arrived in New York in 1929, he focused primarily on sculpture. His work also includes portraits of famous actors and racial allegories. Beauford Delaney's *Street Scene* typifies his exuberant style in its use of vibrant colors and thickly impastoed pigment. Joseph Delaney worked in an Expressionist style fueled with energy and emotion.

Both James Amos Porter (1905–70) and Lois Mailou Jones (b. 1905) helped mold the philosophy and direction of the nation's first African American school of art, established at Howard University. In 1935 Porter, an art historian as well as a painter, received a Rockefeller Foundation grant to study in Europe. In 1943 he published his influential text, *Modern Negro Art.* During the last twenty-three years of his life, he chaired the department of art at Howard University and gave exposure to a whole generation of artists. A skillful painter, Porter was influenced by French Impressionism and Fauvism. His still lifes and landscapes employ the fluid line and bright light of Matisse. Among Porter's pupils were David Driskell, Mildred Thompson, and Lloyd McNeil.

Artists who emerged during the late 1930s reaffirmed their commitment to Afrocentric themes and subjects. However, they did not share the preceding generation's interest in Impressionism and Post-Impressionism. In the works of Romare Bearden, Claude Clarke, Eldzier Cortor, Hughie Lee-Smith, Jacob Lawrence, Elizabeth Catlett, Ernest Crichlow, and Charles White we can see the influence of Cubism, Fauvism, Surrealism, Social Realism, and non-Western cultures.

Romare Bearden (1911–88) was one of the most original talents to emerge in the late thirties. He gained notice first as a writer and then as an

JAMES A. PORTER. *When the Klan Marches By.* 1944.
Oil on canvas, 21 x 29 inches, signed.
Courtesy of Michael Rosenfeld Gallery, New York.

artist, and is now considered one of the foremost American artists of the twentieth century. Bearden grew up during the 1920s in the midst of writers and artists of the Harlem Renaissance. Over the years he worked in a variety of styles. His work from the early forties shows the strong influence of African art in its depiction of biblical scenes. From 1945 to the late 1950s Bearden began to emphasize the two-dimensionality of the picture plane, as in *The Warriors* and *The Bullfighter*. During the fifties Bearden also painted abstractions. It wasn't until the 1960s that he began to work in collage, the style he is best known for. Because his work is autobiographical, its expressive, colorful images and shapes highlight the African American experience.

Claude Clarke's (b. 1915) canvases depict images of everyday rural and urban life. Employing a decorative neoprimitive or Fauvist style, he applies layers of paint with a palette knife to create a highly tactile surface.

HOPE OF THE WAR YEARS, 1940–1946

African American artists entered the 1940s with a strong sense of optimism. Inspired to a great extent by their participation in the Federal Arts Projects of the 1930s, they carried their enthusiasm and expectations for full membership in the art community to the commercial galleries and art museums.

Horace Pippin, Richmond Barthé, and Jacob Lawrence were at the forefront of this move toward active participation in the art world. Unlike their European American counterparts, they had not yet come under the influence of Abstract Expressionism. Richmond Barthé's ideal but naturalistic portrait busts and full sculptural figures were widely appreciated.

Barthé chose as his subjects nonspecific, romantic character types and recognized celebrities from New York's theater world, and so was assured a prominent place in the small but progressively competitive New York art market.

Horace Pippin, a disabled veteran, originally turned to painting for its recreational and therapeutic aspects. But after being "discovered" by a Philadelphia art critic in the late 1930s and proclaimed shortly thereafter "the first important Negro painter to appear on the American scene," this self-taught painter became a professional. Following his New York debut in the Masters of Popular Painting exhibition at the Museum of Modern Art in 1938, his work received unprecedented acclaim. His unsophisticated but charming paintings of scenes from American history and rural life differed dramatically from the polished and visually literate works of Barthé. Yet the vogue for naive, folk, and "primitive" art fueled Pippin's success. Numerous group and solo exhibitions and the honor of being one of the first African American artists to be the subject of a full-length monograph, earmarked him for accolades during and after the war years.

In 1940 the precocious talents of the twenty-three-year-old Jacob Lawrence were known only by a handful of people beyond the African American community. By the end of 1941 Lawrence had become the wunderkind of the art world. His sudden fame came about as a result of his critically acclaimed migration series, several of which were published in the November 1941 issue of *Fortune* magazine. In December of that same year Lawrence's first one-man show at the Downtown Gallery clinched his reputation. Important museum purchases and exhibitions followed that signal event, including a solo show at the Museum of Modern Art in October 1944. As with Pippin's art, Lawrence's wholly original, elemental, and narrative style of painting was

JACOB LAWRENCE. *Strength*. 1952. Gouache on paper, 22 x 17½ inches.
Courtesy of D. C. Moore Gallery, New York.

CHARLES SEBREE. *Untitled*. N.d.
Oil on board, 16 x 12 inches.
Courtesy of Sacks Fine Art, New York.

often categorized as a modern and primitive hybrid, and his youth, race, and cultivated naiveté encouraged this perception.

As a young prodigy, Lawrence was strongly influenced by the older members of the Harlem Renaissance. He studied at the Harlem Art Workshop, the Harlem Community Art Center, and the American Artists School. In 1939, when Lawrence was twenty-one, his work *Touissant L'Ouverture* was exhibited at the Baltimore Museum of Art. In 1940 it was received with great acclaim at the Chicago Negro Exhibition. These series of paintings portray the struggle for Haitian independence. His other series—*The Migration, John Brown, Frederick Douglass,* and *Harriet Tubman*—all stemmed from his interest in and dedication to the history of African Americans. Lawrence's style is characterized by simplified directional forms and strong, flat color patterns. Although his work is distinctive, the works of Orozco, Daumier, Goya, Brueghel, and the early modernist Arthur Dove are apparent influences.

The perceived message in the collective success of Lawrence, Pippin, and Barthé seemed to be that the art world was ready to accept African American painters, sculptors, and graphic artists as equals to Euro-American artists. But it was not until the onslaught of all-Negro art shows that mainstream American attitudes would really begin to broaden. Between 1940 and 1946 there were at least twenty major, all-Negro art exhibitions nationwide.

In the 1940s, several other important art events in the African American community echoed the optimistic spirit of former times. The first of these events was the opening of Chicago's South Side Community Art Center in January 1941. The Art Center was a working symbol of President Roosevelt's belief in government that was responsive to the average citizen's cultural needs. It featured a good-size art gallery, where local artists like Charles Sebree (1914–85), Eldzier Cortor (b. 1916), William Carter (b. 1919), Margaret Goss Burroughs (b. 1917), and Charles White (1918–79) displayed their most recent work.

Another big event of the period was the June 1943 unveiling of Charles White's *The Contribution of the Negro to American Democracy,* a mural created for Hampton Institute (now Hampton University) in Hampton, Virginia. The work portrays the African American's struggle for full citizenship, with images of Crispus Attucks and the Boston Massacre, the activist Ferdinand Smith, and blacks active in America's labor unions. The Julius Rosenwald Fund, well known throughout the 1930s and 1940s for lending support to socially relevant causes pertaining to African Americans, financed White's project.

James Porter's *Modern Negro Art* was published in 1943 and has since become a classic in the literature on African American art. African American artists were filled with pride about finally being a recorded part of American history. Prior to *Modern Negro Art* most literature on African American art ignored important information about the culture and environment in which art was made.

A flurry of art events in 1945 and 1946 attested to the exhilarating tenor of the times. The Whitney Museum of American Art took a progressive step by not only featuring Barthé, Lawrence, and Pippin in its 1945 and 1946 annual exhibitions, but also introducing to audiences an emerging artist from Harlem, Romare Bearden. In 1944 Bearden had his first one-man show, at the G Place Gallery in Washington, D.C. In 1945 he was included in the Whitney annual and the Museum of Modern Art acquired its first Bearden. One of Bearden's paintings, along with the works of eleven other African American

SAMELLA LEWIS. *STIMULANT*. 1943.
Oil on canvas board, 24 x 18 inches.
Collection of Hampton University. Courtesy of Eugene Foney/Artcetera, Houston.

CLAUDE CLARKE. *THE BATH*. N.d.
Oil on canvas, 24 x 24 inches.
Courtesy of Third World Art Exchange, Los Angeles.

artists, was published as a four-page spread in the 22 July 1946 issue of *Life* magazine. In addition to Barthé, Pippin, and Lawrence, artists who had first achieved recognition during the twenties and thirties, like Palmer Hayden, Sargent Johnson, and William H. Johnson, as well as relative newcomers like Romare Bearden, Eldzier Cortor, John Wilson (b. 1922), and William Artis (1914–77), were featured.

Also in 1946, the appointment of Jacob Lawrence as a visiting artist at Black Mountain College and Hale Woodruff as an art instructor at New York University signaled the emerging presence of African American artists as teachers at Eurocentric educational institutions. While African Americans had previously broken barriers as students in predominantly white art schools, the notion of African American art instructors was still rare.

By the end of World War II African American artists had achieved a good measure of representation in America's burgeoning art scene. Of course, in certain parts of the country (and occasionally in New York City), there still existed

REX GORELEIGH. *UNTITLED LANDSCAPE.* Circa 1950.
Oil on canvas, 24 x 32 inches.
Courtesy of Bellevue Gallery, Trenton.

large pockets of segregation. But the overall tenor was one of active participation in the exhibitions, economics, and aesthetics of the times.

INTEGRATION AND PARTICIPATION

The call for integration in the period 1947–57 marked a major turning point for African American artists. The decade of the 1950s saw the beginnings of a more tolerant European American art community, due in part to expansion in the market, the economy, and education. Charles White, Beauford Delaney, Romare Bearden, Hale Woodruff, and Jacob Lawrence had become fix-

tures in the New York art scene, with frequent appearances in the Whitney annuals and numerous solo exhibitions to their credit. In the years that immediately followed, more attention was directed toward individual advancement, with hardly any references to race. Norman Lewis (1909–79), Merton Simpson (b. 1928), John Wilson, John Rhoden (b. 1918), Hughie Lee-Smith (b. 1915), and Walter Williams (b. 1930) began to appear in the art magazines under the rubrics "emerging artists" and "new talents," with rarely a "Negro" qualifier.

Eldzier Cortor was one of the most talked about painters in the 1940s. During the Depression he worked as an easel painter with the

ELDZIER CORTOR. *In These Troubled Times.* 1940.
Oil on canvas, 6 x 4 inches.
Courtesy of Robert Henry Adams Gallery, Chicago.

WPA. In 1945, after a decade of modest success, Cortor suddenly started receiving high praise for his paintings. In 1947 Cortor was awarded an honorable mention in the Carnegie Institute's Annual Art Exhibition. Cortor's entry, a painting of a full-length black female nude entitled *Americana*, touched off a small controversy even before the show opened. Shortly after the work was uncrated at the institute, vandals singled it out for defacing and slashing. Through quick restoration work Cortor's painting was allowed to go on view, but the obvious "jab" at his unique approach to black subject matter left him with a bitter feeling long after the incident.*

The influence of Surrealism is apparent in Cortor's disquieting images of urban life. His interest in non-Western art led him to study African art, which in turn led him to the South Carolina Sea Islands and the Gullah people, who have kept much of their African culture intact.

Like Cortor, Hughie Lee-Smith sought to depict African American subjects in a style neither Academic nor neoprimitive. He developed a surreal, personal, psychological style that used the city as a metaphor for isolation and apathy, as seen in *Portrait of a Boy*. Ernest Crichlow (b. 1914) also portrays daily urban life and black subjects. He uses a realist style.

While the works of Lee-Smith, Cortor, and Bearden look inward, the works of Elizabeth Catlett (b. 1919) engage in explicit social commentary and create heroic African American imagery. Considered a virtuoso sculptor and printmaker, Catlett has been concerned with social issues affecting African Americans, the Third World, and women. For more than forty years she has lived in Mexico City, and her art shows both African and Mexican influences. Her style is characterized by strong, simple forms and forceful symbolism. She reduces natural forms to expressive geometric shapes that create poignant images and unusually readable meanings.

Charles White was an accomplished painter and graphic artist. Like Catlett, he clung to an interest in realism and the figure. His paintings and drawings typically have strong contrasts of light and dark and a powerful dynamism stemming from an almost sculptural form. Much of his early work is full of social content like Lawrence's and Catlett's. In his later work he seems to have turned inward in the manner of Cortor and Bearden. White created images of love and prophecy with great psychological intensity. His major work, completed in 1940, is *Five Great Americans*. Created for the Chicago Public Library, the mural, with its idealized images of Frederick Douglass, Sojourner Truth, and Booker T. Washington, seeks to uplift the African American spirit by portraying the struggle for survival in America.

While some artists of the 1950s opted for Social Realism, or left the country to find their own way, others were swept up in the new movements that came to dominate the American avant-garde. The hotbed of experimentation was New York City, and the style of the time was Abstract Expressionism. Among its major exponents were Adolph Gottlieb, Mark Rothko, Robert Motherwell, Jackson Pollock, Theodore Stamos, and William Baziotes. Few African American artists followed this path at the time because institutional racism made it difficult for them to pursue such a seemingly frivolous pastime as producing abstract art. Furthermore, the majority of the white art world expected African American artists to stay with socially oriented work.

Norman Lewis was one of the first African Americans to embrace Abstract Expressionism. Lewis frequently exhibited in the late 1950s and found a ready audience for his art among members of influential art groups.

---

* Eldzier Cortor to Homer St. Gaudens, 15 September 1947, Eldzier Cortor Papers, Archives of American Art, Smithsonian Institution, Washington, D.C.

ELIZABETH CATLETT. *The Black Woman Speaks*. 1960.
Lithograph, 13¼ x 9 inches.
Courtesy of Sragow Gallery, New York.

NORMAN LEWIS. *Untitled.* 1947.
Oil on canvas, 30 x 36 inches.
Courtesy of Michael Rosenfeld Gallery, New York.

Norman Lewis is credited with laying the foundation for abstraction within the African American art community. A fine example of his early work is *Fantasy* (1936), a Kandinsky-like landscape of surreal abstract forms. Lewis paved the way for making abstract painting based on jazz. In *Street Music, Jenkins Band* (1944) he portrayed the same band found in Malvin Gray Johnson's *Orphan Band* (1934). Lewis had already abandoned the human figure of the thirties to find a visual equivalent to music in abstraction. Although the majority of Lewis's work from the 1940s on was not strictly abstract, he did use many visual metaphors and references to jazz.

The first generation of African American artists to seriously move toward abstraction were Romare Bearden, Norman Lewis, Hale Woodruff, and Beauford Delaney. Delaney is less known because he became an expatriate in France. However, an impressive body of his work exists in the United States.

Like many African American artists in the 1950s, these abstractionists did not merely seek to identify with the 1950s modernism but wanted to create works whose imagery was abstract yet understood by their African American public. They viewed themselves as African American *and* American. They sought to maintain their ties to black people.

Black consciousness rose again as a powerful force in the visual arts in the 1960s, and this time as a vital component of the civil rights movement. While the issues were basically the same forty years earlier at the time of the Harlem Renaissance, the tone was different. In the age of Black Power, anger, determination, and a revolutionary ardor prevailed, and the work of many African American artists during this time reflected this intensity. It was bold and confrontational, and paralleled developments in American art after World War II. African American artists participated in aesthetic schools like Abstract Expressionism, Color-Field, installation sculpture, and performance art, diverting their creative energy to fuel the black consciousness of the sixties and seventies.

Identification with Africa reemerged in the sixties, this time with even stronger intensity, as the term *Afro-American* suggests. As artists examined African culture—some even traveled to Africa—they found a significant quality that the artists of the Harlem Renaissance had not noticed: the spirituality of African art. Traditional art had largely been made for religious purposes and possessed sacred properties. The artists of the sixties chose to exploit this religious dimension rather than the physical symbolism favored by artists of the Harlem Renaissance.

THE NEW ART MARKET

Perhaps it was inevitable that in the period between 1958 and 1967 the rumblings of the civil rights movement and the changing nature of the art scene would coalesce and, in turn, provide the

African American artist an altogether new set of circumstances. While artists continued to integrate the art scene, a rapidly expanding art milieu offered any number of options to African American artists. Their works began to appear in other venues, such as the Museum of Modern Art, the American Academy in Rome, and new African American–run art organizations like the Ebony Museum (later renamed the DuSable Museum) in Chicago and the Studio Museum in Harlem.

The civil rights movement encouraged African American people to positively discover themselves. For the artist this meant freedom to explore diverse subject matter and aesthetic issues that could supersede race.

In 1958 Charles White's portraits of the cast members for the motion picture *Anna Lucasta* were used in the film's opening credits. These drawings, along with his portraits of the gospel singer Mahalia Jackson and the singer and actor Harry Belafonte, made him a favorite among the growing contingent of collectors and among African American performing artists in New York City and Hollywood.

In the same year a number of other African American artists, whose works were closely linked to the current abstract orientation of American art, came into prominence. The most important of these newcomers, sculptor Richard Hunt (b. 1935), had the honor of having both the Museum of Modern Art and the Whitney Museum acquire his work that year. Like White and Cortor, Hunt hailed from Chicago, where his reputation had first been established at the Art Institute. Beginning in the late 1950s (and continuing through the nineties) Hunt's sculptural innovations with welded metal secured for him a key position in the expanding American art scene.

Collage artist Sam Middleton (b. 1927), painter Richard Mayhew (b. 1924), and sculptor Barbara Chase-Riboud (b. 1936) are just a few of the many African American artists who, at this time, worked in the abstract mode. A few stalwarts in the late 1950s and early 1960s, however, continued to think in terms of humanism in art, among them collage artist Al Hollingsworth (b. 1928), sculptor and ceramist Earl Hooks (b. 1927), and painters Walter Williams and Bob Thompson (b. 1937). Thompson's colorful paintings of mysterious landscapes and mythical figures were especially sought after by major collectors, despite the prevailing tastes for abstract art and, later, Pop art. Thompson's premiere at the Delancey Street Museum in 1960, his affiliation with the Martha Jackson Gallery, and his overall success with the critics and collectors virtually ensured him artistic longevity, but his early death in 1966 halted what otherwise appeared to be a vital career on the rise.

Thompson, Hunt, White, and other African American artists greatly benefited from the nationwide emphasis on the arts in the 1960s, characterized by a growing market. From the middle of the decade on there was a steady increase in the number of viable art dealers in Manhattan, so much so that New York would surpass Paris and London to become *the* economic center of the art world.

In 1964 Raymond Saunders (b. 1934) received the Prix de Rome and a Ford Foundation Purchase Award for his painted transcriptions of urban walls, graffiti-covered sidewalks, and signage. As with other African American artists in Saunders's age group (Thompson, Hunt, et al.), the racial climate of the mid-sixties was less a catalyst for Saunders's imagery and more a proselytizing agent for a greater African American presence in the nation's museums and galleries.

Additional painters of this period include Joe Overstreet (b. 1934), Faith Ringgold (b. 1930), Jeff Donaldson (b. 1932), Kay Brown, Vincent Smith (b. 1936), David Hammons (b. 1943), Howardena Pindell (b. 1943), Vivian Browne (b. 1942), Benny Andrews (b. 1930), Ademola

Olugebefola (b. 1941), Al Hollingsworth, and Merton Simpson. These artists used African color and design as a vehicle to work single images in as many patterns and colors as possible, a technique that provided a conceptual parallel for the overlaying of complex rhythms and melodies found in jazz.

There were artists who focused on abstract painting without intentionally taking into account their African American background. This second generation of African American artists included Delilah Pierce (b. 1904), Alma Thomas (1891–1978), Sam Gilliam (b. 1933), Thomas Sills, Charles Alston, Richard Mayhew, Al Loving (b. 1935), Bill Hutson (b. 1936), Betty Blayton (b. 1937), Emilio Cruz (b. 1938), William T. Williams (b. 1942), Mary Lovelace O'Neal (b. 1942), Mildred Thompson (b. 1936), Jack Whitten (b. 1939), Frank Bowling (b. 1936), Ed Clark (b. 1926), Oliver Jackson, David Driskell (b. 1931), Sam Middleton, and Bill T. Rivers.

Sam Gilliam was one of the first African American artists to focus completely on form rather than content. His success was based on his application of structuralist methodologies to the possibilities of color stains and cloth supports. Like Gilliam, Richard Mayhew, Delilah Pierce, and Alma Thomas worked within the Color-Field school. Among their European American contemporaries are Helen Frankenthaler, Ellsworth Kelly, Jules Olitski, Larry Poons, and Kenneth Noland. This aesthetic addresses two components of painting—color and field. Painters apply color in swaths that often span the entire canvas, suggesting that it is a detail of a larger field. There is a deliberate intent to eliminate any distinction between a subject and its background, thereby treating the canvas as a single plane. This style of painting, also referred to as Post-Painterly Abstraction, flourished from the mid-1950s to the late 1960s.

The civil rights marches, sit-ins, and demon-

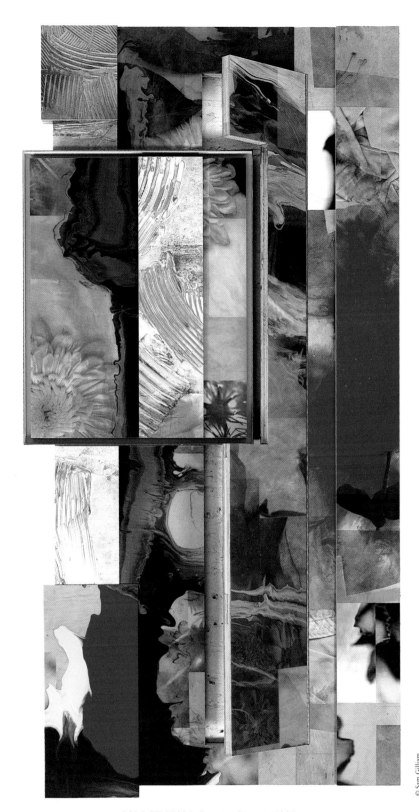

© Sam Gilliam

SAM GILLIAM. *Sesame, Sesame*. 1995.
Acrylic on paper and fabric mounted on hinged wood panels
(closed position), 81 x 41 x 16 inches.
Courtesy of Baumgartner Galleries, Washington, D.C.

ROMARE BEARDEN. *Uptown Sunday Night Session.* 1981.

Mixed media, paper collage on board, 44 x 56 inches.

Courtesy of Joyce and George Wein Collection, New York.

strations of the 1960s forced many professional organizations (including art organizations) to question their complicity in discrimination practices in the marketplace.

The problems facing African American artists in their uphill climb for a place in predominantly Eurocentric and abstract-oriented art centers are addressed at length in a series of letters exchanged among Romare Bearden, John A. Davis (editor of *African Forum* magazine), and William Lieberman (then curator of prints at the Museum of Modern Art). In November 1966 Davis wrote Lieberman to express his concern that an upcoming MoMA-sponsored print exhibition traveling to Africa did not include any African American artists. Lieberman's reply to Davis explained his exclusion of African American artists as "clearly curatorial," having nothing to do with the "race, creed or politics" of the artists. Davis shared Lieberman's response with Romare Bearden, who, in turn, took the opportunity to reflect upon the struggle for more African American representation in the art world:

To my knowledge, [Lieberman] made no inquiries among Negro artists to ascertain whether or not Negro painters like Norman Lewis, Alston, Woodruff, Ray Saunders, Lawrence, Felrath Hines, Hughie Lee Smith . . . are actually doing prints. . . . Had Mr. Lieberman been willing to look beyond the small "in" group that dominate the current art scene, he would have surely found representative artists, some of whom would have been Negro.

If Mr. Lieberman, however, feels that no Negro artist is worthy of being included—that is another thing. He is the curator of prints and drawings, and that is his value judgment —if so. But, you recall, before Jackie Robinson and Jimmy Brown, how often it was written that there were no Negroes of caliber to play baseball and football. Now look!!!

Bearden and Davis were particularly dismayed that this exhibition was destined for Africa, and that it was following on the heels of the historic but controversial First World Festival of Negro Arts, held in Dakar, Senegal, earlier that year. The tense situation, which made itself felt among the festival's black and white U.S. committee members, was, as Bearden pointed out to Davis, sadly being repeated in the MoMA-sponsored exhibition. "What is ironical," Bearden concluded, "is that even in the few events that concern us, we have no say."*

Faced with indifference and invisibility in the art world and a public sector casually responsive to African American artists, many African American artists decided to form their own arts organizations. In 1959 Chicago artist Margaret Goss Burroughs headed the group that organized Chicago's first predominantly black art fair. In 1960 she helped to spearhead the National Conference of Artists, an organization of African American art professionals. Burroughs continued her advocacy of African American artists and African American culture with the founding in 1961 of the Ebony Museum of Negro History and Culture. Ruth Waddy, Burroughs's associate and counterpart in Los Angeles, founded a comparable organization, Arts West Associated, in 1962.

In the summer of 1963 in New York City, several generations of African American artists (Romare Bearden, Norman Lewis, Richard Mayhew, Emma Amos) gathered to discuss their role in the current art scene. Calling themselves Spiral, this group debated the pros and cons of the opportunities and relevance of the visual arts of black America and organized an exhibition in 1965.

---

* John A. Davis to William Lieberman, November 1966.

ERIC PRYOR. *3RD EYE*. 1994. Oil on canvas, 32 x 47 inches.
Courtesy of Sande Webster Gallery, Philadelphia.

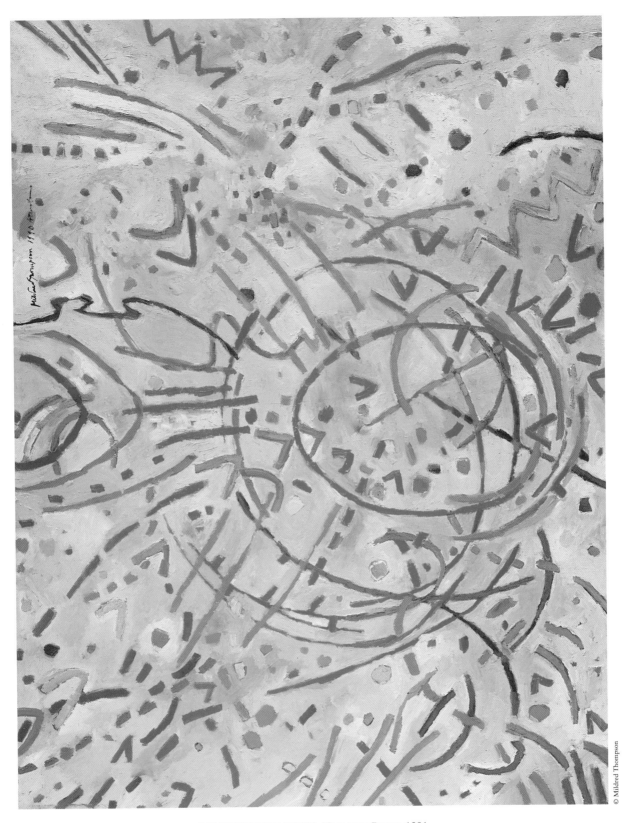

MILDRED THOMPSON. *MAGNETIC FIELDS.* 1991.

Oil on canvas, 62 x 47¾ inches.

Courtesy of Kenkeleba Gallery, New York.

JEFF R. DONALDSON. *JAM-PACKED/JELLY-TIGHT.* 1988.
Mixed media on linen, 36 x 50 inches.
Courtesy of Ayaso International Fine Art, Washington, D.C.

By 1964 a number of institutions and individuals began to respond in a favorable way toward African American artists. For example, the Martha Jackson Gallery hosted several benefit exhibitions around this time for the Congress of Racial Equality. In 1964 Bowdoin College in Maine organized an exhibition entitled *The Portrayal of the Negro in American Painting.* But the most racially conscious exhibition during this time was *The Negro in American Art,* jointly organized in 1966 by the California Arts Commission, UCLA Art Galleries, and the Dickson Art Center.

A major event of 1967 was the transferal of over a thousand works by African American artists from the recently closed Harmon Founda-

tion to the Smithsonian Institution's National Collection of Fine Arts (now the National Museum of American Art). The Smithsonian's acceptance of these works signaled a new commitment on the part of the government to African American cultural preservation. The Harmon Foundation had first approached both the Whitney Museum and the Museum of Modern Art about accepting these historic works, but predictably, neither New York museum, in this period of hard-edged abstractions and Pop dominance in art, was willing to receive them as gifts.

The increased politicization of African American artists and the concurrent distaste, on the part of the art establishment, for any art that smacked of sentiment, humanism, or expression

BENNY ANDREWS. *THE ENCOUNTER*. 1968.
Oil on canvas, 16 x 12½ inches.
Courtesy of Michael Rosenfeld Gallery, New York.

LARRY POTTER. *UNTITLED*. Circa 1965.
Oil on linen, 64 x 51 inches.
Courtesy of June Kelly Gallery, New York.

E. J. MONTGOMERY. *Fall Winds.* 1993.
Offset lithograph, 22½ x 30 inches.
Courtesy of Parrish Gallery, Washington, D.C.

gave the idea of an independent black institution greater urgency. These were the seeds from which sprouted the Studio Museum in Harlem in 1967, which subsequently became the first and only African American museum to be accredited by the Museum Association.

African American polarization continued to be a primary issue in 1967 with the founding of the Nyumba Ya Sanaa Gallery by Weusi, a group of Harlem artists. Ruth Waddy's Los Angeles–based organization was joined that year by a San Francisco branch, Arts West Associated North, founded by E. J. Montgomery (b. 1933). Chicago's Organization of Black American Culture made headlines when the artists in that group—Eugene Eda (b. 1939), Jeff Donald-

son, and others—painted a multipaneled mural on the side of a building in Chicago's African American community. This mural, entitled *The Wall of Respect,* and its raison d'être were firmly grounded in an aesthetic that was, without qualification, by, about, and for black people.

In 1967 City University of New York staged the exhibition *The Evolution of Afro-American Artists, 1800–1950.* Organized by Romare Bearden and historian Carroll Greene, this exhibition, along with *The Negro in American Art* show in California, ushered in for contemporary audiences the genre of the all-Negro art exhibition: something that had not been done since the 1940s. With their educational and historic thrust, these shows were generally well received.

But in the years that followed, such exhibitions would take on a whole new meaning and elicit very different responses from blacks and whites.

BLACK CONSCIOUSNESS, 1968–1976

Alain Locke's contention that artists must study and extract stylistic elements of African art, and incorporate them into their own work, came full circle in the late 1960s and early 1970s.

Richard Mayhew was both a landscape painter and an Abstract Expressionist. He is known for the use of lyrical colors that seem to occupy a fluid space that suggests poetry and music.

William T. Williams, Al Loving, Jack Whitten, and Bill Rivers each focused on geometric abstractions, employing a range of techniques that reflected a shared preoccupation with process and shape as form.

Howardena Pindell worked figuratively in the late 1960s. In the 1970s her aesthetic shifted, and she began to assemble small dots of paper pasted onto paper or canvas, creating subtly textured and delicate images that attached her to other movements of the period, including Process art and Conceptual art.

The period 1968–76 may come to be viewed by cultural historians as an extremely important period in African American art history. The increased amount of artistic activity and the flourishing of new arts organizations and careers were unprecedented. Although signs that there was a change in the attitudes of many African American artists were in evidence as early as 1960, in 1968 we see the first examples of widespread activism, as well as a new racial consciousness, among African American artists.

Obviously, the political assassinations, urban unrest, international conflicts, and domestic issues of this period easily played into this radicalization process. Even when these sociopolitical factors were not blatant elements of the artworks, they nonetheless made their presence felt in the contexts in which works were seen. The proliferation of black art exhibitions in the late sixties and early seventies focused the audience's attention on these racial matters.

Governmental policies pertaining to the arts created a situation in which the new philosophies could prosper. After the National Endowment for the Arts was established in 1965, congressional appropriations for the arts increased on an average of $1.5 million per year. In 1970 these appropriations almost doubled (from $8.25 million to $15.09 million), and they continued to escalate dramatically for much of the 1970s. For African American artists the endowment had the greatest impact in museum programs, in programs placing artists in the public schools, in individual fellowships for artists, and in programs specifically designed to support community art endeavors and other "expansion arts" ventures.*

Between 1968 and 1976 at least thirty major exhibitions focused on African American artists and their works. Many of these exhibitions were surveys and not very different from the 1966 UCLA show or the 1967 CUNY exhibition. On the other hand, many veered away from a strictly survey format, examining instead specific topics under the rubric of African American art and culture. In 1971 Rice University in Houston presented *Some American History,* a multidimensional art exhibition on African American history, which included the works of William T. Williams, Peter A. Bradley, Frank Bowling, Joe

---

* National Endowment for the Arts, *New Dimensions for the Arts, 1971–1972* (Washington, D.C.: National Endowment for the Arts, 1973).

HOWARDENA PINDELL. *Autobiography: Earth Undersea Tolland.* 1987.
Acrylic, gouache, oil stick, tempera, poly-photo transfer on sewn canvas, 70 x 105 inches.
Courtesy of G. R. N'Namdi Gallery, Chicago.

Overstreet, and European American Pop artist Larry Rivers. The High Museum in Atlanta followed a more historic approach with a 1973 exhibition featuring past annual award winners and other works from Atlanta University's art collection. *West Coast '74: The Black Image,* an exhibition consisting solely of works by California-based African American artists, was organized in 1974 by Crocker Art Gallery Association and the E. B. Crocker Art Gallery in Sacramento. Winston Kennedy and Ed Love, two art professors at Howard University, assembled in 1976 *Migraciones,* a print exhibition for the Museo de Arte Moderno la Tertulia in Cali, Colombia.

But the most important exhibition featuring the works of African American artists during this period was *Two Centuries of Black American Art,* curated by David C. Driskell. A former student of James Porter's at Howard University, Driskell was the first historian since Porter to provide fresh historical data on the colonial and antebellum antecedents of African American art.

Another important exhibition of this period was the 1971 *DeLuxe Show* in Houston, curated by Peter Bradley, an artist and associate director of the Perls Gallery. Bradley was interested in exhibiting the work of nineteen artists in an unusual, out-of-the-way place where people who usually do not attend art shows could be

AL LOVING. *Perpetual Motion #2*. 1993.
Rag paper and acrylic paint on plexi back, 34 x 31 inches.
Courtesy of G. R. N'Namdi Gallery, Detroit.

exposed to the work. It was after two bars and a few after-hours clubs had been considered and discarded that the abandoned DeLuxe Music House became the selected site for this major exhibition. After renovation, publicity, and the arrival of artwork, John de Menil, at the suggestion of Peter Bradley, invited critic Clement Greenberg to the show. The DeLuxe Show, according to Greenberg, was not the first show where art had been brought to a poor neighborhood, but the first place where "hard" contemporary art was exhibited in a poor region. "Nor was [there] any ethnic-cum-artistic demagoguery indulged in. The Black artists included were there on the same basis of quality or ambition as the white ones. I cannot praise the De Luxe Show enough on these scores. It sets a unique example, and one that I hope will be much imitated from now on."* The African American artists included in this show—Peter Bradley, Edward Clark, Sam Gilliam, Robert Gorden, Richard Hunt, Al Loving, and William T. Williams—represented the second generation of serious African American nonrepresentational artists to be included in a quality exhibition of American art.

Works of artists like Faith Ringgold, Cliff Joseph (b. 1921), and Black Panther Party artist Emory Douglas (b. 1943) had an overt political slant to them. Similarly, Boston artists Dana Chandler (b. 1943) and Gary Rickson (b. 1942) collaborated in 1968 on one of the more striking of these murals, *Stokely Carmichael/H. Rap Brown*. Chandler and Rickson, along with African American muralists in Chicago, Detroit, and New York, were heirs to a mural tradition in Afro-American art that dates back to Charles White's and John Biggers's work and to even earlier murals of the Harlem Renaissance artist Aaron Douglas.

Although the Whitney Museum of American Art was criticized for its limited support of African American artists in the sixties, between 1968 and 1976 the number of African American artists who appeared in annuals, biennials, and solo exhibitions rose considerably. In the 1970 Whitney Museum Sculpture Annual, eight of the ninety-nine sculptors exhibited were African American. Also in 1970, sculptor Frederick John Everley and painter Al Loving both had solo exhibitions in the Whitney's first-floor gallery. In 1972 Washington, D.C., painter Alma Thomas became the first black woman to have a solo exhibition at the Whitney, followed in 1975 by Betye Saar (b. 1929) and folk artist Minnie Evans (1892–1987).

The year 1971 proved to be a major one for African American art, as seen in the solo exhibitions given to Romare Bearden, Richard Hunt, and Sam Gilliam at the Museum of Modern Art. Bearden's exhibition, *The Prevalence of Ritual,* was both a critical success and one of the more popular exhibitions that season, thereby firmly establishing the artist as a major figure in modern art. In the spring of that year, the Museum of Modern Art looked in retrospect at the direct-metal sculpture of Richard Hunt. The usually acerbic Hilton Kramer perhaps enhanced the art establishment's already high estimation of Hunt when he described the artist as a "virtuoso practitioner of open-form sculpture."*

Sam Gilliam's 1971 installation of dyed, splashed, and draped canvases introduced to Modern Art's clientele and the New York public his theatrical and innovative forms. Gilliam's exhibitions that year and in the following year at

---

* Clement Greenberg, *DeLuxe Show Catalogue,* Houston, Texas, 1971.

* Hilton Kramer, "From Open-Form to the Monolithic Cube," *New York Times,* 4 April 1971.

the Museum of Modern Art Galerie Darthea Speyer in Paris and at the Venice Biennial extended his reputation far beyond that of most other American artists, black or white.

Visibility and successes aside, African American artists still struggled with the critical establishment when the subject of an African American aesthetic arose. As long as their art was seen as either a highly personal vision or part of current mainstream art, it was a serious endeavor. But as soon as the tag "black" appeared on the art or a group exhibition, this immediately sent the uninitiated into an ideological tailspin, damning the artistic efforts as "political," "propagandistic," and/or just plain "inferior." A classic case of this universal blindness in recognizing an independent and vital African American sensibility in contemporary art was Robert F. Moss's essay "The Arts in Black America," published in the 15 November 1975 issue of *Saturday Review*. Moss assesses artistically successful works by African American artists as usually approximating a white model.

Among the many irate letters to the editor that the *Saturday Review* published following Moss's article, several mentioned the populist aspect of African American art as an element that Moss largely ignored.* These respondents foreshadowed the primary concerns in the following years: redefining and revising the prevailing notions about African American art.

REVISION AND REASSESSMENT, 1977–1980

The dominant presence of African Americans in the Second World Black and African Festival of

---

* "Letters from Readers," *Saturday Review,* 7 February 1976, 6–7.

Arts and Culture—held in Lagos, Nigeria, in January and February 1977—represented the first visible sign of cultural revision in the latter half of the 1970s. Artists, curators, and critics of the late seventies—exponents of a "post-black consciousness" point of view—sought out specific themes within African American art.

The trend continued in 1978 when the Cleveland Museum of Art mounted a very ambitious and different African American art exhibition. Entitled *The Afro-American Tradition in the Decorative Arts,* this exhibition examined wood carving, boat building, basket weaving, quilting, and pottery making by African American folk artisans. Curator John Vlach made distinctions between crafts that were derived from a European American tradition, and those works on exhibit that carried in their forms and uses a particular African American quality.

In 1979 the Studio Museum in Harlem, in conjunction with Howard University's Gallery of Art, presented *Impressions/Expressions: Black American Graphics.* Looking at African American contributions to the printmaking medium over several centuries, the exhibition raised provocative questions concerning graphics and its propensity for social commentary.

In 1980 *Forever Free: Afro-American Women Artists* opened at Illinois State University. This exhibition explored the feminist vision in African American art from a variety of perspectives.

Also in 1980, the traveling exhibition *Afro-American Abstraction* presented nonrepresentational works by black artists. Painters Raymond Saunders and Sam Gilliam, the curator turned collagist Howardena Pindell, wood sculptor Martin Puryear, conceptual artist David Hammons, and fourteen other artists were included in this exhibition. On the whole, *Afro-American Abstraction* challenged the racial hegemony of a recognizable African American figure in art by articulating the racial and cultural possibilities of color usage, geometric forms, and popular concepts. David Hammons's *Victory Over Sin*—an installation comprising a spacious room, with the walls and floor covered with podlike drawings, tall, swaying reeds, and patches of kinky human hair—was hailed by *Time* magazine art critic Robert Hughes as possessing "the sort of obsessive intensity that signals the presence of a real talent."

But the most important event for African American art at this time was the opening in 1979 of the Museum of African American Art in Los Angeles, which joined that city's Museum of Afro-American History to form the westernmost link for African American art.

In an essay about the African American artistic presence on the West Coast, art historian Allan Gordon describes the artistic ascendancy of black California as an "improvisational" act, operating outside the art "mainstream" or, at best, existing on the mainstream's edge. Gordon's "improvisation" metaphor for black art in California actually served as a code for all African American art on the eve of the 1980s. In the throes of institution building as well as protests against racism, African American art activists of the late 1970s had to think and act quickly in order to better their lot.

As African American artists moved through the 1980s, their emphasis was redirected to defining their personal direction and improving organizational skills. Major cutbacks in federal arts appropriations (beginning in fiscal year 1982) caused a large number of publicly funded art programs either to close down or to limit their offerings. Likewise, job opportunities for African American art professionals dwindled. Visual artists worked in an essentially private capacity while the art world's deep immersion in a "marketplace" mentality pushed most African American artists away from full participation in the art scene.

The 1980s saw a revitalization of the black visual arts through critical and institutional support. There were major retrospective exhibitions of groups of African American artists as well as individuals. The historian Sharon Patton defines this decade as a "time marking the co-option and appropriation of black culture by Euro-American society."

Within the last decade of the twentieth century African American artists have begun to break away from the superficial isms and categories that have been imposed on them. A new sense of psychological freedom has enabled them to explore, redefine, and assert a collective culture and society through an individual perspective.

Extensive documentation is available for many of the artists mentioned here, and you are encouraged to refer to the Selected Bibliography.

As you familiarize yourself with the history of African American art and its aesthetic movements, you will begin to identify artistic influences and recognize each artist's distinctiveness.

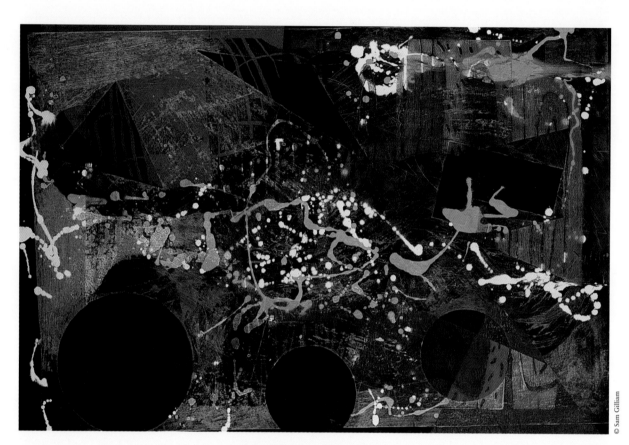

SAM GILLIAM. *CHEHAN.* 1989.
Original monoprint, 44 x 30 inches.
Courtesy of Essie Green Galleries, New York.

6
PRINTS

Printmaking can be a very communal activity.

The medium is not the thing in and of itself. It's what the

artist does with it that matters. It's simply a vehicle for

conveying a creative impulse. It's merely an extension of the

idea. The artist is always shaping space. The work evolves as

a part of himself. It parallels his development.

ROBERT BLACKBURN

Original prints have been made in the United States since the colonial period. Before the American Revolution (1775–81) prints were portraits of important figures or political cartoons. None of these earlier prints were what we would understand an original print to be today: a limited edition made, signed, and numbered by an artist. Modern concepts of authenticity became universal after the success of commercial printmaking, which threatened to drive most fine artists from the field at the end of the nineteenth century. Limiting the production of a print to a few copies ensured that each was made unique with the addition of the artist's signature, while encouraging the idea that art prints were scarce and desirable.

The origins of printmaking can be traced to the ancient Near East. Over five thousand years ago the Sumerians, the earliest known printers, were creating relief impressions in clay using stone seals and carving them with pictures and inscriptions. The use of seals spread from Mesopotamia to India

EVE SANDLER. *ABYDOS*. 1986. Chinecole etching, 22 x 30 inches.
Courtesy of Printmaking Workshop, New York.

and eventually made its way to China. The Chinese applied ink to their seals in order to impress them on wood or silk. By the second century A.D. they had invented paper. The art and products of printmaking, traced to eighth-century China, reached the medieval West through the Arabs, who were known as great traders. By the ninth century books and prints were being done on paper using wooden blocks carved in relief. Two hundred years later the Chinese developed movable type.

It was not until the early 1400s that Europe focused on developing printing technology, and this period of development elevated the printing process to another standard of excellence. Gutenberg invented the printing press, and later lithography was developed in the late 1700s by Alois Senefelder. The majority of printmakers in the late fifteenth and early sixteenth centuries received their training as goldsmiths, and most of the printing shops retained the structure of medieval guilds. After 1500 there was little else that was done to perfect this process until the Industrial Revolution, beginning in 1830.

Historically, most prints were made to convey information, thus ushering in an era of general literacy. By definition, prints are multiple originals. Prints were usually bought by people who could not afford "unique" works of art, which diminished the medium's standing in a hierarchy where the wealth of the patron and the preciousness of the object carry great weight. Fur-

CAROL M. BYARD. *THOUGHTS: MAY YOUR ASPIRATIONS UNFOLD IN ASCENSIONS WAY*. 1984.
Lithograph, 16½ x 20 inches.
Courtesy of Printmaking Workshop, New York.

VINCENT SMITH. *The Masquerade Is Over*. 1995.
Monotype, 22 x 30 inches. Courtesy of Printmaking Workshop, New York.

thermore, the finished print was rarely the work of a single hand. Although some great printmakers, like Rembrandt, were intimately involved in every stage of their works—the conception, execution, and printing—many more relied on expert craftsmen to make the plates and run the presses. Throughout the eighteenth century and much of the nineteenth century most American prints served as advertising or political posters. Few early printers had the skill or interest to work with artists to achieve the level of quality necessary for fine art printmaking. Between the mid-nineteenth and the mid-twentieth centuries, the strictly commercial relationship between artists and printers gradually evolved into a more creative interaction among skilled individuals.

Although most American models for collaborative printmaking were based on European precedents, the fascination with Japan prevalent in the late nineteenth and early twentieth centuries introduced European and American artists to the centuries-old tradition of Japanese color woodblock printing, a method requiring the close cooperation and interdependence of artist, carver, printer, and publisher.

In comparison to European and Asian artists, Americans came late to fine art printmaking and artistic collaboration. The process of collaboration has always involved the artist and the printer. The artist creates the image, and the printer transfers the image to a printing matrix (a metal plate or woodblock; later a stone, a screen, or other surface). In many cases there is also a publisher who initiates the project, a person who approves the print, and another, usually the publisher, who distributes it. Some artists fulfill all these roles, but more frequently, they work together with at least one other person.

There are few recorded historical antecedents of African American printmakers in the United States because of the anonymity of slave artisans. Yet African American printmakers are known to have existed as early as 1724. The only known portrait of the slave poet Phillis Wheatley was engraved by Scipio Moorehead, another Boston slave, in 1773. Fifty years later, a father and two sons are known to have been active in the Boston printing shop of Thomas Fleet, who had arrived in Massachusetts in 1821, seeking refuge from the religious persecution he had suffered in England. Only the two sons are identified by name, Caesar and Pompey, but all three were said to have been "bred to press." These artisan slaves were trained in Fleet's shop to set type and to do woodblock engraving. According to Fleet, the father was an exceptional artist, "who cut on wooden blocks, all the pictures which decorated the ballads and small books of his master."*

Patrick Reason (1817–ca. 1850), known to have been an engraver, draftsman, and lithographer, was apprenticed as a youth to an engraver in New York. Grafton Tyler Brown (1841–1918) owned and operated his own lithography firm in Oakland, California. During the first three decades of the twentieth century, African Americans who followed this profession found outlets

for their works in magazines, newspapers, journals, and other popular publications. The majority of the work by African American artists was confined to articles that focused on race relations. Magazines like *Crisis, Survey Graphic,* and *Opportunity* provided these artists the greatest amount of exposure.

Through the early twentieth century lithography largely remained out of favor among American artists as a medium for fine art printmaking, not because of its commercial associations, but because few professional printers had the ability or patience to work with artists. There was no money to be made from small editions, and artists tended to demand high-quality work. Those who wanted to make fine art lithographs usually had been introduced to the medium in Europe, and often printed their editions there. Making an image on a lithographic stone was much more direct and autographic than any other printmaking technique, because the printing itself was a delicate procedure requiring great technical skill. Many artists found the printing process frustrating and the results poor.

Among the few professionally trained American lithographers in New York City was George C. Miller. He opened his own workshop in 1917 and would later politely refuse Robert Blackburn the opportunity to study with him. He did, however, produce lithographs for artists Thomas Hart Benton, Arthur B. Davies, Stuart Davis, Childe Hassam, Louis Lozowick, Charles Sheeler, and Grant Wood, among others. He was one of the finest printers of the time.

During the 1920s African Americans became glamorous to mainstream white audiences for the first time. Interest in African American life and culture was evoked by the popularity of black-inspired music and Harlem's allure as a thrilling, seductive place with faintly degenerate entertainment. Yet none of this interest displaced

---

* Isaiah Thomas, *The History of Printing in America with a Biography of Printers, and an Account of Newspapers, to Which Is Prefixed a Concise View of the Discovery and Progress of the Art in Other Parts of the World* (Worcester, Mass.: Press of Isaiah Thomas, Isaac Sturtevant, Printer, 1810).

any of the negative images and stereotypes about African Americans.

While the Harlem Renaissance produced major writers and artists, their words and images penetrated the minds of relatively few white Americans. In the same way, the works of African American printmakers were largely ignored by white critics and even less often marketed and collected. Fortunately, two exhibitions exposed the value of their work. The first was curated by American art historian, scholar, and educator Leslie King Hammond's *Black Printmakers of the WPA* and collector-historians Reba and Dave Williams's *Alone in a Crowd: Prints of the 1930s–1940s by African-American Artists from the Collection of Reba and Dave Williams.*

The images that white artists of this period produced of African Americans were not monolithic: Every medium had its own version of stereotypes. The artists of the period included Marion Greenwood, Prentiss Taylor, James Barre Turnbull, Palmer Schoppe, Isac Friedlander, Joseph Hirsch, Meyer Wolfe, Reginald Marsh, Paul Cadmus, Philip Evergood, and Thomas Hart Benton. Among the subjects of interest was lynching, which became a symbol for liberal sympathy for the "Negro condition" and an icon of evil and injustice that was at a safe distance in the benighted South. The other theme was black worship, which fascinated privileged white artists because of its "authentic and natural flavor," so different from the worship of white revivalists. There was also a fascination with Gullah stories and dialects of the isolated African American coastal communities in the Carolinas. These communities preserved African language and customs more purely than anywhere else in the country, just as certain mountain dialects in the Smoky Mountains seemed to have preserved Elizabethan speech perfectly. In these instances

African Americans were accepted and held up as worthwhile subjects, because they were perceived as less constrained by "civilization" and closer to nature. Artist Julian Bloch, who made a career of creating respectful depictions of African Americans in the 1930s, described his motives: He was "attracted by the rich color, rhythmic movement, laughter, and religious fervor so characteristic of the race. . . . Most of my people have been humble workers."

It was not until the WPA Federal Arts Projects that African American artists found viable conditions to explore their own creativity, develop printmaking processes, and gain access to new technologies. Hughie Lee-Smith states, "We artists got along . . . as human beings creating art. There were no black projects or white projects, and that was one of the good things about that whole period."* The WPA thrived over an eight-year period, from 1935 to 1943, and had a phenomenal impact on the African American art community. Without this opportunity, many black artists would not have been able to pursue their art careers. More important, the artists of this period provided history with a visual legacy of their time, culture, and ideals. These artists include Charles Alston, John Thomas Biggers, Robert Blackburn, Elmer Brown, Hilda Brown, Samuel Joseph Brown, Jr., Calvin Burnett, Margaret Burroughs, Elizabeth Catlett, Claude Clarke, Eldzier Cortor, Ernest Crichlow, Allan Rohan Crite, Charles Clarence Dawson, Aaron Douglas, Carl G. Hill, Louise E. Jefferson, Wilmer Jennings, Sargent Johnson, William H. Johnson, Henry Bozeman Jones, Lawrence Arthur Jones, Lois Mailou Jones, Ronald Joseph, Hughie Lee-Smith, James E.

---

* "Black Printmakers and the WPA, A Symposium," *The Tamarind Papers*, volume 13 (New York Public Library, Prints section, 1990).

ALLEN L. EDMUNDS. *HFA II*. 1992. Offset lithograph, 21½ x 30 inches.
Hariston family album. Courtesy of Brandywine Workshop, Philadelphia.

ERNEST CRICHLOW. *WAITING*. 1968.
Second-edition print, 16 x 14 inches.
Courtesy of Janet M. Harrison, New York.

Lewis, Norman Lewis, Samella Saunders Lewis, Richard William Lindsey, William McBride, Hayward Louis Oubre, Georgette Seabrook Powell, David Ross, Charles Sallee, William E. Smith, Raymond Steth, Dox Thrash, James Lesesne Wells, Charles White, Clarence Williams, John Woodrow Wilson, and Hale Woodruff. Hale Woodruff and Robert Blackburn were able to utilize the opportunities afforded by the WPA as a springboard to later establish institutions that helped preserve and promote the African American artist.

JOHN T. SCOTT. *BEHOLD THE LAMB*. 1970. Etching, 8 x 10 inches.
Courtesy of Tim Francis, Esq. Collection, New Orleans.

BARBARA WESSON. *LADY IN BLUE SARONG*. 1992.
Oil on canvas, 56 x 43 inches.
Courtesy of Third World Art Exchange, Los Angeles.

RON ADAMS. *PROFILE IN BLUE*. 1989.
Lithograph, 56 x 43 inches.
Courtesy of Lewallen Contemporary Gallery, Santa Fe.

DOX THRASH. *INTERMISSION.* 1940.

Etching, $8\frac{7}{8}$ x $5\frac{7}{8}$ inches.

Courtesy of Dolan/Maxwell, Philadelphia.

The WPA Graphic Arts Division of the Federal Arts Project centered in Philadelphia became the springboard for four noteworthy artists: Dox Thrash, Claude Clarke, Raymond Steth, and Samuel Brown. These artists were directly assigned to the printmaking division. Brown was officially attached to the watercolor division but found the time to expand the print medium. Dox Thrash was the head of the graphics division.

The Carborundum print can be directly attributed to Thrash. Carborundum is the trade name for a coarse, granular industrial product made of carbon and silicone that is used for grinding and polishing. The Carborundum print developed out of Thrash's use of Carborundum crystals to resurface used lithographic stones. Thrash experimented by manipulating various grades of Carborundum crystals until he achieved a wide range of tints and tonal variations in the final print. Although shop mates Michael J. Gallagher and Hubert Mesibov deserve credit for helping to perfect this process, this pursuit was initiated and, for the most part, developed by Dox Thrash. Because Carborundum was a commercial trade name, Thrash called his prints carbographs and later Opheliagraphs, after his mother.

Community art centers emerged in various urban centers, and black colleges also served as major catalysts for creativity. Community art centers provided young artists with new experiences in the arts, and in particular, experiences that they had been excluded from because of America's racism. Consequently, unique relationships between artists, teachers, and students evolved. One of the benefits of community art centers was that they provided many artists with their first exposure to the printmaking process. They also provided exhibition opportunities for art students. Without these centers, many artists would not have had an opportunity for creative experimentation and artistic growth.

Karamu House, founded in 1915 in Cleveland, Ohio, was one of the most active centers. Karamu is a Swahili word meaning "center of community." Prior to receiving funding from the WPA/FAP, Karamu House was known for its theater group. The artists who were hired as teachers eventually formed the Cleveland Karamu House Artists Association, Inc., in 1935. Artists Hughie Lee-Smith, Elmer Brown, and Charles Sallee were members. These artists, with their technical mastery and their dedication to making art, influenced numerous younger artists.

Because of the prolific activity in the literary, performing, and visual arts during the Harlem Renaissance, Harlem was coined the cultural capital of black America. The Harlem Community Art Center became a focal point for the WPA community center projects. In the imagery and thematic aesthetics of the artists associated with it we see the influence of the Harlem Renaissance, evident in references to African heritage, African American history, music, religion, social injustice, folklore, heroes, legends, and daily life.

The Harlem Community Art Center was directed by painter Gwendolyn Bennett. Among its many accomplished alumni are Selma Burke, William H. Johnson, Aaron Douglas, Palmer Hayden, Jacob Lawrence, and Augusta Savage. Among the center's influential artist-teachers were Charles Alston, Ernest Crichlow, Norman Lewis, and Robert Blackburn. Riva Helford was the artist-teacher credited for teaching Robert Blackburn how to make the lithographs. A great teacher is by definition a perpetual student, and these artist-teachers exemplified this quality. Although there were periods of great productivity during this time, many of the prints have not survived. One of the reasons for this is that there were no African American curators sixty years ago. There were no curators who cared about this work. Consequently, it was not properly catalogued and was lost or damaged.

Another community art center of great significance is the South Side Community Art Center in Chicago. Founded in 1941, it was a latecomer to the roster of WPA facilities. Much of its success resides in the presence of artists like Charles White, Gordon Parks, Archibald Motley, Jr., Charles Sebree, and Margaret Burroughs. Burroughs has the distinction of being one of the few women to experiment with prints at a time when most women were assigned to sculpture and easel projects.

Colleges and universities were also instrumental in nurturing the development of African American printmakers. One of the most important of these institutions was Atlanta University, which included Spelman College and Morehouse College. Hale Woodruff was hired in 1931 to develop a fine arts curriculum for Atlanta University, as well as to teach painting and drawing. Under his direction a gallery opened in 1932 to showcase faculty and student artists. While working for the university, Woodruff was hired by the WPA/FAP. One of his students was Wilmer Jennings, who worked with lithography and wood engraving. Jennings was among the United States' greatest wood engravers.

Although the most significant activities of the WPA/FAP took place in black communities on the East Coast and in the Midwest, Sargent Johnson, who lived in the San Francisco Bay area, was one of the only artists to be assigned to the WPA/FAP sculpture division and the only African American to achieve the position of senior sculptor, assistant supervisor, assistant state supervisor, and, ultimately, unit supervisor. While his primary focus was ceramics and sculpture, he developed his interest in printmaking in the 1930s. The prints he produced during this period expressed his racial consciousness and pride.

In 1941 Hale Woodruff became the force behind the Atlanta School of African American Artists, and he established the first competition for artists at Atlanta University. The result of these efforts is the Atlanta University Art Collection. By 1948 Robert Blackburn had started the Printmaking Workshop in New York City. This workshop, an invaluable center for artistic and technical development of the print process for African American artists, has received national and international recognition. Typical to the medium, artists who were especially interested in it offered to serve as assistants to the printers in order to observe their technical secrets. Robert Blackburn was introduced to lithography at the Harlem Community Art Center by Riva Helford. When Blackburn sought professional instruction in the medium from George C. Miller, who was one of the few professionally trained lithographers willing to work with artists in New York City, he was told, "Young man, if you want to learn anything from me you'll have to spend a hundred dollars a week, and I'll teach you something." A hundred dollars was a fortune at that time, so Blackburn gleaned what he could from painter and printmaker Will Barnett.

It was with Barnett's assistance, in 1948, that Blackburn established his workshop, which offered classes in lithography. It was an open studio for printing and experimentation where artists and students could work together and share their knowledge and discoveries.

In 1953 Blackburn left the workshop for a number of years to study in France as a Whitney Fellow. He also served as master printer at the National Academy of Design and as a graphics instructor at the New School for Social Research. In 1957 he joined Tatyana Grosman at Universal Limited Art Editions, where he printed for Robert Rauschenberg, Robert Motherwell, Larry Rivers, and Helen Frankenthaler. Some of the most exciting developments in American printmaking took

ROBERT BLACKBURN. *A Walk in the Shade.* 1983. Woodcut, 22 x 30 inches.
Courtesy of Printmaking Workshop, New York.

place at ULAE at that time. After five years at ULAE, Blackburn returned to his Printmaking Workshop with renewed energy and vitality. Known as the dean of printmaking within the African American art community and beyond, Blackburn developed a reputation as an extraordinary printer who could entice anyone to attempt his first work in the collaborative process. The workshop was incorporated as a nonprofit organization and has established one of the most remarkable educational, exhibition, and printmaking facilities. One of the guiding principles of the Printmaking Workshop has been to give opportunities to students and artists of all nationalities and economic status to learn lithog-

raphy and other print media and have access to a competent printer. It is a remarkable place where a community of artists explores the potential of printmaking, sharing technical expertise and creative ideas. Hundreds of artists at various stages of their careers, and from all around the world, have spent time working with Bob Blackburn. His workshop has trained numerous printers who have gone on to develop their own printmaking facilities.

Among them is the Sudanese artist Mohammed Omer Khalil. In 1964 Khalil met Blackburn during his second visit to the United States. Bob encouraged him to resume their relationship should he return to the States. Khalil subse-

TARLETON BLACKWELL. *HOG SERIES CXXXV: Cinderella Section XVIX.* 1995.
Graphite, prismacolor, and watercolor, 20 x 16 inches.
Courtesy of Lewallen Contemporary Gallery, Santa Fe.

GERALDINE McCULLOUGH. *CONFRONTATION*. 1992.

Ink resist on paper, 11 x 8½ inches.

Courtesy of Essie Green Galleries, New York.

quently worked at Pratt Institute with Michael Knigen, and when a position became available at the Printmaking Workshop, he worked and studied with Blackburn for a year before opening his own workshop in 1969.

Among the artists whose prints can be purchased at the Printmaking Workshop are Emma Amos, Benny Andrews, Ellsworth Ausby, Carol Byard, Camille Billops, Willie Birch, Robert Blackburn, Betty Blayton, Kabuya Bowen, Bob Broner, Marion Brown, Marvin Brown, Vivian Brown, Nanette Carter, Edward Clark, Melvin Clark, Houston Conwill, Jayne Cortez, Eldzier Cortor, Adger Cowans, Ernest Crichlow, Roy DeCarava, Nadine Delawrence, Melvin Edwards, Elton Fax, Michelle Godwin, Lawanda Graves, Maren Hassinger, Curlee Raven Holton, Manuel Hughes, Margo Humphrey, Noah Jemison, Ronald Joseph, Jacob Lawrence, Spencer Lawrence, Norman Lewis, James Little, Whitfield Lovell, Al Loving, Richard Mayhew, Valerie Maynard, Joanne McFarland, Ademola Olugebefola, Mary Lovelace O'Neal, Laurie Ourlicht, Lee Pate, Lawrence Philip, Stephanie Pogue, Aaron Ibn Pori-Pitts, Hugh Lawrence Potter, Richard Powell, Doris Price, Debra Priestly, Mavis Pusey, Helen Evans Ramsaran, Calvin Reid, Pat Richardson, Faith Ringgold, Aminah Robinson, Moses Ros, Betye Saar, Eve Sandler, Lorna Simpson, Michael Singletary, A. J. Smith, Vincent Smith, Willie Stokes, Maxwell Taylor, Mildred Thompson, Luther Vann, Charles White, Stanley Whitney, Michael Kelly Williams, and William T. Williams.

The Print Council of America was formed in 1956 by a group of museum curators, dealers, artists, collectors, and scholars with a goal to "foster the creation, dissemination, and appreciation of fine prints, old and new." It was the advocacy of the Print Council that did much to legitimatize collaborative printmaking and bring it to the attention of wider audiences. New prints were the focus of many of the council's discus-

sions, as were such topics as the lack of recognition for contemporary printmaking and for printmaking as a medium, the confusion between original and reproductive prints, the lack of standards of quality for new prints, and the lack of publications devoted to prints and printmaking. New publications emerged that gave attention to prints, such as *Artist's Proof, Print Review, The Tamarind Papers,* and, in 1970, *The Print Collector's Newsletter.* Eventually museums added staff and broadened their scope to acquire, exhibit, and publish catalogues of new prints. Traditional collectors of prints generally stored their prints in portfolios to be brought out for study and appreciation. In the 1960s new collectors began to frame and display their prints. Like new collectors in general, these print collectors were educated and displayed their acquisitions to signify both cultivation and social status. As print sales began to compete with paintings, presses invested in larger machines to accommodate the market for large-scale works. Museums and corporations began to purchase large works for gallery and boardroom walls.

The efforts of June Wayne to establish the Tamarid Lithography Workshop in 1959 successfully nurtured the development of master printers in the United States. The impact of the workshop was evidenced by a revival in print interest, which inspired art dealers and publishers to recognize new markets for prints. In New York during the late 1960s Pace, Marlborough-Gerson, Leo Castelli, Richard Feigen, Irwin Hollander, and Gimpel and Weitzenhoffer were pioneers in the market for prints, and published print editions. The Ken Tyler Workshop was also significant to the artists and the marketplace. One of the developments of the 1960s was the practice of publishing prints of several artists together in portfolios. In fact, the Wadsworth Atheneum in Hartford was one of the earliest museums to publish contemporary prints with its

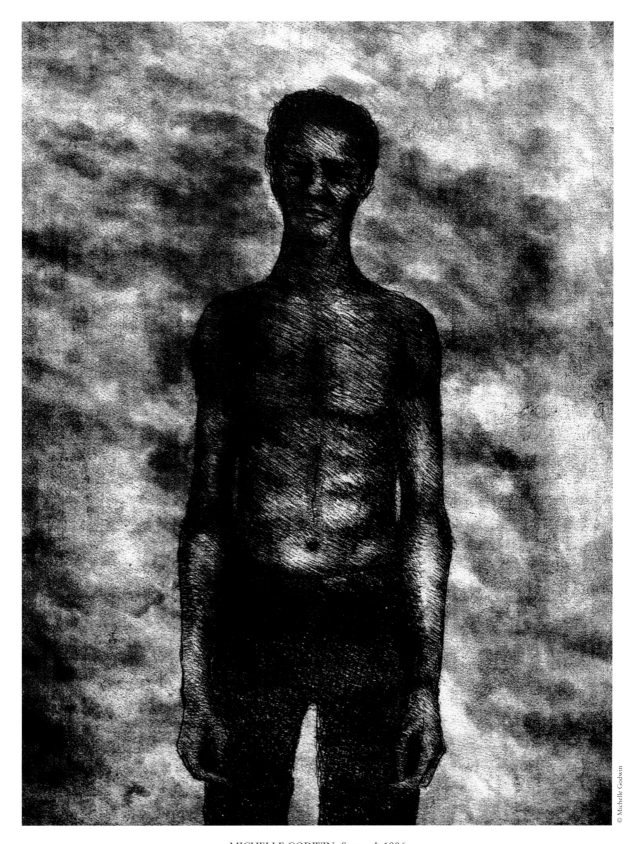

MICHELLE GODWIN. *Smoke I.* 1986.
Etching, 22 x 30 inches.
Courtesy of Printmaking Workshop, New York.

14/30   *Lovers*   *Ernest Crichlow*

ERNEST CRICHLOW. *LOVERS.* 1938. Lithograph, 14 x 12 inches.

Courtesy of Janet M. Harrison, New York.

ELIZABETH CATLETT. *Jackie*. 1985.

Lithograph, 30 x 22¼ inches.

Courtesy of Sragow Gallery, New York. Photo by Sarah Wells, 1996.

Ten Works + Ten Painters Portfolio, setting an example that would be followed by many other nonprofit institutions.

Throughout the 1960s and early 1970s the market for prints was vigorous, and prices rose steadily. As the political events and economic recession of the late sixties dampened the nation's optimism, the art world lost much of its fascination with Pop, Op and Happenings.* There was renewed interest in art that was formal, intellectual, and cooler in spirit.

In essence, the decade of the 1960s was committed to developing an audience for prints. While many artists made stylistic breakthroughs in this period, they continued to explore ideas and formats in their printmaking, including new aesthetic and intellectual concerns that were nurtured by the politics of the time and an array of styles of expression. Many artists rejected the Pop artist's fascination with mass-produced works. The New Realism, Photorealism, Conceptual art, and Minimalism of the early 1970s approached printmaking with renewed objectivity and formalism emphasizing shape, size, structure, scale,

---

* Pop Art draws on the subject matter of advertising and media for its visual celebration of postwar consumerism; the movement, which flourished in the early 1960s, was a reaction against Abstract Expressionism. Op, or optical art, creates the illusion of movement. A Happening is an assemblage of events, including the act of painting, performed or seen at more than one time and place.

TERRY ADKINS. *Djuka Suite.* 1996. Photogravine and aquatint, 22 x 26 inches.
Courtesy of Janet M. Harrison, New York.

DEWEY CRUMPLER. *GIVERNY DUSK #122.* 1990. Acrylic on paper, 38 x 50 inches.
Courtesy of Porter Troupe Gallery, San Diego.

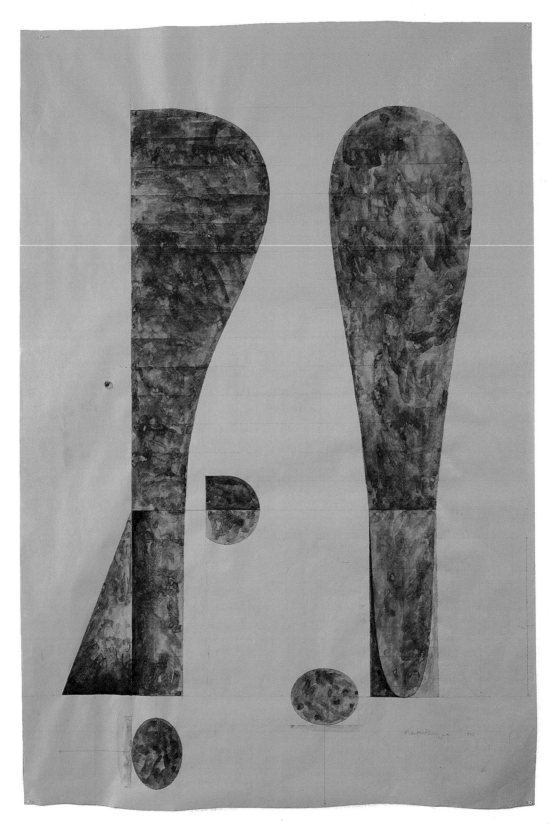

MARTIN PURYEAR. *STUDY FOR OUTDOOR SCULPTURE.* 1995.
Ink wash and pencil on brown paper, 80 x 22 inches.
Courtesy of Donald Young Gallery, Seattle.

GLEN LIGON. *WHITE #1*. 1995. Aquatint and etching, 19½ x 14½ inches.
Courtesy of Betsy Senior Gallery, New York.

composition, and color.* An exciting aspect of this period was that printmaking became a vehicle for exploring the meaning of art and a medium for resolving the conflicts between the intellectual, political, and visual worlds.

Although the Pop and Op styles of the 1960s featured the transferring of images, and the systematic laying down of lines and flat areas of color with the machinelike precision of lithography and screenprinting, the 1970s ushered in a renewed interest in intaglio processes. Etching, aquatint, and drypoint, which could express every linear or tonal nuance of the hand, became a favored medium for many artists. The 1970s also represented a period of development and expansion in the marketplace for prints. Established presses worked with many of their original artists and with new talent, new print shops developed their own relationships, and a growing number of dealers and publishers promoted editions with increasingly sophisticated marketing techniques.

Among the new print shops that emerged after Robert Blackburn's Printmaking Workshop was Workshop, Inc., under the direction and skill of Lou Stovall. Born in Athens, Georgia, Stovall grew up in Massachusetts, studied at the Rhode Island School of Design, and graduated from Howard University. A master printmaker, Stovall is also a noted artist, craftsman, poet, and curator specializing in Washington, D.C.–area artists. Arthur Wheelock, Jr., writes of the sense of joy and celebration infusing Stovall's prints,

which, he says, "comes not just from [the artist's] lyrical transformations of the natural born, but also from the care with which he has approached his craft." Workshop, Inc., has grown from a small but active studio, primarily concerned with community posters, into a professional printmaking facility. Recognition of Stovall's craftsmanship has gained him commissions to print the works of such noted artists as Josef Albers, Peter Blume, Alexander Calder, Elizabeth Catlett, Gene Davis, David Driskell, Sam Gilliam, Gwen Knight, Jacob Lawrence, Robert Mangold, Mathieu Mategot, Pat Buckley Moss, Paul Reed, Reuben Rubin, A. Brockie Stevenson, and James Lesesne Wells.

The American artists of African descent whose work can be purchased from Workshop, Inc., include Elizabeth Catlett, William Buck Clark, Jeff Donaldson, David Driskell, Sam Gilliam, Sterling Hykes, Lois Mailou Jones, Walter Lattimore, Jacob Lawrence, Ed Love, Lloyd McNeil, Anita Philyaw, Joe Ross, Sylvia Snowden, James Lesesne Wells, and Franklin White.

Another important print shop is Brandywine Workshop, founded in 1972 as a not-for-profit institution dedicated to printmaking and bringing culturally diverse artists and audiences together to pursue innovative, quality fine art. Brandywine was founded by master printmaker Allen L. Edmunds, whose mission has been to enhance the role of people of color as both visual artists and audiences in contemporary society. Artists are encouraged to share their cultural awareness and talents in all media in ways that benefit youth and the community.

Edmunds's experience in the fine and graphic arts and in institutional development has earned him international stature. He received a BFA from the Tyler School of Art and an MFA from Temple University, where he majored in printmaking and minored in education. Brandywine

_____

* New Realism, a figurative alternative to Abstract Expressionism, is characterized by a psychological, cerebral, and nonexpressionistic handling of paint. Photorealism is a style of painting that takes as its subject the photograph and the photographic vision of reality. Conceptual art places emphasis on the idea, not on the object. Minimalism eliminates representational imagery and illusionistic pictorial space in favor of a single unified image, often composed of smaller parts arranged according to a grid.

LOU STOVALL. *FOR ASCENDING LARKS*. 1980. Silkscreen, 28 x 28 inches.
Courtesy of Workshop, Inc., Washington, D.C.

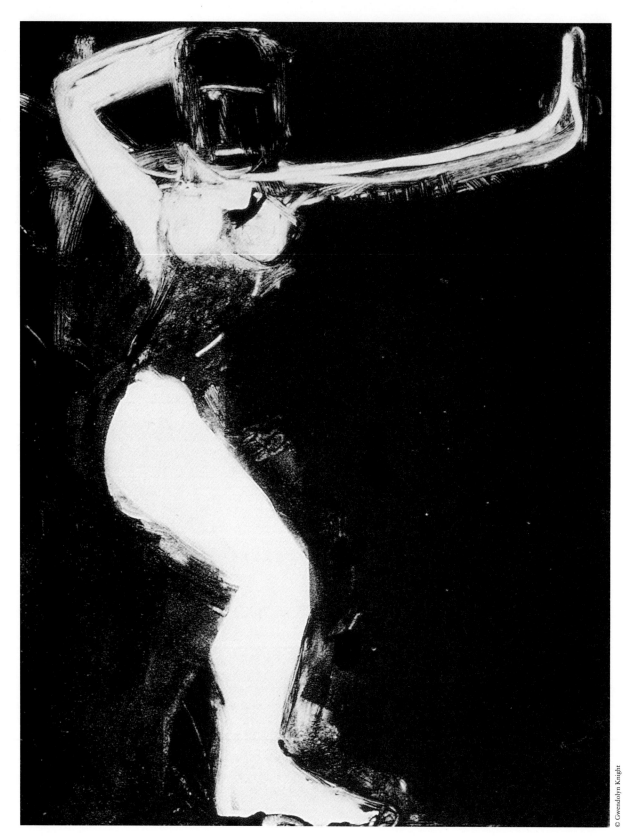

© Gwendolyn Knight

GWENDOLYN KNIGHT. *BLACK DANCER*. 1994.
Monoprint on paper, 26 x 19 inches.
Courtesy of Francine Seders Gallery, Seattle.

MARGO HUMPHREY. *Dorothy's Flowers.* 1997.
Nine-color lithograph, 25 x 32⅞.
Courtesy of Murphy Rabb, Inc., Chicago.

hopes to change the face of Philadelphia's arts community by serving as a point at which cultural currents converge and diverse collaboration is realized. Brandywine is affiliated with the Pennsylvania Academy of Fine Arts, the Museum of Contemporary Hispanic Art, the Pennsylvania Council on the Arts, and the Philadelphia Redevelopment Authority's One Percent for Art Program. Artists of African descent whose work has been printed and can be purchased at Brandywine include Ron-Akili Anderson, Benny Andrews, Romare Bearden, Orisegun Bennett-Olomindom, John Biggers, Camille Billops, Willie Birch, Berrisford Boothe, James Brantley, Moe Brooker, Marvin Brown, Samuel Brown, Selma Burke, Weldon Butler, Elizabeth Catlett, Barbara Chase-Riboud, Edward Clark, Nanette Clark, Adger Cowans, Louis Delsarte, John Dowell, David Driskell, James Dupree, Walter Edmonds, Allen Edmunds, Melvin Edwards, Agboola Folarin, Sam Gilliam, Simon Gouverneur, Estella Gullant, Bill Harris, Michael Harris, Napoleon-Jones Henderson, Barkley Hendricks, Leon Hicks, Vandorn Hinnant, Margo Humphrey, Richard Hunt, Bill Hutson, Martha Jackson-Jarvis, Wadsworth Jarrell, Lois Mailou Jones, Paul Keene, Gwen Knight-Lawrence, Jacob Lawrence, Hughie Lee-Smith, Al Loving, Deryl Mackie, Jimmy Mance, Percy Martin, Valerie Maynard, Quentin Morris, Keith Morrison, Floyd Newsume, Mary Lovelace O'Neal, Magdalene Odundo, Martin Payton, James Phillips, Howardena Pindell, Michael Platt, Leo Robinson, Alison Saar, Betye Saar, John Scott, Charles Searles, Gary Smalls, A. J. Smith, Frank Smith, Sylvia Snowden, David Stephens, Kaylyan Sullivan Two Trees, Hubert Taylor, Evelyn Terry, Phyllis Thompson, John Wade, Pat Ward Williams, Richard Watson, James L. Wells, Stanley Whitney, Clarence Wood, and Shirley Woodson.

Collaboration is primary within these master workshops. Traditional collaborative printmaking requires three stages: the creation of the image by the artist; the preparation and proofing of the printing matrixes; and the production of the edition. An artist might come to a print shop with a preliminary drawing and create an image on a plate, block, or stone. The printer then proofs the images, corrects and adjusts the plates, and provides the artist with various ink colors and paper types to choose from. When the artist approves a prototype, a right-to-print proof (bon à tirer) is signed and the printer then produces a uniform edition of impressions that the artist then approves and signs.

Today, the artist and printer often work and experiment jointly in the preparation of the matrixes, proofing through many stages to arrive at the final stage to be editioned. Clearly, in these relationships the printer is often more than a mere translator or replicator of the artist's vision. For example, an artist may arrive at a press with no preconceived idea of what they will make, and plates and proofing may be prepared as the image is being created. In the making of unique works such as monotypes, monoprints, or hand-colored prints, creation and production often take place simultaneously, with artist and printer working in tandem. The role of the printer has expanded as more research and experimentation is undertaken independent of actual projects at hand. The result is that the printer, often an artist or someone with a strong background in art, has become a colleague who can assist and inform projects, and the workshop becomes both a laboratory and a production facility.

Throughout the 1970s shops bought presses that allowed them to print larger sheets of paper and to work with multiple processes. Fascination with paper, as a support for the printed image and as material that could be manipulated on its own, reflected a new interest in craft and the physicality

ALISON SAAR. *Black Snake Blues*. 1994.
Offset lithograph, 22 x 30 inches.
Courtesy of Brandywine Workshop, Philadelphia.

ARTIS LANE. *Emerging into Spirit.* 1996.
Lithograph, 36 x 24 inches.
Courtesy of Satori Fine Art, Chicago.

of the print. Some artists produced editions of embossed paper that did not include any actual printing.

The contemporary printmaking market saw, in the 1980s, a renewal of interest in relief processes. Inspiration came from early-twentieth-century German Expressionist prints, traditional Japanese woodblocks, contemporary Minimalist art, and international folk art. Abstract and representational artists enthusiastically explored relief prints, some combining relief with lithography, screenprinting, and intaglio processes.

It can be said that collecting prints in America has been a specialized pursuit, with the majority of collectors concentrating on etchings, engravings, and woodcuts by old masters. The prints produced under the Federal Arts Project were not intended for private collections because they were distributed to public institutions. In the postwar years the market for specialist prints was limited until large-scale prints accompanying advertisements began to appear in major art magazines. Collaborative prints looked different from the recent American prints people were accustomed to seeing. They conveyed the aesthetic of painters, not that of specialist printmakers. They also looked effortlessly professional. Many artists use prints to further develop images that already exist in paintings or to explore ideas that lend themselves more to printmaking than to painting. Some artists see printmaking as a continuum, and others see it as a separate activity of their aesthetic development. By the end of the 1980s the print market had become firmly established in America, and almost every important artist had made some contribution to the medium. It was throughout the 1980s that more contemporary African American artists produced a great deal of work on paper. Artists no longer made one or two prints at a time but spent extended periods at workshops involved in projects. This can be explained in part by the revival of interest in Minimal or Conceptual work at the end of the decade as Neo-Expressionism (a revival of interest in the traditional formats of easel painting and carved sculpture) ebbed from the scene. The nature of the imagery required sequential presentation. Some prints had entered the mainstream to the extent that private collectors and museums were buying in volume. The print market, however, functions in concert with the rest of the general economy. This could be seen during the print market crash of 1990, in which the spring auctions at Sotheby's and Christie's were not as successful as they had been. With a major recession in the country, art was perceived as a nonessential luxury. Print publishing was curtailed as publishers and workshops tried to survive on their inventory.

It has taken thirty years for printmaking to become a part of the fabric of the American art scene. It is no longer a subordinate aesthetic process. The influence of printmaking has exceeded technological innovation because it has been both immediate and future oriented. As we approach the end of this century, changes in the demands of higher education, in the ability to raise significant resources for nonprofit art organizations, and in the market for contemporary prints will ensure that nonprofit and university-affiliated workshops will continue to metamorphose into different and more challenging structures with greater business and marketing acumen, fund-raising skills, and educational prerogatives. All of this, combined with a parallel interest by collectors, ensures greater opportunity for both artists and collectors.

© Don Camp

DON CAMP. *YOUNG MAN #2, MILLION MAN MARCH.* 1995.
Earth pigment in casein, 30 x 42 inches.
Courtesy of Sande Webster Gallery, Philadelphia.

7

PHOTOGRAPHY

The symbol is not the thing symbolized

The map is not the territory

The word is not the thing

S. I. HAYAKAWA

hotography is involved, directly or indirectly, in almost everything we experience visually. It's hard to imagine a world without photographs and photographic processes. We take for granted television, motion pictures, and magazine and newspaper illustrations, but these are only the more obvious signs of the influence of photography on our lives.

Photography critic, historian, and educator A. D. Coleman affirms that "photography is so thoroughly interwoven into the fabric of our culture that the warp of our culture and the loom of history are absolutely dependent upon it for stability."* It wasn't always like this. Newspaper and magazine reproductions of photographs were still a novelty at the beginning of the twentieth century. Color photography was in its infancy in 1910. As we approach the twenty-first century we have CD-ROM, video, Web sites, and Internet imagery to increase our dependence on the image. Instead of restating the history of the photographic medium, I encourage the collector to read the books listed in the Selected Bibliography (see Coleman, Rosenblum, Willis-Thomas).

Of all the markets, photography may offer the most opportunity and excitement for the collector.

---

* A. D. Coleman, *Light Readings: A Photography Critic's Writings, 1968–1978* (New York: Oxford University Press, 1979).

ANDRES SERRANO. *Blood Cross*. 1985.
Cibachrome print, 30 x 40 inches.
Courtesy of Fay Gold Gallery, Atlanta.

Although prices have risen dramatically in recent years, you can still buy the work of almost any photographer, no matter how famous, for less than $1,500. Photographs by the best new photographers sell for as little as $200. No other field of collecting offers so much quality for so little money.

One of the reasons that photography has taken a long time to gain acceptance as an art form is that people doubted the expressive potential of the "little brown box" and believed that because anyone could take a photograph, it did not require the skill of an artist. Since 1839 there has been a fearful disdain and lack of regard for the medium beyond its being a tool to assist painters. It was never considered equal in

creativity to drawing and painting. This view is supported by the belief that since the photograph utilizes a mechanical device and chemical phenomena, it should not be considered art. However, the camera itself, without a human agent, is a "dumb" machine. And yet, like etching and lithography, photography has replicable techniques and is as significant as handmade works of art. Others consider photography to be too literal to be art; the photograph, they argue, requires narrative, allegorical, or genre images in order for it to have value. Skeptics wonder how a photograph can be valuable if the negative can yield an infinite number of prints. In the case of fine art photographs rarely are more than a few to a dozen of the same image ever

ROLAND CHARLES. *THE LIVING BIBLE*. 1993.
Cibachrome print, 16 x 20 inches. Courtesy of Black Gallery, Los Angeles.

© Albert Chong

ALBERT CHONG. *Self-Portrait with Eggs from the I-Trait Series.* 1985.
Silver gelatin print, 30 x 30 inches. Courtesy of Porter Troupe Gallery, San Diego.

printed. There are four basic kinds of photographs available in the marketplace: early one-of-a-kind photographs, nineteenth-century paper prints, twentieth-century master prints, and contemporary photographs.

Early one-of-a-kind photographs Some of the first photographs include daguerreotypes, ambro-types, and tintypes. All were printed, without a negative, directly on the surface of a sheet of copper, glass, or tin. As a result, each photograph was unique. The plates were typically leather-bound glass cases and are so attractive they are collected in their own right. Photography was a popular art from the very beginning. Between 1840 and 1860 more than thirty million daguerreotypes and other one-of-a-kind photographs were made in the United States alone. Because the supply of these objects is vast and the demand is relatively small, early one-of-a-kind photographs are generally inexpensive, often costing as little as ten to fifteen dollars. The vast majority of early one-of-a-kind photographs were portraits of unknown people. If you want to assemble a good but inexpensive collection of early photographs, look for unusually appealing anonymous portraits. Some early photographs command higher prices because of the specific historical significance of the subject or the standing of the artist/photographer.

Nineteenth-century paper prints The majority of prints produced at this time were daguerreotypes, tintypes, and albumin prints. Among the nineteenth-century photographers of African descent are James Presley Ball, Sr., of J. P. Ball and Son; Thomas Ball and Alexander Thomas; Glenalvin Goodridge, the Goodridge brothers, Wallace and William; Harry Shepard; Jules Lion; James Conway Farley; and Henry Ossawa Tanner, to name a few.

Twentieth-century master prints The three basic categories of twentieth-century master prints are fine art photography, documentary photography, and photojournalism, although many photographs fall into more than one category.

Traditionally, **fine art photography** is defined by the constructs of academia and art history, in which visual and historical references are used to define the criteria for strong and weak aesthetics. When photographs transcend literal images by reason of their visual power, symbolic resonance, and sublimity, they have the attributes of fine art photography. In essence, the images often go beyond the literal idea of the subject that is being photographed. Content is a quality that is universally recognizable.

Documentary photography and **photojournalism** can describe any given image. Both styles can achieve the greatness and brilliance to move

from their specific realms into art. Documentary photography is self-defining: Photographs, as documents, are "truthful" renderings of the world the photographer sees before him.

Photojournalism is a visual expansion of journalism. But whereas the concept of journalism is related to the area of the daily newspaper, photojournalism is, generally speaking, the main support of the illustrated weekly magazine. Contemporary photojournalism, however, is chiefly manifested in photo reportage, photo stories, and photo essays. In many ways photojournalists are documentary photographers. Often photographic styles overlap and intertwine, so it is important not to limit yourself to the "idea" of a particular style.

It is equally important to know the types of prints that are in the market regardless of the style of photography.

Vintage print A print made by the photographer, or directly under his supervision, about the time when the negative was taken.

Series print A print made by the photographer, or under his supervision, but some time after the negative was taken. Because the negative may have altered with time, or the photographer may have used different printing papers or chemicals, the surface of the image may be significantly different from that of vintage prints.

Posthumous print A print made after the death of the photographer, perhaps by someone he or she designated.

Copy print If a negative is destroyed or is unsuitable for printing, it is possible to make a copy negative from a print. Prints made from the copy negative are called copy prints and are not considered to be original photographs.

Combination print A print that combines more than one image on a single sheet of photographic paper. Techniques for making composite images include multiple exposures, the layering of negatives, and collaging. The print may also be referred to as a photomontage.

Contact print A print made by passing light through a negative that has been placed in direct contact with sensitized paper. A positive image is produced in the same size as the negative.

Dye transfer print A highly involved method of printing that can produce very stable color prints of unequaled quality. Three separate negatives of the original subject matter are produced through red, green, and blue filters. The negatives are then exposed to special matrix film and are subsequently dyed yellow, magenta, and cyan. The matrixes are then carefully registered and individually contacted onto a receiving paper, and the color dyes are transferred to form a full-color print.

Clearly not all images are limited to the modernist canon of the straight silver print. The ease of mechanical printing processes is seen in work by photographers who have explored etching, engraving, lithography, and silk screen. Photo etchings retain an aura of realism while avoiding strict verisimilitude. This is a recognized technique among photographers and graphic artists. There are also straight photographs, collages, and montages on a variety of materials using digital imaging, printing, and photography.

PHOTOGRAPHERS TO SEE

Roy DeCarava is a fine art photographer who works in a documentary style. It may not be his intention to literally translate everything he photographs; rather, his work is more about mood, atmosphere, and sublimity. In 1955 DeCarava became the first African American to receive the prestigious Guggenheim Fellowship. The second African American recipient was Don Camp, who was honored in 1995. Additional fine art photographers include Elisabeth Sunday, Beuford

Smith, Anthony Barboza, Fern Logan, Coreen Simpson, Conrad Barclay, Jeanne Moutoussamy-Ashe, Lorna Simpson, Jules Allen, Carrie Mae Weems, Eli Reed, Roland Charles, Dawoud Bey, Ming Smith, Frank Stewart, Charles Martin, and Louis Draper.

Gordon Parks has worked in many different areas of photography, but he is most known for his black and white photography, which can be defined as documentary. Park's most significant contribution to the medium is his ability to impart to his images a certain visionary quality that transforms the ordinary into the iconographic.

Other documentary photographers are P. H. Polk, James VanDerZee, Morgan Smith, Marvin Smith, Chuck Stewart, Roland Freeman, Robert Sengstacke, Marilyn Nance, Bill Gaskins, Ozier Muhammad, Eli Reed, Moneta Sleet, Chester Higgins, Jr., Ovie Carter, Roy Lewis, Michelle Agins, Salimah Ali, Lenore Davis, Barbara Dumetz, Sharon Farmer, Alex Harsley, Renee Hannans, David Lee, Odell Mitchell, and Bob Black, to name a few. Between 1969 and 1986 Ovie Carter, Michel duCille, Matthew Lewis, Ozier Muhammad, Moneta Sleet, and John White won the coveted Pulitzer Prize for photography. Although most of these photographers are known for one particular style, none of them is limited to any one. This classification is solely intended to provide a reference, which may assist you in assembling a collection.

The contemporary photography market provides the best buys in photography by living photographers who have not yet achieved master status. So, do ask the photographers you meet about their colleagues. Regionally they tend to know one another and will make referrals to others whose work they admire. Prices range from $150 to $1,000 for most photographers.

As a general rule, the highest prices in photography are paid for twentieth-century master prints, especially for good rare work. Excellent

© Renee Cox

RENEE COX. *YO MAMADONNA AND CHILE*. 1994.
Silver gelatin print, 40 x 60 inches.
Courtesy of Christinerose Gallery, New York.

works remain available to the budget-conscious collector for $1,000 or less. You simply have to avoid frequently reproduced images.

Currently the most prominent photographers with works available in the marketplace include James VanDerZee, P. H. Polk, Gordon Parks, Roy DeCarava, Lorna Simpson, Carrie Mae Weems, Pat Ward Williams, Dawoud Bey, Albert Chong, Andres Serrano, Renee Cox, Clarissa T. Sligh, and Lyle Ashton Harris.

SEEING PHOTOGRAPHS AS ART

Not enough attention is paid to the criteria for looking at photographs and a specific visual vocabulary for "reading" photographs as objects of art. Also overlooked is the historical context of black photography, that is, the framework in which the photographers have worked, and how it corresponds to the body of work they produce.

The basis of all aesthetics is rooted in the relationship between the brain and the senses (sight, hearing, taste, smell, and touch), which enables us to experience stimuli in our environment. Covering our eyes when the sun is too bright and moving our hand away from a hot object are responses completely based on habit. Similarly, when our eye sees an image, it is naturally inverted. Like a camera, our brain automatically adjusts the image right side up, which is the way we think we see things.

All art operates inside a "framework" that exists in our brain. This framework includes an artistic form, vocabulary, and syntax that are universal. There are always changes happening within the framework because our expectations are or are not met. Once the photographer resolves an aesthetic challenge, you, the viewer, enter a "dialogue" with the image the photogra-

pher creates. You have an opportunity to discover and reacquaint yourself with familiar experiences through this image. This personal dialogue enables you to come to terms with the image in a negative or positive way. You may like it or dislike it, or find it strange, interesting, disturbing, or thought-provoking.

The most basic, but significant, aspect of photography is that it is simply the process for the *articulation of light on a surface.* For example, the image of you and your family can only be seen because you were the surface for the light to highlight. The detection of light and shadow is essential to the survival of all living things. Photosynthesis is the interaction between the sunlight and the chlorophyll from the leaves. The *photo* in photosynthesis and in photography means "of or produced by light." Plants require light to grow, and people and animals use light and shadow to detect the presence or absence of danger. Light is particularly important to photography because our eyes are continually reacting to it. Light reveals the unfamiliar and alters the symbols of our reality. It can make something that is very ordinary appear unusual. Light can create patterns with shadow that provide order or chaos in a picture. It can evoke moods, associations, and emotion by imbuing the subject with meaning, atmosphere, and poetic qualities.

There are several considerations that a photographer keeps in mind. One of the first basic properties of photography is **time.** The photographer's ability to capture a fleeting instance on film makes the difference between a great image and a mediocre image. Similar to other arts, photography is completely dependent on the materials it uses. Film records light streaking a surface. Time addresses the issue of controlling that light. Time and light are both important tools of the medium and are a major area of concern for a photographer. You might want to ask yourself

DAWOUD BEY. *Lakesha, Jackie, and Crystal.* 1996.
Eight panels, 60 x 92 inches overall.
Courtesy of David Beitzel Gallery, New York.

how an artist uses his materials. How many ways is time important to the photographs you encounter? Both the photographer and the viewer are fascinated with the way time conveys a sense of change and permanence. This is because time presents reality in a way the mind does not usually perceive it. The mind relies on its sensory perceptions. What happens when your mind responds to something it thinks it saw but actually has not? You become captivated by an image of a frozen motion. The ability to catch a fleeting moment in photography is referred to as the "decisive moment." Within the 170-year history of photography, French photographer Henri Cartier-Bresson is best known for his ability to capture a fleeting moment without compromising the elements of an organized, well-composed picture.

Another characteristic of a good photograph is that it evokes associations from our own experience. **Symbolism** in photography highlights references to a familiar object, yet provides new meaning to that object. This is similar to a caricature, which distorts a person's features, exaggerating the size of the nose, chin, or mouth. We see a person whose face is all nose, chin, or mouth. The range of symbolism in photographs is vast. Therefore, any object or situation can be recorded by the camera in a way that enhances its normal meaning, making it symbolic instead of realistic. Our perception of the impact of this change is based on a familiar reference about the subject or object.

There are many ways for a photographer to organize a photograph. Like a painter, a photographer uses traditional methods of organization —perspective, balance of shapes, triangles, and lines. Compared with a painter, a photographer

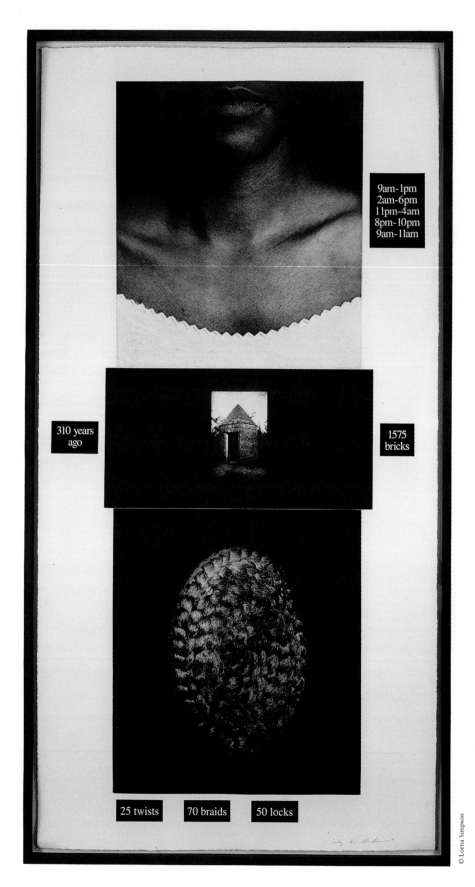

9am-1pm
2am-6pm
11pm-4am
8pm-10pm
9am-11am

310 years
ago

1575
bricks

25 twists   70 braids   50 locks

LORNA SIMPSON. *COUNTING*. 1991. Photogravure with silkscreen,
76 x 40¼ x 2¼ inches. Courtesy of Dr. Robert H. Derden Collection, Chicago.

has a much more difficult task of organizing his picture. Part of this has to do with eye and hand coordination. Another factor is how the photographer selects the forms in his image. Specific forms that are included or excluded from a picture are paramount to the organization of a photograph.

One reason the concept of **abstraction**—not representing things realistically—pleases the mind is that it provides the satisfaction of solving a puzzle. Our brain automatically creates meaning in everything we see based on our references and memories. Our brain sees things as a whole, not as pieces of something. In photography the movement of the camera above or below eye level alters the way a subject appears on the surface of the film. The lens flattens a spatial relationship into a pattern that looks abstract. This destroys the usual clues and symbols of identity our brain requires to create order and understanding. Ambiguity of spatial relationships and content arouses our curiosity about the object. It also creates tension between what we expect to see and the unexpected dimension of what we actually see before our eyes.

Have you ever had a dream in which familiar faces and places look different from reality? This is **surrealism,** where the unconscious mind is brought into the photograph. Surrealistic photographs contain mysterious qualities addressing issues beyond the reality you experience every day. Simply put, surrealism is the opposite of symbolism in photography. Symbolism enhances the normal meaning of an object in reality. Surrealism distorts the usual meaning of an object as if it were a part of a dream. Surrealism fascinates us. Surrealistic photography is full of innuendo and suggestion. We respond more emotionally to a surreal image than to a realistic one, because a logical response to the story described is difficult. Surrealism can explore humor, a dream, non-

sense, and is a link to the subconscious mind. Objects and ideas in these images shock us, surprise us, and intensify our response to them.

Pictorialism is a quality in photography that stresses the content of a picture over its form. It provides the viewer with an accurate and subjective description of the subject of an image. The subject matter is realistic.

Many people unfamiliar with photography as art ask what makes a photographer "see" things differently from others? What makes a photographer take a particular photograph? How does a photographer use a camera to describe what he sees? To chart out the birth of a photograph: A photographer has to recognize the image, and take the picture. It sounds simple, but it is not. Imagine that you are walking down the street or on vacation. You suddenly witness an extraordinary event or you see something that excites you. You have a camera and decide to take a picture. However, one of the forms in your image is moving, like an animal, a person, a flag. In order for you to photograph what you see, the movement of this form must stay the same. Since you are an observer, you cannot go up to a stranger and say, "Hey, don't move, I'm taking a picture and you are a part of it." Form is an unavoidable element in all traditional art. The way in which photographs are taken proves there is not only a form of observation but also a form of action. For instance, in other art forms the issue of how to reconcile "form of observation" with "form of action" arises. Should the poet write the revolutionary hymn at home or mount the barricade in person? In photography there is no escape: The photographer must be present where the action is.

Photographers have to see the image and take the picture simultaneously. This requires eye and hand coordination. This ability is not the same for everyone, which is why some people are

LYNN MARSHALL-LINNEMEIER. *The Family Jewels #3.* 1994.
Illuminated photo, 20 x 28 inches. Courtesy of Fay Gold Gallery, Atlanta.

better athletes, dancers, and musicians than others. It is because of eye and hand coordination that a photographer takes a hunter's pride in capturing the spontaneity of life without leaving traces of his presence. The photographic process is based on selection, not synthesis. The distinction between the two is that synthesis, as applied to painting, is constructed from traditional skills, schemes, and references. A painting is made; photographs are taken.

One of the first things that a photographer learns is that the medium addresses tangible subject matter. The photographer recognizes that the world itself is a backdrop to the subject matter. It is up to the photographer to find the subject matter between the backdrop and the camera. In order to identify the best image, the photographer must anticipate, clarify, and record it. Yet he recognizes that the subject and the "thing,"

otherwise known as the photograph itself, are not the same.

At this point, recall the photograph you imagined taking earlier. That photograph is an illusion of a literal description of how the camera recorded what you saw. Based on this understanding the following holds true:

- Any and all physical things are photographable.
- A photograph can only look like what the camera records.
- There is no "right" way for a photograph to look, beyond being an illusion of a literal description.

In essence, a photographer's talent lies in eye and hand coordination and in the ability to see what reality will look like on a piece of paper (otherwise known as a print). The creation of a photograph rests in a chemical and mechanical process referred to as the gestation of a print. The illusion of literal description is what photography can do better than any other graphic medium. Photography demonstrates that there is nothing so mysterious as a fact clearly described. However, many contemporary photographers are also manipulating chemical processes to achieve the spontaneity and inventiveness of the graphic arts while preserving the replicative aspects of the medium and the tactile quality of the silver print.

With regard to the conceptual and biographical photography of Lorna Simpson, Carrie Mae Weems, Deborah Willis, Renee Cox, Dawoud Bey, Albert Chong, Lyle Ashton Harris, Clarissa T. Sligh, and others, there is a combination of technical and conceptual talent. While utilizing the same formalism of earlier portrait photographers, these photographers are shaping, defining, and challenging ideas of form, content, and society's norms and mores with their imagery. And they continue to apply all the basic principles of the photographic process. According to photography historian Naomi Rosenblum, "The new attitudes toward mechanical and electronic printing can also be viewed as an aspect of a new Pictorialism, in that the images are meant neither as utilitarian objects—that is, advertising or political posters—nor as windows into exterior or private realities, but primarily as unique aesthetic artifacts."*

Clearly it takes time to develop a sensitivity to photographs outside of the snapshots we all take. As a collector of photography, you want a print that is in good condition—with no scratches or nicks on the surface and no dents in the emulsion, which is the light-sensitive coating on the film or printing paper. Resist anything that has yellowed or suffers from browning or foxing. Before you buy a work that is in less than perfect condition, just remember that the science of conserving photographs is still evolving. Conservation is expensive, uncertain, and sometimes ineffective. Equally important, when looking at the print, examine the tones in between black and white. See if the tones in the print are balanced. Is the print gray and fuzzy or clear and bright? Look at a body of a given photographer's work because he may want different effects in his prints. You will be in a better position to tell the relative quality of a particular print if you know something about the photographer's work as a whole.

Signed photographs are desirable, but don't make a signature an absolute requirement. Some photographers do not make it a habit to sign their work.

Another thing to consider in collecting the work of contemporary photographers is color. It has only been in the past fifteen years that photographers have begun to take color seriously, despite the added dimension it obviously brings to a work. One reason for the delay is that many photographers actually prefer the elegance and stark contrasts of black and white. The other reason is technical: All photographs are ephemeral, but color photographs are so ephemeral you practically have to keep them locked up in an air-conditioned closet if you want them to last as long as thirty years. There are three color processes currently used:

1. **Type C.** A subtractive process, meaning that the necessary dies are embedded in the printing paper and respond proportionately to the colors in the negative or transparency.
2. **Dye transfer.** An additive process, meaning that three different negatives are required

---

* Naomi Rosenblum, *A World History of Photography* (New York: Abbeville Press, 1989), 609.

to print the photograph. The process permits good control of balance and contrast, and it is much more stable than Type C, especially when kept in dark storage.

3. **Cibachrome.** The most stable of the three processes, Cibachrome is appreciated by some—but shunned by others—for the saturated and glaring quality of the color. It is more widely accepted among commercial photographers than it is in fine arts circles.

The relative instability of color photographs should not deter you from collecting them. If a print lasts thirty years and you paid less than $1,000 for it, it would cost $30 annually for the life of the print.

It is not uncommon for a photographer to select a group of related images and issue them in the form of a limited-edition portfolio. The initial advantage of buying a portfolio of prints is that you spend less per print than you would buying them individually. Also, the value of a portfolio rises more rapidly than that of an individual photograph.

If you cannot afford to buy an original print by a photographer you admire, consider buying a well-made illustrated book of the photographer's work. The photo plates rarely convey the full richness of the original prints, but you will be surprised how beautiful they can be. Photography books can also be meaningful additions to your collection, especially ones that are signed by the photographer.

It is a good idea to purchase photographs from a specialist, say, a photographer or photography dealer. A photography dealer knows more about the medium technically and aesthetically. Dealers who carry photographs along with other items generally exhibit photographs that look like paintings, or else the best-known images of the best-known photographers. Galleries generally exhibit fewer American photographers of African descent than they do painters. Photography is not fully appreciated by collectors of African American art or in the overall photography marketplace.

Since few galleries are featuring meritorious work by American photographers of African descent, do not assume that museums and gallery directors are unaware of their work. Curators are always looking at an abundance of work and are interested in supporting the artist and the art establishment by disseminating information. Do make use of this valuable resource.

The following institutions regularly exhibit works of African American photographers: the California Museum of Afro-American History and Culture (Los Angeles), the Afro-American Historical and Cultural Museum (Pennsylvania), the Studio Museum in Harlem (New York), the Texas Institute of Culture, the Banneker Douglass Museum (Annapolis, Maryland), the University Museum at Hampton Institute (Virginia), the National African American Museum Project of the Smithsonian Institution (Washington, D.C.), the Los Angeles Afro-American Art Museum, En Foco (Bronx, New York), the Fourth Street Gallery (New York), the Black Gallery (California), the Urban League's Gallery 62 (New York), and the New York Public Library's Schomburg Center for Research in Black Culture and Countee Cullen Branch Library.

Photography Resources (page 257) lists people to contact about exhibitions that include and/or highlight the work of African American photographers. It is best to make your inquiries in writing—and do so only if you are sincere about your interest. Curators are generally happy to be helpful, but they often have demanding schedules. So do respect their time.

Although people began collecting photographs almost as soon as they began taking

DEBORAH WILLIS. *No Man of Her Own*. 1995.
Photolinen and fabric, 44 x 41 inches. Courtesy of Steinbaum Krauss Gallery, New York.

This quilt is a symbolic reference to my aunt Annie. I made this photograph of her when I was 12 years old. She worked seven days a week, twelve to eighteen hours a day, as a domestic. She was a proud woman and died at the age of 52 in 1969, the year I began studying photography. I saved the negatives and upon reading recently an essay by Zora Neale Hurston, "How It Feels to Be Colored Me," was reminded of our late night chats about segregation and service jobs in the 1950s and 1960s. Zora writes, "I have not separate feelings about not being an American citizen and colored. I am merely a fragment of Great Soul that surges within the boundaries. My country, right or wrong. Sometimes, I feel discriminated against, but it does not make me angry. It merely astonishes me. How can any deny themselves the pleasure of my company? It's beyond me."

My aunt was married to Uncle Nate, who was a mechanic. Uncle Nate and I would often alternate trips to pick up Aunt Annie on Saturdays so that she could go to church on Sunday. The images of wooden washtub and scrub-board were made recently and I feel they represent her dual existence. She often met with other maids at church and encouraged them to organize. She taught them how to negotiate with their private employers in private homes. She taught them how to communicate. She worked for $15 a day and carfare. She got a raise after telling Miss Paul about the cost of living in her community. This quilt is about placement and displacement, sharing experiences and memory.

HERVÉ COUER-AMIABLE. *April*. 1998.
Silverprint. 11 x 14 inches.
Courtesy of Denise Andrews, Miami.

© Hervé Couer-Amiable

them, serious collectors discovered photography relatively recently. According to most experts, the photography boom dates to 1969, when Lee D. Witkin opened his specialty gallery in New York. Although Witkin was not the first person to sell photography exclusively, he was the first to succeed. Alfred Stieglitz, a leading figure in the vanguard movement known as Photo-Secession, curated *The New American School of Photography*. Following his success in Paris and London, he and Edward Steichen opened Little Galleries of the Photo-Secession in New York in 1902, with the hope of compelling serious recognition of photography as a medium of pictorial expression. His goals were "to hold together those Americans devoted to pictorial photography...to exhibit the best that has been accomplished by its members or other photographers, and above all, to dignify that profession until recently looked upon as a trade."* They neglected to include African Americans in their exhibitions until Steichen's discovery of Roy DeCarava, whom he included in his pivotal *Family of Man* exhibition at the Museum of Modern Art. Unlike Witkin, Stieglitz failed to persuade collectors to value this medium as an instrument for fine art. Fortunately, Witkin and others persevered, and now there are over 150 photography dealers across the country.

OVERVIEW

People of African descent have been involved in photography since its inception. The camera obscura has been documented in the literature of tenth-century Arab scholars as having origins in Africa. Photography was not invented; rather, it was a process that evolved into an artistic tool

---

* Naomi Rosenblum, *The History of Photography* (New York: Abrams, 1944).

for expression. The camera was inspired by the observation of a naturally formed pinhole image. Aristotle of Stageira (384–22 B.C.), known as a philosopher and advocate of reason and moderation, mentioned the images of a solar eclipse formed on the ground by sunlight passing through little gaps in the foliage of a tree. His comments indicate that he had some grasp of photographic principles and exposure to earlier Egyptian texts. His influence can be traced one thousand years later to Roger Bacon's discussion of the camera obscura in 1267. The word *camera obscura* means "dark chamber room."

The daguerreotype was first seen in America in New Orleans, in 1837, two years before Louis-Jacques-Mandé Daguerre received a patent for his invention. The photographer responsible for this introduction was Jules Lion, a black man from France. Portraiture, which dominated American painting in the middle of the nineteenth century, influenced photographers' choice of subject matter. Naturally, the daguerreotype stimulated the popularity of the genre. Concurrent with the invention of photography was the emergence of a white middle class with the discretionary income to create a record of itself and its possessions.

It is remarkable that many of the images by African American photographers have survived from this early period. The two earliest African American photographers, Jules Lion and J. P. Ball, were among the first American daguerreotypists of any ethnic background. Both had successful studios throughout their lives, photographing black and white subjects, and both men frequently moved their operations, as daguerreotypy was largely an itinerant profession to assure a steady influx of new clients. Both photographers went to Europe in the 1850s and 1860s undoubtedly to escape the insupportable political situation in America at that time. The

CHESTER HIGGINS, JR. *VOYAGE. MALI*. 1993.
Silverprint, 16 x 20 inches.
Courtesy of ACA Galleries, New York.

Civil War marks one of the bleakest periods in African American history, a time of ravaging poverty, widespread illiteracy, and social dismemberment. There are no known photographs by African American photographers of this period. In addition, the participation and involvement of African American soldiers from the North and South was not documented by well-known white photographers of the period like Mathew Brady or George Barnard.

The significant African American photographers of the 1850s were portraitists C. M. Battey, Addison Scurlock, and A. P. Bedou. All were southerners and owners of commercial portrait studios, and at some point in their illustrious careers, they were affiliated with black educational institutions like Howard University and Tuskegee Institute. As the official photographers of these institutions, they created portraits of the black elite of the time. Black photographers' primary concerns were for income, family support, and business advancement. Traditionally, these photographers were also interested in their subjects in ways that reflected dignity and personal pride, qualities that were generally of less concern to white photographers in their images of African Americans. The family and community—its celebrations, grieving, and contributions to the workplace—were thoroughly documented. These photographers were the first self-appointed visual ambassadors of African American culture, promoting the culture at its best through photography.

Historically, the majority of early women

ROLAND FREEMAN. *Nellie G. Morgan and granddaughter Tammie Pruitt Morgan. Mississippi, 4 July 1976.*
Black and white photograph. Courtesy of Roland Freeman.

JAMES VANDERZEE. *FUTURE EXPECTATIONS (WEDDING DAY)*. 1926. 8½ x 11 inches.
Courtesy of Donna Mussenden VanDerZee, New York.

ROLAND CHARLES. *BETWEEN THE SHADOW AND THE LIGHT*. 1992.
Silverprint, 16 x 30 inches.
Courtesy of Black Gallery, Los Angeles.

photographers worked in anonymity with their husbands. Therefore, access to their work is either limited or undocumented. The primary record of their contributions to American photography rests in newspaper clippings, advertisements, and references to their husbands' studios. However, there were three women who worked independently and successfully: Mary Warren, who was based in Houston, Texas, and worked as a photographic printer in the 1860s; Mary Flenoy, who had a successful studio in Danville, Illinois, between 1893 and 1909; and Jennie Louise VanDerZee Welcome, who was active from 1910 through the 1920s.

Welcome opened her own studio and school for the arts, the Toussaint Conservatory of Art and Music, in 1910. She used her husband's name professionally and so was known as Mme. E. Toussaint Welcome. She taught courses in photography, portraiture drawing, painting, cartooning, and "artistic" painting on screens, lamp shades, and piano and mantel covers. She also taught piano and string, brass, and reed instruments at a time when being a black woman pro-

prietor of a business in Harlem, where the majority of people were affluent whites, was not the norm. It is possible that her talents and sphere of interest influenced her younger and better-known brother, the photographer James Van-DerZee, whose integration of painting and scenic design is a hallmark of much of his portraiture.

Addison Scurlock had the most successful studio in the country. Harry Truman, Herbert Hoover, and Booker T. Washington are among the more publicly known subjects who sat for him. Scurlock passed his craft to his sons, George and Robert, who continued to operate his studio in Washington, D.C.

P. H. Polk photographed rural working-class people in the South and Midwest. His work examines the inherent strength of poor blacks, which is one reason why Polk is so significant. Also a trained painter, Polk studied under C. M. Battey at Tuskegee and brought a painterly sensibility to his work.

Like Scurlock, James VanDerZee had a formalized style, but his aesthetic sensibilities were less commercial. Polk photographed the rich

GORDON PARKS. *EMERGING MAN.* 1952.
Silver gelatin print.
Courtesy of Howard Greenberg Gallery, New York.

and poor in Alabama, while VanDerZee photographed the common and uncommon in New York, in and out of his Harlem studio.

Job opportunities increased the migration of African Americans from the South to the cities of the North in the early decades of the twentieth century. It was in the liberating landscape of Harlem that VanDerZee would record the most complete documentation of the evolution of an urban African American lifestyle. There is hardly a major figure of the Harlem Renaissance who was not photographed by VanDerZee. In fact, VanDerZee's work has informed Americans of the existence of a moneyed gentry among African American New Yorkers between the world wars. And yet VanDerZee's images are considered to be more than mere photographic documents, because of his fascination

with textures, composition, and the lighting of his subjects. He often painted extraordinary backdrops and consciously included many personal references in his portraiture through the use of props.

VanDerZee was also a photojournalist and created a body of work that records the daily happenings in Harlem life: schoolchildren, streetside religious leaders, and supporters of Marcus Garvey's Back-to-Africa movement. VanDerZee also produced a series of female nudes, making him the first African American photographer to address this subject.

By the beginning of the late 1920s the aesthetics of the photographic image were influenced by the coverage of on-the-spot news in newspapers and periodicals, which preferred the unselfconscious image. The era of commercial portrait photography was replaced by Edwin Land's "instant" Polaroid pictures in 1947.

Among the first African American photographers to gain recognition for bringing to their images of Harlem an aesthetic sensibility informed by cultural biography were Gordon Parks and Roy DeCarava. Both photographers have been at the forefront of exploring the aesthetic limits of the camera and have achieved a level of universality in their work that renders the designation "black photographer" meaningless. Unintentionally, both photographers later became the deans of two aesthetic schools of photography within the African American community that flourished in the 1960s and 1970s. These aesthetic schools evolved in two cities, New York and Chicago, and developed the aesthetic vision for black photographers of the period.

One reason why these informal schools emerged was that it was not until the early 1970s that photography gained public acceptance as an art form. The primary effort to provoke interest in photography as an art was made by Edward Steichen, who curated the 1955 *Family of Man* exhibition at the Museum of Modern Art. Roy DeCarava was the only African American photographer included in this groundbreaking exhibition. Soon after, museums throughout the United States began to consider collecting, buying, and exhibiting photographs. And collecting photographs became a trend. Auction houses like Sotheby's and Christie's, both in New York

ROY LEWIS. *WILLIE LOVES ALICE.* 1967.
Silver gelatin print, 8 x 11 inches.
Courtesy of Parish Gallery, Washington, D.C.

and London, held their first photography auctions. Similar to the print market in the 1970s, photography became an accepted and collected art form, and was soon regarded as an investment. African American photographers recognized that for their work to be appreciated, exhibited, and valued, they themselves would have to act collectively. A by-product of this consciousness was *The Black Photographer's Annual,* which showcased the work of many photographers. The first edition was published in 1973; the second in 1974; the third in 1978; and the fourth in 1980. Due to financial difficulties, publication ceased after 1980.

In 1955 Roy DeCarava's *Sweet Flypaper of Life,* with the prose of Langston Hughes, marked the beginning of the New York school. This book, which powerfully merges a poet's spirit and an artist's vision, presents, in Deborah J. Johnson's words, an extraordinary "insider's view by an artist committed to the interpretation of the black urban experience." In 1961 the Kamoinge Workshop was formed by Louis Draper, Ray Francis, and DeCarava. A committee led by Edward Steichen was formed to investigate allegations of discrimination within the industry. Due to organizational and public politics, the issue was never seriously addressed. Simultaneously, Draper was involved in informal discussions with other photographers and was contacted by Ray Francis. Together with Roy DeCarava they formed Kamoinge. In 1963 DeCarava was chosen as its chairman. Annointed "Kamoinge" by Draper, a Kikuyu (East African) word that means "a group of people working together," the group's mission was

© Frank Stewart

FRANK STEWART. *Boob Tube.* 1982.
Courtesy of Halima Taha Collection, New York.

ADGER COWANS. *Silk & Shadow.* 1985.
Silver gelatin print.
Courtesy of Kamoinge Workshop, New York.

to establish a rapport among other working African American photographers and to be a mirror for the community by exclusively exhibiting within the African American community. Among the original members were Roy DeCarava, Ray Francis, Louis Draper, Al Fennar, Calvin Wilson, Herb Randall, Jimmie Mannas, Herman Howard, Larry Stewart, and Herb Robinson. Later members included Beuford Smith, C. Daniel Dawson, Anthony Barboza, Adger Cowans, and Ming Smith. In the 1970s Cowans was the most active in international fine art photography circles and regularly exhibited. He was also a member of an exclusive group called Heliographers, who advocated the concept of photography as art for personal expression, not commercialism. George Love and Cowans were the only two African American members of Heliographers. Current members include Anthony Barboza, Adger Cowans, C. Daniel Dawson, Louis Draper, Albert Fennar, Ray Francis, Steve Martin, Toni Parks, John Pinderhughes, Herb Randall, Herb Robinson, Sa Rudolph, Beuford Smith, Ming Smith, Frank Stewart, and Shawn Walker. The group remains active and is pursuing more publishing and exhibition opportunities.

Hugh Bell was one of the leading photographers of beautiful white women in the 1960s, a time when black photographers generally were not chosen for high-profile jobs. Photographer Anthony Barboza was commercially influenced by Hugh Bell, whom he worked with as an assistant in his early years of photography. Currently

ROBERT A. SENGSTACKE. 1967.
Archival silverprint.
Courtesy of Murphy Rabb, Inc., Chicago.

Barboza is one of the most successful African American advertising and fashion photographers in the country. His less commercial approaches to the medium were heavily influenced by painter-photographer Adger Cowans. During the 1970s the commercial photographer Owen Brown was among the most sought after and financially successful black photographers.

African American photographers in New York in the 1960s and 1970s benefited from living in an international center for communications and exchange that nurtured an appetite for diverse subjects and approaches to their work. In the more isolated environment of Chicago photographers looked to the microcosm of African American culture in making images that highlighted the cold, harsh realities of Chicago life. Despite the differences in their respective milieus,

photographers in Chicago and New York shared the common goal of documenting and making art out of the African American experience in the United States.

The first mentor for many contemporary photographers is Gordon Parks, who arrived in Chicago from Kansas and later moved to New York, where he worked for *Life* magazine. Parks's poignant imagery of the black experience in America documents the early years of the civil rights struggle of the 1950s. His images also synopsize a bitter and ironic past, from 1942 to just before the first civil rights demonstrations of 1956. As in the case of the Civil War, no large body of photographs by African American photographers exists to document the early years of the civil rights struggle. Few images record the time and its heroes. Parks has influenced and

FRANK JACKSON.
MILLION MAN MARCH. 1995.
Courtesy of Black Gallery, Los Angeles.

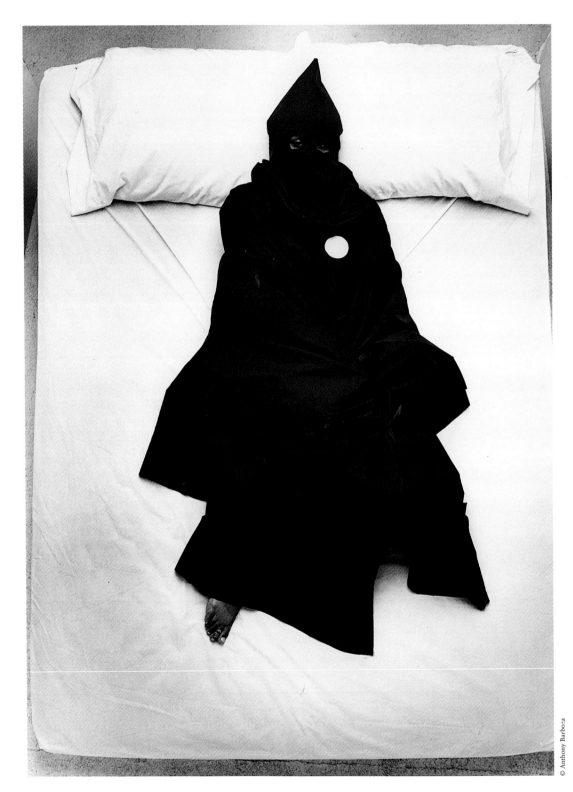

ANTHONY BARBOZA. *Kulture/Black Dreams/White Sheets* series. 1997.
11 x 17 inches. Courtesy of Anthony Barboza, New York.

BEUFORD SMITH. *EVELYN #16*. 1994. Silver gelatin print, 11 x 17 inches.
Courtesy of Césaire Photo Agency.

JEFFREY. *EYE ON L.A.* 1992.
Silver gelatin print, 20 x 24 inches.
Courtesy of Black Gallery, Los Angeles.

encouraged photographers Jim Taylor, Bob Green, and Adger Cowans.

At this time in Chicago Ted Williams was developing his career and taught photography classes in which Bill Grant, Roy Lewis, Chester Sheard, and Mikki Ferrill were students. Inspired by Williams, Ferrill moved to Mexico and worked as a freelance foreign correspondent. Her works have been published in *Time, Ebony, Jet,* the *Chicago Tribune,* and the *Chicago Defender.* She was also influenced by other Chicago photographers like Billy Abernathy, who began photographing in the 1950s. He gained greater recognition in the 1970s with his book *In Our Terribleness,* with text by Imamu Baraka. This book best illustrates the conceptual influence of the Chicago aesthetic. Abernathy inspired Robert Sengstacke, who photographed

for the *Chicago Defender.* Jim Hinton, a native of Atlantic City, grew up in Chicago. An admirer of the work of Robert Wilson (Adeoshun Ifalade), he actively participated in the shaping of the consciousness of the 1960s. He later moved to New York and became a cinematographer. The Chicago school was an informal group of photographers who shared their works to provide themselves with a support system. In 1967 a more formal group, the Organization of Black American Culture, was organized in Chicago among painters, writers, and photographers who worked on the historic *Wall of Respect* mural. The photographers who participated were Bill Abernathy, Darryl Cowheard, Roy Lewis, and Robert Sengstacke.

There are two more recent Atlanta-based groups. Zone III Photography Workshop (the

© Coreen Simpson

COREEN SIMPSON. *Untitled*. 1989.
Silver gelatin print, 16 x 20 inches.
Courtesy of Coreen Simpson.

© Lou Draper

LOU DRAPER. *UNTITLED*. 1973. Silver gelatin print.
Courtesy of Kamoinge Workshop, New York.

JAMES VANDERZEE. *HARLEM COUPLE*. 11 x 14 inches.
Courtesy of Donna Mussenden VanDerZee, New York.

name, taken from the Zone System of photography, means "black with detail") was founded in 1990 by Gerald Straw, D'Bora Emory, and Bill Moore, whose goal was to encourage the advancement of photography enthusiasts, from novice to professional, and to provide an atmosphere conducive to their growth and development. The workshop sponsors annual members' exhibitions. Members include Ralph Bains, Rick Banks, Ken Benjamin, Del Brown, Harold Brown, Keith Brown, Michael Carr, Brian Chrisitan, Connie Cross, Ercel Danies, Leon Davis, James Debro, Shawn Dowdel, D'Bora Emory, Warren O. Fletcher, Denise Gray, Steve Greenige, Carolyn Hallmon, Al Harbison, Jarrod Harris, Horace Henry, Livingston Jackson, M. D. Jackson, Alex Jones, Jena P. Jones, Jonathan Kelly, Sa'longo Lee, Carlton Lewis, J. Fountaine Lewis, James Long, Bernard Little, Dwayne Mack, Joe Marable, Larry McGee, Amanda Morris-May, Debra Mosley, Lisa Norfleet, William Partee, Lamar Reed, Treva L. Reed, Michael Reese, Susan J. Ross, Robert Rostick, Fran Scott, Stanley Searcy, Gerald Straw, Lydia Swain, Charter Taylor, Marvin Taylor, Vincent Thomas, Luther Tolliver, Lee Towner, Sheila Turner, Don Wells, Lawrence Wells, Doyle Whitaker, Mona Lisa Whitaker, Don Whitener, Carleton Wilkinson, Iria Williford, and Inye Wokoma.

The second Atlanta group is Sistagraphy, which was founded in 1993. Its mission is to exhibit the work of African American women; to foster dialogue on the art of photography particularly, though not exclusively, among African American women; and to pursue other activities that will benefit artists and educate the general public. Since 1993 Sistagraphy has expanded its network of members to include women photographers living in New York and California. The group's members are Catherine Alston, Nia Anderson, T. Major Bey, Edith Biggers, Barbara Bishop, Melody Clark, Connie Cross, Sharon Dobson, D'Bora Emory, Mikki Ferrill, Allison Gay, Denise Gray, Carolyn Hallmon, Rachel Hill, Jena P. Jones, S. Renee Kennedy, Iris King, Penny Lawrence, Edith "Chickie" Lewis, Lynn Marshall-Linnemeier, Sylvia McAfee, Cheryl Miller, Amanda Morris-May, Debra Mosley, Lisa Norfleet, Maisha Peterson, Treva L. Reed, Susan J. Ross, Wakeeta Rosser, Francesca "Fran" Scott, Valita Shefiff, Lydia Swain, Lee Towner, Sheila Turner, Franita Ware, and Julie Yarborough.

Many of the photographers mentioned in this chapter are trailblazers who have documented and recorded the world in which they live—its influences, challenges, and inspiration—for the benefit of all audiences. These technical and aesthetic pioneers have allowed many contemporary photographers in the marketplace to participate in a process of beauty, purpose, and style.

It is ironic that many of these photographers are not active within the photography market. (And by no means is this an all-inclusive citation of talented and collectable photographers.) It is the author's hope that collectors will reconsider or continue to explore photography as collectible art. As with prints and paintings, it is because of collectors who have explored images about or by themselves and who have taken risks that the marketplace for African American art has finally piqued the art establishment's interest in African American photography as a "new American commodity." Photography as a medium and market may have a move readily achieved potential for aesthetic democracy than painting. Only time will tell. The move toward change and enrichment of American culture rests, in part, in the hands of collectors.

Start collecting images of photographers who live in your neighborhood, and write to local institutions to request that they curate exhibitions that include African American photographers of every theme and style. In essence, force the curators to do their homework and move beyond the perpetual promotion of safe, historical, and well-known photographers. As collectors, you have no reason not to exert your financial, cultural, and aesthetic clout. There is no need to be intimidated by this power. This, too, is a part of the art market at large. When you see exhibitions, contact any writers and critics you know and ask them to write about the exhibitions. A sterling example of the impact that you can have may be found in the writings of A. D. Coleman, arguably one of the most sensitive and pivotal writers on photography as art during the late 1960s and 1970s. One of the few early critics to seriously look at the images of contemporary African American photographers, Coleman taught a generation of readers how to look at a photograph. He, like many people, regardless of their race or ethnicity, has been underrated, in part because of his humility.

The market for most African American photographers—those who are not using mixed media or sensationalist gimmicks—is still in its infancy. The more you educate yourself about the history of the medium and the various philosophical and practical discourses it has inspired, the greater the likelihood that your appreciation will develop into a contagious quest for the acquisition of photography as art.

VIVIAN E. BROWN. *The Sun Has Always Been Red.* 1985.
Oil on canvas, 60 x 57¾ inches.
Courtesy of June Kelly Gallery, New York.

Afterword by June Kelly

African Americans have been a vital force in American art for nearly three hundred years, from colonial times to the present. But in today's art world more African American artists are at work—and many more have received critical recognition—than has ever been the case in the past.

African American artists are creating some of the most challenging and compelling work of our time. At the same time, there has been a growing audience for the work of these artists, as well as significant growth in the number of black-owned galleries and museum exhibitions focusing on or including the works of African American artists.

There is also a steadily rising interest in collecting the works of these artists. Yet many people who might want to acquire art by African Americans find the art scene daunting. They want to collect but don't know how to begin. Here are some guidelines for aspiring collectors that should prove useful.

Aspiring collectors must recognize that it is impossible to become an expert overnight. Collecting is a long-term commitment and requires careful self-education.

Aspiring collectors must train their eyes and ears to absorb information about art and artists. They must rely on their instincts and develop their eye for art and their own aesthetic judgment and taste—that is, what they like and what they don't like in art. They must listen carefully to a few trusted dealers, curators, and other collectors.

Aspiring collectors should visit museums, attend lectures, and perhaps join a museum and participate in its programs. They should also visit art galleries in their communities (unlike many museums, galleries charge no admission) and attend gallery openings (the artist is normally present to greet guests). The dealer is an excellent source of information about the artists shown by the gallery. Art fairs are another opportunity to see a broad cross section of art styles and talk with knowledgeable dealers and collectors.

Aspiring collectors will also want to read books about art and art history, which can be found in all public libraries. Another option is to take a course in art appreciation at a local college or university.

When aspiring collectors have done their homework and research, a time will come when they want to take the first step and buy a work of art. One rule of thumb: Aspiring collectors should not buy the first piece that attracts their eye. They should hold off, because they will undoubtedly find another work that they like better.

For all purchases, aspiring collectors should set an absolute top limit on what they will spend and then try to find an appealing work within that range. Good drawings, watercolors, and limited-edition etchings and lithographs may be available for as little as $500.

Living with art is the ultimate test. Collectors may become more and more enraptured by a work, or sadly discover that it is not as exciting as they thought when they first saw it. But collecting art is a trial-and-error adventure.

After someone has been collecting for a while, he or she will want to start thinking about specializing in one or two areas in this vast ocean of art. This will enable the collector to achieve a higher level of expertise and comfort in the collecting process. Among the areas of specialization are specific artists, specific styles, or, more broadly, watercolors, drawings, paintings of a certain style or period, and limited-edition prints. A collector might also consider specializing in the works of women artists, emerging artists, or established artists.

Aspiring collectors should keep in mind that the work of established artists is likely to carry a higher price tag. They should also remember that their taste may change or broaden, and that they may want to devote their energy to another specialty down the road.

Collectors should also familiarize themselves with auctions, which may be a good source of information about art and may offer an opportunity to acquire art at a reasonable price. Most auction houses publish catalogues that provide detailed information about the art they are offering. The catalogues also provide information about the bidding process and the terms of sale. The best advice to collectors is to attend several auctions and observe carefully what goes on before being tempted to bid. They should not be intimidated when entering an auction house. Above all, collectors must remember that they should not let themselves get carried away by the excitement of the sale.

Is art an investment? There are many people who look upon art as an investment, and in many respects it is, but collectors who buy a work of art hoping to sell it in a few years at a greatly increased price are likely to be disappointed. Art should not be bought as an investment. It should be bought because the collector loves the work and finds great pleasure in living with it.

Collecting art is a rewarding journey of discovery and adventure. It will add a rich, satisfying dimension to the life of the serious and studious collector.

June Kelly is the owner and director of the June Kelly Gallery in New York City. She is a member of the Art Dealers Association of America and vice president of Art Table, Incorporated, a national organization for professional women in the arts.

Postscript by
Evangeline J. Montgomery

The preceding pages attest to the fact that African American art can be acquired by anyone who seeks the enrichment offered by this unique visual culture. It is important for the collector to recognize that art is educational, decorative, and provocative; it provides information and insight into the past and instills hope for the future as an icon, artifact, and cultural investment.

The 1980s and 1990s saw both a virtual explosion in the production of visual arts and a steady decline in government support for the arts. And yet, even in this uncertain climate, a significant number of African American artists were invited to participate in arts programs sponsored by the National Endowment for the Arts, the State Department, and the United States Information Agency (USIA), and earned in the process outstanding international recognition.

The elitism of the international art establishment has required aggressive and productive collaborations among those African American artists, curators, dealers, and art historians who were the beneficiaries of government patronage. In 1989 the sculptor Martin Puryear was chosen to represent the United States at the 20th International Bienal in São Paulo, Brazil, the first African American to be accorded this honor. Puryear's installation, which was curated by Kellie Jones, earned first place. At the 1992 Dakar International Biennale abstract painters Joe Overstreet, Mary Lovelace O'Neal, Mildred Thompson, Frank Bowling, and Leonardo Drew represented the United States; Corrine Jennings was the curator. The sculptor and mixed-media artist Betye Saar and John Outterbridge were selected to participate in the 22d São Paulo International Bienal; this exhibition, curated by Lizzetta LeFalle-Collins, was also selected to represent the United States at the inaugural South African Biennale in Johannesburg in 1995. The 1997 Venice Biennale marked the first time that the artist chosen to represent the United States in the American Pavilion was an African American, the painter Robert Colescott.

Throughout the 1980s and 1990s the USIA sponsored special workshops and speakers programs, which sent the following artists abroad: sculptors Fred Wilson, Mel Edwards, Richard Hunt, Camille Billops, and Terry Adkins; printmakers Robert Blackburn, Allen Edmunds, and Margo Humphrey; painters Emilio Cruz, Donald Locke, Whitfield Lovell, Pheoris West, Philemona Williamson, Jacob Lawrence, Gwen Knight, Samella Lewis, and Freida High-Tesfagiorgis; photographers Roy DeCarava, Deborah Willis, and Roland Freeman; master textile printer Robert Smith; and weaver Napoleon Jones-Henderson.

Abstract painter Sam Gilliam created three major installations in Korea, Finland, and Germany, and Betye Saar created five installations in Taiwan, Malaysia, the Philippines, and New Zealand. Brandywine Workshop, an African American–owned and –operated international print workshop, was invited to exhibit its print collection in over fifty countries.

Curators and art historians have played important roles in the globalization of African American art. Dr. Samella Lewis, curator of *Caribbean Visions*, the first major exhibition of contemporary Caribbean art, has toured internationally. Kellie Jones will curate the exhibition of selected works of African women artists worldwide for the 1998 South African Biennale. Dr. Richard Powell, David Driskell, and Lizzetta LeFalle-Collins, as curators and historians, have shaped and documented the increasing African American presence in international art circles.

Major American art dealers now include blacks from other countries in their stables and exhibitions. Major lectures, conferences, and symposia occur regularly in key cities, and recent books like *Black Artists*, with its listing of four hundred international artists, reflect the even broader range of artistic expressions among blacks worldwide.

All these accomplishments, events, and opportunities have sparked enthusiasm for, and interest in, collecting African American art. The good news is that new paradigms for selection and inclusion in the art collections, festivals, and biennials have begun to shape a new global aesthetic consciousness. In the new millennium collectors of African American art will be important advocates for art produced by African American and other black artists worldwide.

Evangeline J. Montgomery is a Program Officer in the Cultural Programs Office of the United States Information Agency. She is an accomplished sculptor, jewelry designer, printmaker, and mixed-media artist.

The statements expressed herein are those solely of the writer and do not in any way reflect the views of the artists listed or governmental agencies mentioned.

Appendices

Black art has always existed. It just hasn't been looked for in the right places.

ROMARE BEARDEN

Art Dealers

† = specialize in African American art   * = African American–owned gallery or private dealer   Δ = represent African American artists

CALIFORNIA

†*Diara Basley
Third World Art Exchange
2016 Hillhurst Avenue
Los Angeles, CA 90027
323-666-9357 (also fax line)

†*Asake Bomani
Bomani Gallery
251 Post Street, Suite 600
San Francisco, CA 94108
415-296-8677; fax: 415-296-8643

†*Roland Charles
Black Gallery
P.O. Box 8778
Los Angeles, CA 90008
323-294-9024; fax: 323-933-2447
e-mail: BPC @ LaBridge.com

†*Eric Hanks
M. Hanks Gallery
3008 Main Street, Suite 100
Santa Monica, CA 90405
310-392-8820; fax: 310-392-3968

†*Thelma Harris
Thelma Harris Art Gallery
5940 College Avenue
Oakland, CA 94618
510-654-0443; fax: 510-654-4251

ΔBenjamin Horowitz
Heritage Gallery
718 North La Cienega Boulevard
Los Angeles, CA 90069
310-652-7738

†*Alitash Kebede
Alitash Kebede Gallery
1295 Ridgeley Drive
Los Angeles, CA 90046
323-549-0003, 323-549-0004;
   fax: 323-876-7248

†*Claude Lewis
United Works Gallery
P.O. Box 1202
Los Angeles, CA
213-931-7732

†*Margaret Porter
Porter Troupe Gallery
301 Spruce Street
San Diego, CA 92103-5626
619-291-9096; fax: 619-291-9098

†*Joyce Thigpen
The Gallery Tanner
5271 West Pico Boulevard
Los Angeles, CA 90019
323-933-0202

COLORADO

†*Ernest Bonner
Mosadi's Collections Art Gallery
1670 York Street
Denver, CO 80206
303-331-0700 or 800-843-7370;
   fax: 303-331-0300

DISTRICT OF COLUMBIA

ΔAnnie Gawlak
Baumgartner Galleries
2016 "R" Street, NW
Washington, DC 20009
202-232-6320

†*Ruth Cooke Gibbs
Ayaso International Fine Art
1100 Constitution Avenue, NE
Washington, DC 20002
202-546-1667; fax: 202-546-4865

ΔJane Haslem Gallery
2025 Hillyer Place NW
Washington, D.C. 20009
202-232-4644; fax: 202-387-0679

†*Helen Jackson
Capital East Graphic Gallery
600 East SE
Washington, DC 20003
202-547-8246

†*Norman Parish
Parish Gallery
Canal Square
1054 31st Street, NW
Washington, DC 20007
202-944-2310

†*Lou Stovall
Workshop, Inc.
3145 Newark Street, NW
Washington, DC 20008
202-966-4202 or 202-362-0116

FLORIDA

†*Denise Andrews
A+ Resources
3084 Jefferson Street
Coconut Grove, FL 33133
305-860-0591 (also fax)

ᐃMarilyn Mars
Art Impact, Inc.
2623 Jetton Avenue
Tampa, FL 33629
813-251-3688

GEORGIA
ᐃFay Gold
Fay Gold Gallery
247 Buckhead Avenue
Atlanta, GA 30305
404-365-8633

†*Montanette T. Jones
Montanette T. Jones Gallery
500 Bishop Street, Suite C-1
Atlanta, GA 30318
404-355-2783 or 404-351-3311

ᐃLouise McIntosh
McIntosh Gallery
One Virginia Hill
587 Virginia Avenue
Atlanta, GA 30306
404-892-4023

†*Ed Spriggs
Hammonds House Galleries
503 Peeples Street SW
Atlanta, GA 30310
404-752-8730; fax: 404-752-8730

ILLINOIS
ᐃRobert Henry Adams
Robert Henry Adams Fine Art
715 North Franklin
Chicago, IL 60610
312-642-8700; fax: 312-642-8785

ᐃRhona Hoffman
Rhona Hoffman Gallery
312 North Main Street
Chicago, IL 60067
312-455-1990; fax: 312-455-1727

†*Isobel Neal
G. R. N'Namdi Gallery
230 West Huron Street
Chicago, IL 60610
312-587-8262; fax: 312-587-8325

†*Madeline Murphy Rabb
Madeline Murphy Rabb, Inc.
400 South Green Street,
    Unit G
Chicago, IL 60607
312-242-5070; fax: 312-243-5092
e-mail: info @ rabbart.com

ᐃ*Nicole Smith
Nicole Smith Gallery
734 North Wells Street
Chicago, IL 60610
312-787-7716; fax: 312-787-7716

†*Susan Woodson
5121 South Drexel Avenue
Chicago, IL 60615
312-443-3600; fax: 312-443-0849

LOUISIANA
ᐃDenise Berthiaume
Le Mieux Galleries
332 Julia Street
New Orleans, LA 70130
504-522-5988

†*Stella Jones/Harry Jones
Stella Jones Gallery
201 St. Charles Avenue
New Orleans, LA 70130
888-400-9100 or 504-568-9050;
    fax: 504-568-0840

ᐃDonna C. Perret
Gallery Simone Stern
518 Julia Street
New Orleans, LA 70130
504-529-1118

MASSACHUSETTS
ᐃJan Shapiro and Constance Brown
Wendell Street Gallery
17 Wendell Street
Cambridge, MA 02138
617-864-9294

MICHIGAN
†*NCA/Michigan Chapter
National Conference of Artists
    Gallery
301 West Grand Boulevard
Fischer Building
Detroit, MI 48202
313-875-0923; fax: 313-875-7537
www.ncamich.org

†*George N'Namdi
G. R. N'Namdi Gallery
161 Townsend
Birmingham, MI 48009-6001
810-642-2700; fax: 810-642-5630

ᐃEd and Karen Ogul
Paramour Fine Arts
PO Box 760072
Lathrup Village, MI 48076
810-559-4695; fax: 810-559-3101

†*Dell Pryor
Dell Pryor Galleries
Harmonie Park
1452 Randolph
Detroit, MI 48226
313-963-5977; fax: 313-331-2643

†*Sherry Washington
Sherry Washington Gallery
The L. B. King Building
1274 Library Street
Detroit, MI 48226
313-961-4500; fax: 313-961-4584

NEW JERSEY
†*Victor Dawson
Aljira: A Center for Contemporary
    Art
2 Washington Place, 4th floor
Newark, NJ
973-643-6877; fax: 973-643-3594

†*Larry Hilton
Bellevue Gallery
209 Bellevue Avenue
Trenton, NJ 01618
609-695-7976 or 609-292-5003

NEW MEXICO
ᐃArlene Lewallen
Lewallen Contemporary Gallery
129 West Palace Avenue
Santa Fe, NM 87501
505-988-8991; fax: 212-662-7495

NEW YORK
†*Derrick Adams
Rush Arts Gallery
526 West 26th Street
New York, NY 10001
212-691-9552; fax: 212-691-9304

†*Peg Alston
Peg Alston Fine Arts
407 Central Park West, Suite 6C
New York, NY 10025
212-662-5522; fax: 212-662-7495

ᐃDavid Beitzel Gallery
102 Prince Street
New York, NY 10012
212-219-2863 or 212-941-7158

ᐃJeffrey Bergen
American Contemporary Arts
    Galleries (ACA)
41 East 57th Street
New York, NY 10022
212-644-8300; fax: 212-644-8308

†*Robert Blackburn
  Printmaking Workshop
19 West 24th Street
New York, NY 10010
212-989-6125 (also fax)

ΔMary Boone
Mary Boone Gallery
745 Fifth Avenue
New York, NY 10151
212-752-2929; fax: 212-752-3939

†*Lurita Brown
Clinton Hill Gallery
583 Myrtle Avenue
Brooklyn, NY 11205
718-857-0074 or 718-624-5041

†*Loris Crawford
Savacou Gallery
24 East 13th Street
New York, NY 10003
212-473-6904 or 212-220-8446

†*Mark Dabney
Hannibal International Fine Arts
  Services
199 Greene Avenue
Brooklyn, NY 11238
718-399-6106

ΔTerry Dintenfass
Terry Dintenfass with Salander-
  O'Reilly Galleries, Inc.
20 East 79th Street
New York, NY 10021
212-581-2268

ΔDr. John Driscoll
Babcock Galleries
724 Fifth Avenue
New York, NY 10019
212-767-1852; fax: 212-767-1857

ΔThomas Erben
Thomas Erben Gallery
476 Broome Street
New York, NY 10013
212-966-5283; fax: 212-941-0752

†*Essie Green-Edmiston
Essie Green Galleries
419A Convent Avenue
New York, NY 10031
212-368-9635; fax: 212-281-6675

ΔHoward Greenberg
Howard Greenberg Gallery
120 Wooster Street
New York, NY 10012
212-334-0010 or 212-941-7479

ΔPaul Ha
White Columns Gallery
154 Christopher Street
New York, NY 10014
212-924-4212 or 212-645-4764

†*Alex Halsey
Fourth Street Photo Gallery
63 East 4th Street
New York, NY 10003
212-673-1021

†Janet M. Harrison
509 Cathedral Parkway, #2E
New York, NY 10025
212-865-2411; fax: 212-662-8559
e-mail: JMHPRO@aol.com

ΔMartha Henry
Martha Henry, Inc.
Allvyn Court
180 West 58th Street
New York, NY 10019
212-262-0863; fax: 212-262-1009

†*Bill Hodges
Bill Hodges Gallery
24 West 57th Street
New York, NY 10019
212-333-2640; fax: 212-333-2644

†*Julia Hotten
7C Lakeshore Villa
Port Ewen, NY 12466
914-339-9027

†*Corrine Jennings
Kenkeleba Gallery
214-16 East 2nd Street
New York, NY 10009
212-674-3939; fax: 212-505-5080

†*Ruth Jett
Cinque Gallery
560 Broadway
New York, NY 10012
212-966-3464

†*June Kelly
June Kelly Gallery
591 Broadway
New York, NY 10012
212-226-1660; fax: 212-226-2433

ΔSean Kelly
Sean Kelly Gallery
43 Mercer Street
New York, NY 10013
212-343-2405; fax: 212-343-2604

ΔPhyllis Kind
Phyllis Kind Gallery
136 Greene Street
New York, NY 10012-3202
212-925-1200; fax: 212-941-7841

ΔMetro Pictures
150 Greene Street
New York, NY 10012
212-925-8335

ΔBridget Moore
D. C. Moore Gallery
724 Fifth Avenue
New York, NY 10019
212-247-2111; fax: 212-247-2119

†*Christiane Nienaber
191 Chrystie Street
New York, NY 10002
212-358-0577; fax: 212-475-5469
e-mail: CN191@aol.com

ΔMariacristina Parravicini
Christinerose Gallery
529 West 20th Street
New York, NY 10011
212-206-0297; fax: 212-206-8494
e-mail: CRgallery@aol.com

ΔJean K. Pettibone
Pettibone Fine Art
1158 Fifth Avenue
New York, NY 10029
212-289-0045
e-mail: pettibon@interport.net

ΔPenny Pilkington
P.P.O.W., Inc.
532 Broadway
New York, NY 10012
212-941-8642; fax: 212-274-8339

†*Eric Pryor
Bedford Stuyvesant Restoration
  Corporation
1368 Fulton Street
Brooklyn, NY 11216
718-636-6976

†ΔRoger Ricco
Ricco/Maresca Gallery
529 West 20th Street
New York, NY 10011
212-627-4819; fax: 212-627-5117

†*Don Robertson
Ac-baw Gallery
128 South 4th Avenue
Mt. Vernon, NY
914-667-7278

△Juan Rodriguez
130 East 70th Street
New York, NY 10021
212-472-2234 or 212-472-2368

†△Michael Rosenfeld
Michael Rosenfeld Gallery
24 West 57th Street
New York, NY 10019
212-247-0082; fax: 212-247-0402

△Luise Ross
Luise Ross Gallery
568 Broadway
New York, NY 10012-3225
212-343-2161; fax: 212-343-2468

△Mary Ryan
Mary Ryan Gallery
24 West 57th Street
New York, NY 10019
212-397-0669; fax: 212-397-0766

†Beverly and Ray Sachs
Sachs Fine Art
171 West 57th Street
New York, NY 10019
212-333-5577

△Betsy Senior
Betsy Senior Gallery
375 West Broadway
New York, NY 10012
212-941-0960; fax: 212-334-3109

△Tony Shafrazi
Tony Shafrazi Gallery
119 Wooster Street
New York, NY 10012
212-274-9300 or 212-334-9499

△Jack Shainman
Jack Shainman Gallery
513 West 20th Street
New York, NY 10011
212-645-1701 or 212-645-8316

†*Danny Simmons
Corridor Gallery
334 Grand Avenue
Brooklyn, NY 11238
718-638-8416

△*Merton Simpson
Merton D. Simpson Gallery
1063 Madison Avenue
New York, NY 10028
212-988-6290; fax: 212-988-3041

†*Skoto
Skoto Gallery
529 West 20th Street
New York, NY 10011
212-352-8058

†*Debra S. Spencer
117 West 58th Street, 12-D
New York, NY 10019
212-757-5177

†△Ellen Sragow
Ellen Sragow, Ltd.
73 Spring Street
New York, NY 10012
212-219-1793

△Bernice Steinbaum
Steinbaum Krauss Gallery
132 Greene Street
New York, NY 10012
212-431-4224; fax: 212-431-3252

△Jack Tilton
Jack Tilton Gallery
49 Greene Street
New York, NY 10013
212-941-1775; fax: 212-941-1812

△Vinalhaven Press
565 Broadway
New York, NY 10012
212-966-7691

△Joan Washburn
Washburn Galleries
20 West 57th Street
New York, NY 10019
212-397-6780; fax: 212-397-4853

△Wooster Gardens
558 Broadway
New York, NY 10012
212-941-6210 or 212-941-5480

NORTH CAROLINA
△Jerald Melberg
Jerald Melberg Gallery
Morocroft Village
3900 Colony Road
Charlotte, NC 28211
704-365-3000 or 800-748-5221

†*Noel
Noel Gallery/Fine Art Acquisitions,
   Inc.
Trans America Square
401 North Tryon Street
Charlotte, NC 28202
704-343-0050

†*Cheryl Sutton
303 Swiss Lake Drive
Carey, NC 27513
919-468-8800

OHIO
†*Ernestine T. Brown
Malcolm Brown Gallery
20100 Chagrin Boulevard
Shaker Heights, OH 44122
216-751-2955

PENNSYLVANIA
†*Alan Edmunds
Brandywine Workshop
730 S. Broad Street
Philadelphia, PA 19146
215-546-3675 or 215-546-2825
www.blackboard.com/brndyne

†*Steven Jones
4810 Florence Avenue
Philadelphia, PA 19143
215-726-5813

†*Evelyn Redcross
October Gallery
68 North Second Street
Philadelphia, PA 19106
215-387-7177
www.octobergallery.com

△Ronald Rumford
Dolan/Maxwell
2046 Rittenhouse Square
Philadelphia, PA 19103
215-732-7787; fax: 215-790-1866

△Robert Schwarz
1806 Chestnut Street
Philadelphia, PA 19103
215-563-4887; fax: 215-561-5621

†*Barbara Wallace
Barbara Wallace and Associates
544 West Queens Lane
Philadelphia, PA 19144
215-848-8996; fax: 215-848-5791

†△Sande Webster
Sande Webster Gallery
Wallnuts Frame Design
2018 Locust Street
Philadelphia, PA 19103
215-732-8850; fax: 215-732-7850

SOUTH CAROLINA
△*Chuma Nwokike
Gallery Thuma
43 John Street
Charleston, SC 29403
803-722-7568; fax: 803-722-1618

TENNESSEE
†*Carlton Wilkenson
In The Gallery
624A Jefferson Street
Nashville, TN 37208
615-255-0705

TEXAS
†*Kathleen Coleman
Art Ventures
3350 Rosedale #2
Houston, TX 77004
713-526-9552; fax: 713-524-2490

†*Eugene Foney
Artcetera
P.O. Box 131914
Houston, TX 77219
713-270-4319

†*Aaronetta Pierce
Premier Artworks, Inc.
209 Canade Verde
San Antonio, TX 78232
210-490-4084 or 210-491-0402
premierartworks@webtv.net

†*Lana Smith
The Canal Group, Ltd.
3917 Main Street
Houston, TX 77002
713-529-5262; fax: 713-529-5151

∆Emily Todd
Diverse Works
1117 East Freeway
Houston, TX 77002

WASHINGTON
∆Gregory Kucera
Gregory Kucera Gallery
608 Second Avenue
Seattle, WA 98104
206-624-0770 or 206-624-4031

∆Francine Seders
Francine Seders Gallery, Ltd.
6701 Greenwood Avenue
North Seattle, WA 98103-5294
206-782-0355

∆Donald Young
Donald Young Gallery
2107 Third Avenue
Seattle, WA 98121
206-448-9484

WISCONSIN
∆Paula McCarthy Panczenko
Tandem Press
201 South Dickinson Street
Madison, WI 53703
608-263-3437; fax: 608-265-2356

NATIONAL EVENTS
Annually, contact:
Camille Billops
Hatch-Billops Collection, Inc.
491 Broadway, 7th floor
New York, NY 10012
212-966-3231

Joscelyn Wainwright
Wainwright & Smith Associates
The National Black Fine Art Show
68 East 7th Street
New York, NY 10003
212-777-5218

Biannually, contact:
National Black Arts Festival
236 Forsyth Street, SW, Suite 400
Atlanta, GA 30303
404-730-7315 or 404-730-7104

OF RELATED INTEREST
Appraisers Association of America
386 Park Avenue South, #2000
New York, NY 10016
212-889-5404

Art Dealers Association of America
575 Madison Avenue
New York, NY 10022
212-940-8590

International Print Dealers
   Association, Inc.
485 Madison Avenue, 15th floor
New York, NY 10022
212-759-4469

ON THE WEB
African American Museums
   Association
www.artnoir.com/aama.html

Art in Context
www.artincontext.com

Artnoir Showcase
www.artnoir.com

Schomburg Center for Research in
   Black Culture, New York
www.nypl.org/research/sc/sc.html

Photography Resources

ARIZONA
Terrence Pitts, Director
Center for Creative Photography
University of Arizona
Tuscon, AZ 85721

Trudy Wilner Stack, Curator of
   Exhibitions and Collections
Center for Creative Photography
University of Arizona
Tuscon, AZ 85721

CALIFORNIA
Marietta Bernsdorff and Sydney
   Kanlager
Social and Public Resource Center
685 Venice Boulevard
Venice, CA 90291-4897

Edward Earle, Senior Curator
California Museum of Photography
3824 Main Street
Riverside, CA 92501

David Featherstone, Independent
   Curator
1320 Vallejo Street, PH-1
San Francisco, CA 94123

Marnie Gillett, Executive Director
San Francisco Camerawork
70 Twelfth Street
San Francisco, CA 94103

Constance Glenn, Director
California State University Art
    Museum
1250 Bellflower Boulevard
Long Beach, CA 90840-1901

Beth Goldberg, Assistant Director
San Francisco Camerawork
70 Twelfth Street
San Francisco, CA 94103

Jonathan Greene, Director
California Museum of Photography
3824 Main Street
Riverside, CA 92501

Andy Grundberg, Executive
    Director
The Friends of Photography
250 Fourth Street
San Francisco, CA 94103

Therese Thau Heyman, Curator
The Oakland Museum
1000 Oak Street
Oakland, CA 94607

Graham Howe, Director
Curatorial Assistance
113 East Union Street
Pasadena, CA 91103

Judith Keller, Associate Curator of
    Photographs
J. Paul Getty Museum
401 Wilshire Boulevard
Santa Monica, CA 90401-2112

Lynette Molnar, Director
Eye Gallery
1151 Mission Street
San Francisco, CA 94103

Weston Naef, Curator of
    Photography
J. Paul Getty Museum
P.O. Box 2112
Santa Monica, CA 90406

Julie Nelson-Gal
San Francisco Museum of Modern
    Art
401 Van Ness Avenue
San Francisco, CA 94102

Douglas Nickel, Assistant Curator
    of Photography
San Francisco Museum of Modern
    Art
401 Van Ness Avenue
San Francisco, CA 94102

Arthur Ollman, Executive Director
Museum of Photographic Arts
1649 El Prado-Balboa Park
San Diego, CA 92101

Jane Levy Reed, Independent
    Curator
18 Chattanooga Road
San Francisco, CA 94115

Karen Sinsheimer, Curator of
    Photography
Santa Barbara Museum of Art
1130 State Street
Santa Barbara, CA 93101

Joe Smoke, Director
Los Angeles Center for
    Photographic Studies
1048 West 6th Street, Suite 424
Los Angeles, CA 90017

Robert Sobieszek, Curator of
    Photography
Los Angeles County Museum of Art
5905 Wilshire Boulevard
Los Angeles, CA 94607

Abigail Solomon–Godeau
102 Calle Palo Colorado
Santa Barbara, CA 93105

Naomi Vine, Director
Laguna Art Museum
307 Cliff Drive
Laguna Beach, CA 92651

DISTRICT OF COLUMBIA

Philip Brookman, Curator of
    Photography and Media Arts
The Corcoran Gallery of Art
500 17th Street, NW
Washington, DC 20006-4899

Marita Chance, Curator of
    Photography
Library of Congress
10 First Street, SE
Washington, DC 20540

Sue Coliton, Program Specialist
National Endowment for the Arts
1000 Pennsylvania Avenue, NW
Washington, DC 20506

Merry Foresta, Curator of
    Photography
National Museum of American Art
Eighth and G Streets, NW
Washington, DC 20560

Sarah Greenough, Curator of
    Photographs
National Gallery of Art
Fourth Street and Constitution
    Avenue, NW
Washington, DC 20565

David Haberstich, Photographic
    Archivist
National Museum of American
    History
Smithsonian Institution
Washington, DC 20560

Maggie Olvey, Assistant Curator
National Museum of American
    History
Smithsonian Institution
Washington, DC 20560

Stephen Ostrow, Chief of Prints and
    Photographs Division
Library of Congress
10 First Street, SE
Washington, DC 20540

Mary Panzer, Curator of
    Photographs
The National Portrait Gallery
F Street at Eighth Street, NW
Washington, DC 20560

Anne Schumard, Assistant Curator
    of Photographs
The National Portrait Gallery
F Street at Eighth Street, NW
Washington, DC 20560

Joshua Smith, Independent Curator
2219 California Street, NW
Washington, DC 20008

Deborah Willis, Collections
    Coordinator
National African American
    Museum Project
Smithsonian Institution
900 Jefferson Drive, SW
Washington, DC 20560

FLORIDA

Alison Nordstrom, Director
Southeast Museum of Photography
Box 2811
Daytona Beach, FL 32114

GEORGIA

Ellen Dugan, Curator of
    Photography
High Museum of Art
1280 Peachtree Street
Atlanta, GA 30309

ILLINOIS

Martha Alexander, Assistant
    Director
The Museum of Contemporary
    Photography
600 South Michigan Avenue
Chicago, IL 60605-1996

Denise Miller-Clark, Director
The Museum of Contemporary
    Photography
Columbia College
600 South Michigan Drive
Chicago, IL 60605

Diana Rogain, Curator of Prints
    and Photographs
Chicago Historical Society
1601 North Clark Street at North
    Avenue
Chicago, IL 60614-6099

David Travis, Curator of
    Photography
The Art Institute of Chicago
Michigan Avenue at Adams Street
Chicago, IL 60603

Colin Westerbeck, Associate
    Curator
The Art Institute of Chicago
Michigan Avenue at Adams Street
Chicago, IL 60603

KANSAS

Steve Goddard, Curator of Prints
    and Drawings
Helen Spence Museum of Art
1301 Mississippi Street
Lawrence, KS 66044

John Pultz, Curator of Photographs
Helen Spence Museum of Art
1301 Mississippi Street
Lawrence, KS 66044

LOUISIANA

John Lawrence, Photography
    Collection
5333 Royal Street
New Orleans, LA 70130

Steven Maklansky, Curator of
    Photography
New Orleans Museum of Art
P.O. Box 19123
New Orleans, LA 70179

Ted Potter
Visual Arts Office
Contemporary Arts Center
P.O. Box 30948
New Orleans, LA 70190

MARYLAND

Tom Beck and Cynthia Wayne,
    Curators of Photography
Kuhn Library and Gallery
The University of Maryland
5401 Wilkens Avenue
Baltimore, MD 21228

MASSACHUSETTS

Clifford Ackley
Curator of Prints, Drawings, and
    Photographs
Museum of Fine Arts
465 Huntington Avenue
Boston, MA 02115

Curator
Polaroid Collection
119 Windsor Street
Cambridge, MA 02139

Barbara Hitchock, Director
Corporate Cultural Affairs
Polaroid Corporation
575 Technology Square
Cambridge, MA 02139

Stephen Jareckie, Curator of
    Photography
Worcester Art Museum
55 Salisbury Street
Worcester, MA 01609

Pat Johnson, Chair
Simmons College
300 The Fenway
Boston, MA 02115-5898

Deborah Martin Kao, Assistant
    Curator of Prints and
    Photographs
Fogg Art Museum
32 Quincy Street
Cambridge, MA 02138

Barbara Norfleet, Senior Lecturer
    and Curator of Photography
Carpenter Center for the Visual
    Arts
24 Quincy Street
Cambridge, MA 02138

Jock Reynolds, Director
Addison Gallery of American Art
Phillips Academy
Andover, MA 01810

Martha Sandweiss, Director
Mead Art Museum
Amherst College
Amherst, MA 01002

Jim Sheldon, Independent Curator
Phillips Academy
Andover, MA 01810

Brenda Sullivan, Acting Director
Photographic Resource Center
602 Commonwealth Avenue
Boston, MA 02215

Sam Yanes, Director
Corporate Communications
Polaroid Corporation
575 Technology Square
Cambridge, MA 02139

MICHIGAN

Ellen Sharp, Curator of Graphic
    Arts
The Detroit Institute of Arts
5200 Woodard Avenue
Detroit, MI 48202

MINNESOTA

Christian Peterson, Associate
    Curator of Photography
Minneapolis Institute of the Arts
2400 Third Avenue
Minneapolis, MN 55404

MISSOURI

Keith Davis, Director
Fine Art Programs
Hallmark Cards, Inc.
2501 McGee
Kansas City, MO 64108

NEW JERSEY

Peter Bunnell, Curator
The Art Museum
Princeton University
Princeton, NJ 08544

NEW MEXICO

Steven Yates, Curator of
    Photography
The Museum of New Mexico
P.O. Box 2087
Sante Fe, NM 87504

NEW YORK

Miles Barth, Curator of Archives
    and Collections
International Center of
    Photography
1133 Avenue of the Americas
New York, NY 10036

Roy DeCarava
DeCarava Archives
81 Halsey Street
Brooklyn, NY 11016

June First, Associate Curator
Department of Photography
The Museum of Modern Art
11 West 53rd Street
New York, NY 10019

Noriko Fuku, Independent Curator
Noriko Fuku Associates
310 Riverside Drive, #514
New York, NY 10025

Marianne Fulton, Chief Curator
International Museum of
    Photography
900 East Avenue
Rochester, NY 14507

Peter Galassi, Director
The Museum of Modern Art
11 West 53rd Street
New York, NY 10019

Suzanne Goldstein, Manager
Pacific Press Service
60 East 56th Street
New York, NY 10022

Howard Greenberg
Howard Greenberg Gallery
120 Wooster Street
New York, NY 10012

Paul Ha, Director
White Columns Gallery
154 Christopher Street
New York, NY 10014

Alex Halsey
Fourth Street Photo Gallery
63 East 4th Street
New York, NY 10003
212-673-1021

Maria Morris Hambourg, Curator
The Metropolitan Museum of Art
1000 Fifth Avenue
New York, NY 10028-0198

Willis Hartshorn, Executive
    Director
International Center of
    Photography
1130 Fifth Avenue
New York, NY 10128

Robert Hirsch, Acting Executive
    Director
CEPA Gallery
700 Main Street
Buffalo, NY 14202

Rich Hock, Curator of Special
    Projects
George Eastman House
900 East Avenue
Rochester, NY 14607

Jeffrey Hoone, Director
Light Work
316 Waverley Avenue
Syracuse, NY 13244

Colleen Kenyon, Executive Director
The Center for Photography at
    Woodstock
59 Tinker Street
Woodstock, NY 12498

Leica Gallery
670 Broadway
New York, NY 10012

Nathan Lyons, Director
Visual Studies Workshop
31 Prince Street
Rochester, NY 14607

Gail Nicholson, Executive Director
CEPA Gallery
700 Main Street
Buffalo, NY 14202

Geno Rodriguez, Curator
Alternative Museum
594 Broadway, Suite 402
New York, NY 10012

Grant Romer, Director of Education
George Eastman House
900 East Avenue
Rochester, NY 14607

Jeff Rosenheim, Assistant Curator
The Metropolitan Museum of Art
1000 Fifth Avenue
New York, NY 10028-0198

Deborah Smith, Curator of Paper
The Strong Museum
One Manhattan Square
Rochester, NY 14607

Charles Stainback, Associate
    Director of Exhibitions
International Center of
    Photography
1130 Fifth Avenue
New York, NY 10128

Susana Torruella-Leval, Acting
    Director and Curator
El Museo del Barrio
1230 Fifth Avenue
New York, NY 10029

Julia Van Haaften, Photography
    Specialist
The New York Public Library
Fifth Avenue at 42d Street,
    Room 313
New York, NY 10018

Donna Vanderzee
Vanderzee Photography
784 Columbus Avenue
New York, NY 10025

Jeanne Verhulst, Associate Curator
    of Exhibitions
George Eastman House
900 East Avenue
Rochester, NY 14607

Adam Weinberg, Curator
The Whitney Museum of American
    Art
945 Madison Avenue
New York, NY 10021

Carla Williams, Curator
The Schomburg Center for
    Research in Black Culture
515 Malcolm X Boulevard
New York, NY 10037-1801

James Wyman, Exhibitions
    Program Coordinator
Visual Studies Workshop
31 Prince Street
Rochester, NY 14607

Bonnie Yochelson, Consulting
    Curator of Prints and
    Photographs
The Museum of the City of
    New York
335 Greenwich Street, 2C
New York, NY 10013

OHIO
Tom Hinson, Curator of
    Contemporary Art
The Cleveland Museum of Art
11150 East Boulevard
Cleveland, OH 44106

Christine Swenson, Curator of
    Graphic Arts
The Toledo Museum of Art
Box 1013
Toledo, OH 43697

OREGON

Bill Foster
Center of Photography
Portland Art Museum
1219 Southwest Park Avenue
Portland, OR 97202

Chris Rauschenberg, Board
    Chairman
Blue Sky Photography Gallery
1231 Northwest Hoyt
Portland, OR 97209

Susan Seyl, Curator of Photography
Oregon Historical Society
1231 Southwest Park Avenue
Portland, OR 97205

PENNSYLVANIA

Linda Benedict-Jones, Adjunct
    Curator
Carnegie Museum of Art
4400 Forbes Avenue
Pittsburgh, PA 15213

Martha Chahroudi, Associate
    Curator of Photographs
Philadelphia Museum of Art
Benjamin Franklin Parkway
P.O. Box 7646
Philadelphia, PA 19101

Innis Shoemaker, Senior Curator of
    Prints and Drawings
Philadelphia Museum of Art
P.O. Box 7646
Philadelphia, PA 19101

Glenn Willumson, Curator of
    Collections
Palmer Museum of Art
The Pennsylvania State University
University Park, PA 16802-2507

TEXAS

Brown Curator of Contemporary
    Art
San Antonio Museum of Art
200 West Jones Avenue
San Antonio, TX 78299

Jean Caslin, Executive Director
Houston Center for Photography
1441 West Alabama
Houston, TX 77006

Chris Codden, Director
Women and Their Work
1137 West 6th Street
Austin, TX 78703

Roy Flukinger, Curator of
    Photography and Film
The University of Texas
Box 7219
Austin, TX 78713-7219

Caroline Huber, Co-Director
Diverse Works
1117 East Freeway
Houston, TX 77002

Liz Lunning, Conservator
Menil Collection
1511 Branard
Houston, TX 77006

Marti Mayo, Director
Blaffer Gallery
University of Houston
Houston, TX 77204-4891

Barbara McCandless, Curator
Amon Carter Museum of Western
    Art
P.O. Box 2365
Fort Worth, TX 76113-2365

Annegret Nill, Curator
Dallas Museum of Art
1717 North Harwood
Dallas, TX 75201

Wendell Ott, Director
Tyler Museum of Art
1300 South Mahon Avenue
Tyler, TX 75701-3499

Mark Petr, Assistant Curator
The Museum of Fine Arts
1001 Bissonet Street
Houston, TX 77265

Al Scuza, Chair
Department of Art
The University of Houston
Houston, TX 77204-4893

Thomas Southall, Curator of
    Photographs
Amon Carter Museum of Western
    Art
P.O. Box 2365
Fort Worth, TX 76113-2365

Daniel Stetson, Director
Laguna Gloria Art Museum
P.O. Box 5568
Austin, TX 78763

Anne Tucker, Gus Lyndall Wortham
    Curator
The Museum of Fine Arts
1001 Bissonet Street
Houston, TX 77265

Stephen Vollmer, Curator of
    Collections
El Paso Museum of Art
1211 Montana
El Paso, TX 79902

Wendy Watris, Curator/FotoFest
Inova Design Center
20 Greenway Plaza, Suite 368
Houston, TX 77046

Clinton Willour, Curator and
    Executive Director
Galveston Arts Center
2127 Strand
Galveston, TX 77550

VIRGINIA

Brooks Johnson, Curator of
    Photography
The Chrysler Museum
Olney Road and Mowbray Arch
Norfolk, VA 23510

Thomas Moore, Curator of
    Photography
Manners Museum
100 Museum Drive
Newport News, VA 23606

WASHINGTON

Rod Slemmons, Curator
Seattle Art Museum
P.O. Box 22000
Seattle, WA 98129-9700

WISCONSIN

Tom Bamberger, Adjunct Curator
    of Photography
Milwaukee Art Museum
750 North Lincoln Memorial Drive
Milwaukee, WI 53202

Jay Ruby
Center for Visual Communication
P.O. Box 128
Mifflitown, WI 17059

African American Museum
Association Resources

ALABAMA
Birmingham Civil Rights Institute
520 16th Street North
Birmingham, AL 35203
205-328-9696

State Black Archives, Research
  Center, and Museum
P.O. Box 595
Normal, AL 35762
205-851-5846

CALIFORNIA
African American Museum of Fine
  Arts
3025 First Street, Suite 27
San Diego, CA 92102
619-696-7799

The Black Inventions Museum
P.O. Box 76122
Los Angeles, CA 90076-0122
310-859-4602

COLORADO
Black American West Museum and
  Heritage Center
3091 California Street
Denver, CO 80205
303-292-2566

DISTRICT OF
COLUMBIA
Howard University Gallery of Art
2455 6th Street, NW
Washington, DC 20056
202-806-7070

Moorland-Spingarn Research
  Center
Howard University
500 Howard Place, NW
Washington, DC 20059
202-806-7241

National African American
  Museum Project
Smithsonian Institution
900 Jefferson Street, SW
Washington, DC 20560

National Capital Region
1100 Ohio Drive, SW
Washington, DC 20242
202-205-3832

National Museum of African Art
950 Independence Avenue, SW
Washington, DC 20560
202-357-3600

National Museum of American
  History
Washington, DC 20560
202-357-2914

FLORIDA
Black Heritage Museum
P.O. Box 57037
Miami, FL 33257-0327
305-252-3535

Museum of African-American Art
13 North Marion Street
Tampa, FL 33602
813-272-2466

GEORGIA
Herndon Home
587 University Place, NW
Atlanta, GA 30314
404-581-9813

Morgan County African American
  Museum
156 Academy Street
P.O. Box 484
Madison, GA 30650
706-342-9191

ILLINOIS
Chicago Historical Society
Clark Street at North Avenue
Chicago, IL 60614-6099
312-642-4600

DuSable Museum of African
  American History
740 East 56th Place
Chicago, IL 60637
312-947-0600

Museum of Science and Industry
57th Street and Lake Shore Drive
Chicago, IL 60637
312-684-1414

INDIANA
Crispus Attucks Museum
1140 Martin Luther King, Jr., Street
Indianapolis, IN 46202
317-226-4611

Madame Walker Urban Life Center
617 Indiana Avenue
Indianapolis, IN 46202
317-236-2099

KENTUCKY
The Kentucky Derby Museum
P.O. Box 3513
Louisville, KY 40201
502-637-1111

LOUISIANA
Arna Bontemps African American
  Museum and Cultural Center
P.O. Box 533
Alexandria, LA 71309
315-473-4692

Jean Lafitte National Historical
  Park and Preserve
National Park Service
365 Canal Street, Suite 380
New Orleans, LA 70130-1142
504-589-3882

MARYLAND
Banneker Douglass Museum
84 Franklin Street
Annapolis, MD 21401
410-974-2893

The Great Blacks in Wax Museum
1601-03 East North Avenue
Baltimore, MD 21213
410-583-3404

Highland Beach Historical
  Commission
3243 Walnut Drive
Annapolis, MD 21403
410-268-2956

James E. Lewis Museum of Art
Morgan State University
Coldspring Lane and Hillen Road
Baltimore, MD 21239
410-319-3030

Maryland Museum of African Art
5430 Vantage Point Road
P.O. Box 1105
Columbia, MD 21044
410-730-7105

MASSACHUSETTS

The Children's Museum
300 Congress Street
Boston, MA 02210
617-426-6500

Museum of Afro-American History
46 Joy Street
Boston, MA 02114
617-742-1854

Museum of the National Center of
    Afro-American Artists
300 Walnut Avenue
Boston, MA 02119
617-442-8614

MICHIGAN

African American Cultural and
    Historical Museum
1676 Coburn Drive
Ann Arbor, MI 48108
313-769-1630

Kindred Souls
1334 Meyers Road
Detroit, MI 48235
313-342-1683

Motown Historical Museum
2648 West Grand Boulevard
Detroit, MI 48208
313-875-2264

Museum of African American
    History
301 Frederick Douglass
Detroit, MI 48202
313-833-9800

MISSOURI

Vaughn Cultural Center
525 North Grand Street
St. Louis, MO 63103
314-535-9227

NEW JERSEY

Afro-American Historical Society
    Museum
1841 Kennedy Boulevard
Jersey City, NJ 07305
201-547-5262

Newark Museum Association
43-49 Washington Street
P.O. Box 540
Newark, NJ 07101
201-596-6550

NEW YORK

The Brooklyn Children's Museum
145 Brooklyn Avenue
Brooklyn, NY 11213
718-735-4400

Center of African American Culture
537 Post Avenue
Rochester, NY 14619
716-436-6453

Community Folk Art Gallery
2223 East Genesee Street
Syracuse, NY 13210
315-424-8487

The Strong Museum
One Manhattan Square
Rochester, NY 14607
716-263-2700

The Studio Museum in Harlem
144 West 125th Street
New York, NY 10027
212-864-4500

NORTH CAROLINA

Afro-American Cultural Center
401 North Myers Street
Charlotte, NC 28202
704-374-1565

Diggs Gallery at Winston-Salem
    State University
601 Martin Luther King, Jr., Drive
Winston-Salem, NC 27110
910-750-2458

North Carolina Central University
    Art Museum
P.O. Box 19555
Durham, NC 27707
919-560-6211

OHIO

African American Museum
1765 Crawford Road
P.O. Box 22039
Cleveland, OH 44106
216-791-1700

Arts Consortium
1515 Linn Street
Cincinnati, OH 45214
513-381-0645

The Dayton Art Institute
456 Belmonte Park North
Dayton, OH 45405-4700
513-223-5277

The John Malvin Foundation, Inc.
P.O. Box 606033
Cleveland, OH 44106
216-229-9999

National Afro-American Museum
    and Cultural Center
1350 Brush Row Road
P.O. Box 578
Wilberforce, OH 45384
513-376-4944

PENNSYLVANIA

Afro-American Historical and
    Cultural Museum
701 Arch Street
Philadelphia, PA 19106-1557
215-574-0380

The Carnegie Institute
4400 Forbes Avenue
Pittsburgh, PA 15213
412-622-3125

Pennsylvania Historical and
    Museum Commission
P.O. Box 1026
Harrisburg, PA 17108
717-787-2891

Please Touch Museum
210 North 21st Street
Philadelphia, PA 19103
215-963-0667

RHODE ISLAND

Rhode Island Black Heritage
    Society
46 Aborn Street
Providence, RI 02903
401-751-3490

SOUTH CAROLINA

Avery Institute of Afro-American
    History and Culture
P.O. Box 21492
Charleston, SC 29413-1492
803-723-5349

Avery Research Center for African-
    American History and Culture
College of Charleston
66 George Street
Charleston, SC 29424
803-727-2009

McKissick Museum
University of South Carolina
Columbia, SC 29208
803-777-7251

Penn Center of the Sea Islands
Martin Luther King Drive
P.O. Box 126
St. Helena Island, SC 29920
803-838-2432

I. P. Stanback Museum and
Planetarium
South Carolina State College
300 College Street, NE
Orangeburg, SC 29117
803-536-7174

TENNESSEE

Beck Cultural Exchange Center
1927 Dandridge Avenue
Knoxville, TN 37915
615-524-8461

Chattanooga African-American
Museum
200 Martin Luther King Boulevard
Chattanooga, TN 37403
615-267-1076

National Civil Rights Museum
450 Mulberry Street
Memphis, TN 38103
901-521-9699

TEXAS

Museum of African American Life
and Culture
P.O. Box 26153
Dallas, TX 75226
214-565-9026

VIRGINIA

Alexandria Black History Resource
Center
638 North Alfred Street
Alexandria, VA 22314
703-838-4356

Hampton University Museum
Hampton, VA 23668
804-727-5308

Harrison Museum of African
American Culture
523 Harrison Avenue, NW
P.O. Box 194
Roanoke, VA 24002-0194
703-345-4818

Newsome House Museum and
Cultural Center
203 Oak Avenue
Newport News, VA 23607
804-247-2360

Petersburg Museum
15 West Bank Street
Petersburg, VA 23803
804-733-2402

Selected Bibliography

Adams, Clinton. *American Lithographers 1900–1960: The Artists and Their Printers.* Santa Fe: University of New Mexico Press, 1983.

African-American Art: The Harmon and Harriet Kelly Collection. Exhibition catalogue. San Antonio Museum of Art, 1994.

African-American Art: Twentieth-Century Masterworks. Exhibition catalogue. Michael Rosenfeld Gallery, New York, 1994.

African-American Art: Twentieth-Century Masterworks, II. Exhibition catalogue. Michael Rosenfeld Gallery, New York, 1996.

Allen, Cleveland G. "Our Young Artists." *Opportunity* 1 (June 1923): 24–25.

Ashton, Dore. *American Art Since 1945.* New York: Oxford University Press, 1982.

Baraka, Amiri, and Thomas McEvilley. *Thornton Dial: Image of the Tiger.* New York: Harry N. Abrams, 1993.

Barnes, Albert C. "Negro Art and America." *Survey,* 1 March 1925, 668–69.

Barr, Alfred. *Cubism and Abstract Art.* New York: Museum of Modern Art, 1936.

Bearden, Romare. "The Negro Artist and Modern Art." *Opportunity* 12 (December 1934): 371–72.

Bearden, Romare, and Harry Henderson. *A History of African-American Artists from 1792 to the Present.* New York: Pantheon Books, 1993.

———. *Six Black Masters of American Art.* New York: Zenith Books, Doubleday, 1972.

Bearden, Romare, and Carl Holty. *The Painter's Mind.* New York: Crown Publishers, 1969.

Berger, Maurice, and Johnetta Cole, eds. *Race and Representation: Art/ Film/Video.* New York: Hunter College Art Gallery, 1987.

Black American Artists of Yesterday and Today. Black Heritage Series. Dayton: George A. Pflaum, 1909.

Bontemps, Arna, ed. *The Harlem Renaissance Remembered.* New York: Dodd, Mead, 1972.

Bontemps, Jacqueline F. *Forever Free: Art by African-American Women, 1862–1980.* Exhibition catalogue. Alexandria, Va.: Stephenson, 1980.

Boswell, Peyton, Jr. *Modern American Painting.* New York: Dodd, Mead, 1939.

Brawley, Benjamin G. *The Negro Genius.* New York: Dodd, Mead, 1937.

Breeskin, Adelyn D. *William H. Johnson, 1901–1970.* Washington, D.C.: Smithsonian Institution Press, 1971.

Bresler, Judith, and Ralph E. Lerner, *Art Law: The Guide for Collectors, Investors, Dealers, and Artists.* New York: Practicing Law Institute, 1989.

Brown, Sterling. *The Negro Caravan.* New York: Dryden Press, 1942.

———. *Negro Poetry and Drama and the Negro in American Fiction.* Washington, D.C.: Associates in Negro Folk Education, 1937.

Buffalo, Andreen. *Explorations in the City of Light: African-American Artists in Paris, 1945–1965.* Exhibition catalogue. The Studio Museum in Harlem, New York, 1996.

Butcher, Margaret Just. *The Negro in American Culture.* New York: Alfred A. Knopf, 1971.

Caribbean Visions: Contemporary Painting and Sculpture. Exhibition catalogue. Art Services International, Alexandria, Va., 1995.

Cederholm, Theresa Dickenson, ed. *Afro-American Artists: A Bibliographic Directory.* Boston: Trustees of the Boston Public Library, 1973.

A Century of Black Photographers: 1840–1960. Exhibition catalogue. Rhode Island School of Design, Providence, R.I., 1983.

Charles Alston: Artist and Teacher. Exhibition catalogue. Kenkeleba House, New York, 1990.

Charles Ethan Porter (1847–1923). Exhibition catalogue. The Connecticut Gallery, Marlborough, Conn., 1987.

Coar, Valencia Hollins. *A Century of Black Photographers, 1840–1960.*

Providence: Rhode Island School of Design, Museum of Art, 1983.

Coleman, A. D. *Light Readings: A Photography Critic's Writings, 1968–1978*. New York: Oxford University Press, 1979.

Crawford, Joe, ed. *The Black Photographers Annual*. New York: Another View, 1971–77.

Dover, Cedric. *American Negro Art*. Greenwich, Conn.: New York Graphic Society, 1969.

Dream Singers, Story Tellers: An African-American Presence. Exhibition catalogue. New Jersey State Museum and Fukui Fine Arts Museum, 1992–94.

Drewal, Henry J., and David C. Driskell. *Introspectives: Contemporary Art by Americans and Brazilians of African Descent*. Exhibition catalogue. California Afro-American Museum, Los Angeles, 1989.

Driskell, David C. *African American Visual Aesthetics*. Washington, D.C.: Smithsonian Institution, 1995.

———. *Amistad II: Afro-American Art*. New York: United Church Board for Homeland Ministries, 1975.

———. *Hidden Heritage: Afro-American Art, 1800–1950*. Exhibition catalogue. Bellevue Art Museum, Bellevue, Wash., and the Art Museum Association of America, 14 September–10 November 1985.

———. *Two Centuries of Black American Art*. Los Angeles and New York: Los Angeles County Museum of Art and Alfred A. Knopf, 1976.

Du Bois, W. E. B. "Criteria of Negro Art," *Crisis*, October 1926, 297.

Edward Mitchell Bannister, 1901–1928. Exhibition catalogue. Kenkeleba House, New York, and the Whitney Museum of American Art, 1992.

The Evolution of Afro-American Artists, 1800–1950. Exhibition catalogue. City University of New York, Harlem Cultural Council, and New York Urban League, 1967.

Fax, Elton C. *Seventeen Black Artists*. New York: Dodd, Mead, 1971.

Fine, Elsa Honig. *The Afro-American Artist: A Search for Identity*. New York: Holt, Rinehart and Winston, 1973.

Fonvielle-Bontemps, Jacqueline. *Choosing: An Exhibit of Changing Perspectives in Modern Art and Art Criticism by Black Americans, 1925–1985*. Exhibition catalogue. 1985.

Gordon, Allan M. *Echoes of Our Past: The Narrative Artistry of Palmer C. Hayden*. Exhibition catalogue. The Museum of African American Art, Los Angeles, Calif., 1988.

Green, Jonathan. *American Photography: A Critical History: 1945 to the Present*. New York: Harry N. Abrams, 1984.

Gruber, J. Richard. *The Dot Man: George Andrews of Madison, Georgia*. Augusta, Ga.: Morris Museum of Art, 1994.

Haynes, George E. *The Trend of the Races*. New York: Council of Women for Home Missions and Missionary Educational Movement, 1922.

Henry Ossawa Tanner. Exhibition catalogue. Philadelphia Museum of Art, 1991.

Holbrook, Francis C. "A Group of Negro Artists," *Opportunity* 1 (July 1923): 211–12.

Horowitz, Benjamin. *Images of Dignity: The Drawings of Charles White*. Glendale, Calif.: Ward Ritchie Press, 1967.

Igoe, Lynn Moody. *Two Hundred Fifty Years of Afro-American Art: An Annotated Bibliography*. New York and London: R. R. Bowker Company, 1981.

Imagery of Black America: Personal and Political Statements. Exhibition catalogue. Robeson Center Gallery, Rutgers University, N.J., 1987.

The International Review of African American Art. 2, no. 4 (1994).

The Jacob Lawrence issue. Black Art 5, no. 3 (1982).

Janis, Sidney. *They Taught Themselves: American Primitive Painters of the Twentieth Century*. Port Washington, N.Y.: Kennikat Press, 1942.

Johnson, Abby, and Ronald Johnson. *Propaganda and Aesthetics: The Literary Politics of Afro-American Magazines in the Twentieth Century*. Amherst, Mass.: University of Massachusetts Press, 1979.

Lewis, David Levering. *When Harlem Was in Vogue*. New York: Alfred A. Knopf, 1981.

Lewis, Samella S. *Art: African American*. New York: Harcourt Brace Jovanovich, 1973.

Lewis, Samella S., and Richard J. Powell. *Elizabeth Catlett: Works on Paper, 1944–1992*. Hampton, Va.: Hampton University Press, 1993.

Lewis, Samella S., and Ruth G. Waddy. *Black Artists on Art*, 2 vols. Los Angeles: Contemporary Crafts, 1971, 1976.

Livingston, Jane, and John Beardsley.

Black Folk Art in America, 1930–1980. Exhibition catalogue. Jackson: University Press of Mississippi, 1982.

Locke, Alain L. "The American Negro as Artist." *American Magazine of Art* 22 (September 1931): 211–20.

———. "The Concept of Race as Applied to Social Culture." *Howard University Review*, June 1924, 290–99.

———. *Negro Art: Past and Present*. Washington, D.C.: Associates in Negro Folk Education, 1936.

———. *The Negro in Art: A Pictorial Record of the Negro Artist and the Negro Theme in Art*. Washington, D.C.: Associates in Negro Folk Education, 1940.

———. *The New Negro: An Interpretation*. New York: A. and C. Boni, 1925.

———. "A Note on African Art." *Opportunity* 2 (May 1924): 134–38.

McElroy, Guy C.; Richard J. Powell; and Sharon F. Patton. *African-American Artists, 1880–1987*. Exhibition catalogue. Smithsonian Institution, Washington, D.C., 1989.

Martin, Tony. *Literary Garveyism: Garvey, Black Arts, and the Harlem Renaissance*. Dover, Mass.: Majority Press, 1983.

Morrison, Keith. *Art in Washington and Its Afro-American Presence: 1940–1970*. Washington, D.C.: Washington Project for the Arts, 1985.

Moutoussamy-Ashe, Jeanne. *Viewfinders: Black Women Photographers*. New York and London: Writers and Readers Publishing, 1986.

Naifeh, Steven, with the assistance of Gregory White-Smith. *The Bargain Hunters Guide to Art Collecting*. New York: William Morrow and Company, 1982.

Negro Artists: An Illustrated Review of Their Achievements. New York: Harmon Foundation, 1935.

The Negro in Chicago, 1779–1929. Chicago: Washington Intercollegiate Club of Chicago, 1929.

Nell, William C. *Colored Patriots of the American Revolution*. Boston: Robert F. Wallcutt, 1855.

Newhall, Beaumont. *The History of Photography: From 1830 to the Present Day*. New York: Museum of Modern Art, 1964.

Perry, Regina A. *Free Within Ourselves: African-American Artists in the Collection of the National Museum of American Art*. Exhibition catalogue. San Francisco: Pomegranate Art Books, 1989.

Porter, Dorothy B. *A Working Bibliography on the Negro in the United States.* Reproduced by University Microfilms, Ann Arbor, Michigan, for the National Endowment for the Humanities Summer Workshops in the Materials of Negro Culture, 1968.

Porter, James A. *Modern Negro Art.* New York: Arno Press, 1943.

Powell, Richard J. *The Blues Aesthetic: Black Culture and Modernism.* Exhibition catalogue. Washington Project for the Arts, Washington, D.C., 1989.

————. *Homecoming: The Art and Life of William H. Johnson.* New York: Rizzoli International Publications, 1991.

Powell, Richard J., and Jock Reynolds. *James Lesesne Wells: Sixty Years in Art.* Washington, D.C.: Washington Project for the Arts, 1986.

Recherché/Den Flexible. Exhibition catalogue. Charlottenborg, Copenhagen, Denmark, 1986; and Port of History Museum, Philadelphia, 1987.

Reynolds, Gary A., and Beryl J. Wright. *Against the Odds: African-American Artists and the Harmon Foundation.* Exhibition catalogue. The Newark Museum, 15 January–15 April 1990.

Richardson, E. P. *A Short History of Painting in America.* New York: Harper and Row, 1963.

Richings, G. F. *Evidences of Progress Among Colored People.* Philadelphia: George S. Ferguson, 1899.

Robertson, Bruce. *Representing America: The Ken Trevey Collection of American Realist Prints.* Los Angeles: University of California Art Museum, 1995.

Rodman, Selden. *Horace Pippin: A Negro Painter in America.* New York: Quadrangle Press, 1947.

Romare Bearden, 1911–1988: A Memorial Exhibition. Exhibition catalogue. ACA Galleries, New York, 1989.

Rosenblum, Naomi. *A History of Women Photographers.* New York: Abbeville Press, 1994.

————. *A World History of Photography.* New York: Abbeville Press, 1989.

Sandler, Martin V. *The Story of American Photography.* Boston: Little, Brown and Company, 1979.

Since the Harlem Renaissance: Fifty Years of Afro-American Art. Exhibition catalogue. Center Gallery of Bucknell University, Lewisburg, Pa., 1984.

The Studio Museum in Harlem, New York. *Hale Woodruff: Fifty Years of His Art.* Exhibition catalogue. 1979.

————. *Harlem Renaissance: Art of Black America.* New York: The Studio Museum in Harlem, Abradale Press, and Harry N. Abrams, 1987.

————. *Tradition and Conflict: Images of a Turbulent Decade, 1963–1973.* Exhibition catalogue. 1985.

Taylor, William E., and Harriet G. Warhol. *A Shared Heritage: Art by Four African Americans.* Bloomington: Indianapolis Museum of Art and Indiana University Press, 1996.

Thomas, Isaiah. *The History of Printing in America with a Biography of Printers, and an Account of Newspapers, to Which Is Prefixed a Concise View of the Discovery and Progress of the Art in Other Parts of the World.* Worcester, Mass.: Press of Isaiah Thomas, Isaac Sturtevant, Printer, 1810.

Washington, M. Bunch. *The Art of Romare Bearden.* New York: Harry N. Abrams, 1972.

Washington-Chapman, Luisa. *The United American Healthcare Corporation Collection.* Exhibition catalogue. United American Healthcare Corporation, 1993.

Wheat, Ellen Hawkins. *Jacob Lawrence: American Painter.* Exhibition catalogue. Seattle Art Museum, 1986.

William H. Johnson: Works from the Collection of Mary Beattie Brady, Director of the Harmon Foundation. Exhibition catalogue. Michael Rosenfeld Gallery, New York, 1995.

Williams, Dave, and Reba Williams. *Alone in a Crowd: Prints of the 1930s–1940s by African-American Artists from the Collection of Reba and Dave Williams.* Exhibition catalogue. American Federation of Arts, 1993.

Willis-Thomas, Deborah. *Black Photographers, 1840–1940.* New York: Garland Publishers, 1985.

Woodruff, Hale A. *The American Negro Artist.* Ann Arbor: University of Michigan Press, 1956.

Woodson, Carter G. *A Century of Negro Migration.* Washington, D.C.: Association for the Study of Negro Life and History, 1918.

Index

Note: Page numbers in *italics* refer to illustrations